ISHAI SAGI

D1465909

SharePoint®
2007

HOW-TO

SAMS | 800 East 96th Street, Indianapolis, Indiana 46240 USA

SharePoint® 2007 How-To

ISBN-13: 978-0-672-33050-6
ISBN-10: 0-672-33050-4

Library of Congress Cataloging-in-Publication Data:

Sagi, Ishai.

SharePoint 2007 how-to/Ishai Sagi. — 1st ed.

   p. cm.

  ISBN 0-672-33050-4

1. Intranets (Computer networks) 2. Microsoft SharePoint (Electronic resource) 3. Web servers. I. Title.

TK5105.875.I6S24 2009

004.6'82—dc22

                 2009010144

Printed in the United States of America

First Printing May 2009

Trademarks

Warning and Disclaimer

Bulk Sales

Sams Publishing offers excellent discounts on this book when ordered in quantity for bulk purchases or special sales. For more information, please contact

  U.S. Corporate and Government Sales

  1-800-382-3419

  corpsales@pearsontechgroup.com

For sales outside the United States, please contact

  International Sales

  international@pearson.com

Editor-in-Chief
Karen Gettman

Executive Editor
Neil Rowe

Acquisitions Editor
Brook Farling

Development Editor
Mark Renfrow

Managing Editor
Patrick Kanouse

Senior Project Editor
Tonya Simpson

Copy Editor
Chuck Hutchinson

Indexer
Tim Wright

Proofreader
Leslie Joseph

Technical Editor
Thomas Holland

Publishing Coordinator
Cindy Teeters

Book Designer
Gary Adair

Compositor
Bronkella
Publishing, LLC

Contents at a Glance

Table of Contents

Part IV: Appendixes

About the Author

Ishai Sagi is a SharePoint expert who has been working with Microsoft SharePoint since its initial release in 2001. Since then, Ishai has trained numerous end users, administrators, and developers in using Microsoft SharePoint or developing solutions for the platform. He has spoken at Microsoft conferences around the world, including in Spain, Israel, and Australia. Ishai received the Microsoft Most Valued Professional (MVP) award for Microsoft SharePoint in 2007 and 2008 as recognition for his contribution to the Microsoft SharePoint community.

Ishai also is the author of a popular SharePoint blog for developers at http://www.sharepoint-tips.com and manages the Canberra SharePoint User Group website at http://www.sharepointusers.org.au/Canberra/default.aspx.

Currently, Ishai is a SharePoint developer and a solutions architect in Canberra, Australia where he spends his spare time taking pictures of the wildlife. This might help explain the numerous pictures of kangaroos that can be seen in this book.

Acknowledgments

To Anja, who was patient with me spending all my spare time on this book for the past year. To my parents, who taught me that reading books is fun, and to my high school English teacher, Steve, who allowed me to read my own books during class instead of doing boring exercises—which taught me that entertaining books can be educational, but never vice versa.

Thank you all, Ishai Sagi

We Want to Hear from You!

As the reader of this book, *you* are our most important critic and commentator. We value your opinion and want to know what we're doing right, what we could do better, what areas you'd like to see us publish in, and any other words of wisdom you're willing to pass our way.

You can email or write me directly to let me know what you did or didn't like about this book—as well as what we can do to make our books stronger.

Please note that I cannot help you with technical problems related to the topic of this book, and that due to the high volume of mail I receive, I might not be able to reply to every message.

When you write, please be sure to include this book's title and author as well as your name and phone or email address. I will carefully review your comments and share them with the author and editors who worked on the book.

E-mail: consumer@samspublishing.com

Mail: Neil Rowe
Executive Editor
Sams Publishing
800 East 96th Street
Indianapolis, IN 46240 USA

Reader Services

Visit our website and register this book at informit.com/title/9780672330506 for convenient access to any updates, downloads, or errata that might be available for this book.

Introduction

Overview of This Book

The aim of this book is to be your companion as you use Microsoft SharePoint 2007. It lists common tasks that you need to do when you use SharePoint as a working tool and shows how to accomplish these tasks in an easy step-by-step process.

This book is written for people who are unfamiliar with or are unsure how to approach tasks in Microsoft SharePoint 2007. It even covers advanced issues, such as managing sites and security, editing pages, and using some of the more complex functionality available in Microsoft SharePoint 2007. However, this book is not intended as an administration guide, a developer handbook, or a complete and comprehensive user guide. Instead, this book focuses on assisting you with the basics—covering the essentials and making sure you know where to go to do the most common day-to-day tasks that you will encounter as a Microsoft SharePoint 2007 end user.

How to Benefit from This Book

We've designed this book to be easy to read from cover to cover. It is divided into four parts designed to make looking up problems easy.

Part I, "Solutions for Readers," has the most common and basic tasks that do not involve changing anything in SharePoint, but just viewing, browsing, and finding information. This part includes

- ► Chapter 1, "About Microsoft SharePoint 2007"
- ► Chapter 2, "Finding Your Way Around a SharePoint Site"
- ► Chapter 3, "Solutions Regarding Files, Documents, List Items, and Forms"
- ► Chapter 4, "Searching in SharePoint"
- ► Chapter 5, "Personal Sites and Personal Details (Available Only in MOSS)"

Part II, "Solutions for Authors and Content Managers," teaches you how to perform tasks that involve adding content to SharePoint or changing the way it looks. This part includes

- ▶ Chapter 6, "Creating and Managing Files, List Items, and Forms in SharePoint"
- ▶ Chapter 7, "Creating Lists and Document Libraries"
- ▶ Chapter 8, "Creating List Views"
- ▶ Chapter 9, "Authoring Pages"
- ▶ Chapter 10, "Managing Security"
- ▶ Chapter 11, "Workflows"

Part III, "Solutions for Site Managers," has advanced tasks involved in creating and customizing SharePoint sites. This part includes

- ▶ Chapter 12, "Creating Subsites"
- ▶ Chapter 13, "Customizing a SharePoint Site"
- ▶ Chapter 14, "Managing Site Security"

Finally, in Part IV, "Appendixes," you find shortcuts and links that will help you find your way and achieve some tasks faster.

This book is written with the firm belief that to learn, you must do. You can use this book as a reference tool when you are tasked with a certain job that you need help finding out how to perform, or you can use it as a learning guide if you have an environment to perform the tasks outlined in this book one by one. Whatever your choice, it is our hope that this book will be a helpful companion.

How to Continue Expanding Your Knowledge

This book does not claim to cover all of what you can do with SharePoint. If you find yourself in need of more information check out the SharePoint built-in help interface. Almost every page in SharePoint has a Help icon that will open the SharePoint help screen, enabling you to search for the topic you want. Additionally, you can find SharePoint manuals and help articles from Microsoft on the Microsoft help site at http://tinyurl.com/mosshelp.

If you cannot find what you want in the Microsoft help pages, plenty more help is available on the Internet from the SharePoint community, which is big and helpful both in blogs and discussion forums. To find solutions to problems, it is recommended to search using your favorite search engine. Many blogs and websites have information on how to achieve tasks in SharePoint.

If you have a question that you cannot find an answer for, the Microsoft forums are the best place to go to get answers. These forums can be found at http://tinyurl.com/sharepointforum.

PART I

Solutions for Readers

IN THIS PART

CHAPTER 1

About Microsoft SharePoint 2007

IN THIS CHAPTER

- ▶ What Is Microsoft SharePoint 2007?
- ▶ What Is the Difference Between WSS and MOSS?
- ▶ What Is a Site?
- ▶ What Is a Personal Site?
- ▶ What Is a List?
- ▶ What Is a Document Library?
- ▶ What Is a Form Library?
- ▶ What Is a Picture Library?
- ▶ What Is a View?
- ▶ What Are Web Parts?
- ▶ What Are Alerts?
- ▶ What Is a Site Column?
- ▶ What Is a Content Type?
- ▶ What Are Versions?
- ▶ What Does Check-In/Check-Out Mean?
- ▶ What Is a Workflow?

What Is Microsoft SharePoint 2007?

SharePoint is a platform that allows users to build websites. SharePoint 2007 is the third version of this Microsoft product (also known as SharePoint v3) and is very different from the versions that came before it.

SharePoint enables users to create different websites with different content and different purposes. It has many built-in features and components that make it a comprehensive solution that can fit many needs.

One common use of SharePoint in organizations is to create sites that are used for collaborations inside teams. These collaborative sites (also known as *team sites*) enable team members to better work with one another—share documents, assign tasks, track team events on a shared web calendar, and much more. This use is known as a *team collaboration system*.

Many companies use SharePoint as their central document storage, replacing network folders. This use is known as an *electronic document management system*.

Another common use is a corporate portal where the corporate employees can go and download forms, read corporate news, fill in surveys, and search for documents. This use is known as an *electronic content management system*.

Finally, some companies choose SharePoint as the platform for their Internet site, where visitors from around the world can visit the company's website and read about the company's products, register for events, and do whatever the site has been configured to allow them to do. This use is known as a *web content management system*.

All these different possible uses are an indication of the flexibility of the SharePoint platform. It is highly customizable, which means that one SharePoint site might look completely different from another SharePoint site. This book mostly shows basic SharePoint sites (sites that have not been customized), so the sites that you use might look significantly different (see Figures 1.1 and 1.2). It is important to keep this fact in mind when following the instructions in this book because some of the features mentioned in the text and shown in the figures can differ from site to site.

> **NOTE** The SharePoint platform is also known as Windows SharePoint Services, or WSS. This book uses the WSS acronym when referring to a SharePoint site that is built based on that platform.

The SharePoint product family has other products that can be added on top of the platform to enhance the sites in different ways. One of these products is the Microsoft Office SharePoint Server, also known as MOSS. Often the term *SharePoint* is used to refer to either just Windows SharePoint Services (WSS) or to the extended version of Microsoft Office SharePoint Server (MOSS), which can be a bit confusing.

FIGURE 1.1
A standard SharePoint site.

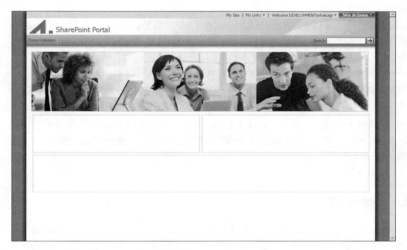

FIGURE 1.2
A customized SharePoint site.

Because MOSS is an extension of WSS, MOSS sites have all the capabilities of WSS sites, but with extra features. The differences between WSS and MOSS are explained later in the following section.

SharePoint sites have many built-in features that make them useful, flexible, and customizable. For example, they have security management, lists of information, document libraries (places to store and manage files and documents), views, alerts, search capability, and much more. All these features and more are explained in this chapter.

What Is the Difference Between WSS and MOSS?

As mentioned in the preceding section, MOSS is an extension of WSS. MOSS sites have features that are not available in WSS sites, while making use of all the features that WSS sites can use.

WSS sites are a good platform for collaboration sites; they enable groups of users to upload and download documents, communicate in discussion boards, assign tasks, share events, and use workflows. However, they do not have enough features to be a good platform for a corporate portal or for a search solution for a corporation. MOSS offers the extra features that upgrade the platform into one that can serve a corporation with enterprise search (search from one location across all the sites that that corporation has). It has features for storing details on people and searching on them. It also has features that allow employees to have their own custom sites where they can store documents (instead of on their machines), and it provides many more features to do with business intelligence, business processes, and forms. For more information about personal sites, see "What Is a Personal Site?" later in this chapter and Chapter 5, "Personal Sites and Personal Details (Available Only in MOSS)," which is dedicated to personal sites.

Finally, a commonly used feature that comes with MOSS is the publishing feature, which adds the ability for site managers to create publishing sites where it is easy to author pages (as opposed to documents) and publish them using workflows. This feature is very important for large corporations that want to, for example, publish corporate news using an approval workflow or build an Internet site where every page must go through a special approval process.

To find out whether the site you are working on is using MOSS or just WSS, see "Determine Whether a Site Is WSS or MOSS" in Chapter 2, "Finding Your Way Around a SharePoint Site."

What Is a Site?

The way SharePoint *sites* (often referred to as *Webs*) are structured is very different from the way you know Internet sites, which contain only pages. In SharePoint a site can house more than just pages; it is a container that holds lists and libraries (see later in this chapter) and can have other sites under it.

An example for the hierarchy of sites is a corporate portal that has a *Home site*, containing information that people see when they browse to that site, and it has a *subsite* called Human Resources that stores (for example) forms such as travel requests, expense claims, and more (see Figures 1.3 and 1.4). The two sites are linked because the Human Resources site is under the Home site. They therefore can share some attributes, such as security (who is allowed to do what in the sites) or navigation (so that visitors to the sites can navigate between the sites), but they have separate contents—for example, different pages, different libraries, and different lists.

Links to Subsites

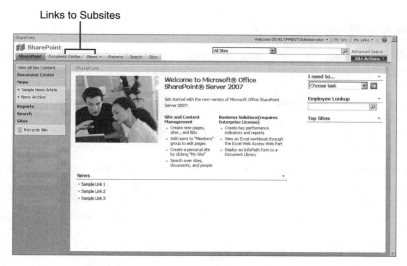

FIGURE 1.3
A site that has subsites. News and Document center are subsites to the SharePoint site.

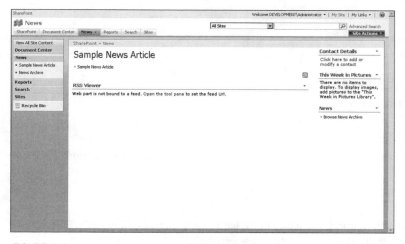

FIGURE 1.4
A subsite. The News site is under the site "SharePoint."

All SharePoint sites are members of a *site collection*, which is exactly what its name implies: Every site collection has a single site as its root site, under which other sites can be built. A site collection has some attributes that are common to all the sites in that collection—for example, some search settings and a recycling bin for deleted items.

What Is a Personal Site?

A *personal site* is a special site that belongs to a specific user and is used to show the information that is personally his or hers. This means the user can upload documents to a personal document library in the personal site, and only that user is able to see and manage the documents. The personal site is also the place where users can manage their personal favorite links that appear throughout SharePoint (see "Use My Links to Manage Your Links" in Chapter 5). Additionally, the personal site is usually the place from which users can modify their personal details in the corporate directory.

A personal site usually has components that display to the users information that is targeted especially for them (see Figure 1.5). For example, it might have a component that shows their email, upcoming meetings from their calendar, as well as a list of documents they have recently worked on and tasks that are assigned to them.

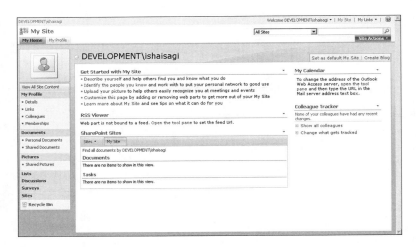

FIGURE 1.5
A personal site.

As mentioned earlier in this chapter in "What Is the Difference Between WSS and MOSS?," personal sites are available only with MOSS.

What Is a List?

A SharePoint *list* is a container for information, similar to a simple database or spreadsheet. A list is the most common way to manage information in a SharePoint site.

In a list, data is gathered in rows; each row is known as a *list item*. A list can have multiple columns, also known as *properties*, *fields*, or *metadata*. So a list item is a row of data filled in those columns.

For example, a list of contacts has the following columns (see Figure 1.6):

- ▶ First Name
- ▶ Last Name
- ▶ Company
- ▶ Phone

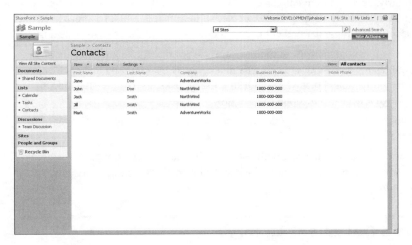

FIGURE 1.6
A contacts list, with sample data.

So a list item in that list is

- ▶ First Name: John
- ▶ Last Name: Doe
- ▶ Company: AdventureWorks
- ▶ Phone: 1800-000-000

More examples for lists are

- ▶ A list of links
- ▶ A list of tasks
- ▶ A list of discussions
- ▶ A list of announcements
- ▶ A list of events (calendar)

In SharePoint, users can create lists and columns, so lists can be extended to other uses, essentially anything that can be described by a group of columns.

The information in the lists can be displayed on pages in the SharePoint site. This way, if the site manager wants to display a list of links on the site's home page, that manager can add a web part (see "What Are Web Parts?" later in this chapter) that shows that list.

Lists can have separate security settings, so list managers can define who is allowed to add items to a list, who is allowed to edit items, who is allowed to read the items, and so on. Similarly, each list item can have its own security settings, so different list items can be visible to different people. For example, an item that is a link to a restricted site can have security settings that prevent users without access to that site from seeing it.

In some lists you can attach files to the list items—very much like attachments in email. Examples for the use of attachments in a contacts list could be that each contact has a picture and resume attached to it. Or in a list of tasks, users may attach documentation of what needs to be done to each task.

A list can hold different types of content, as explained under "What Is a Content Type?" later in this chapter.

For information on how to interact with lists, see Chapter 6, "Creating and Managing Files, List Items, and Forms in SharePoint," and Chapter 7, "Creating Lists and Document Libraries."

What Is a Document Library?

A *document library* is a special instance of a list in which every list item is a file (see Figure 1.7). Files can be Microsoft Office documents, Adobe Acrobat documents (PDF files), or any other type of file that the system administrator allows. In this book this feature is referred to as either a *document library* or simply a *library*.

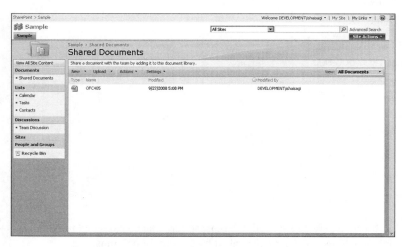

FIGURE 1.7
A sample document library with a single document.

Although most of the attributes of lists exist in document libraries and they are in many ways similar, the fact that each item in a document library is a file does make for some changes. For one, when creating a new item in a document library, you must either upload a file or create one. This process is explained in Chapter 6.

Additionally, unlike in lists, in document libraries each row can hold only one file; there isn't an option to attach more files to the row. Essentially, the file itself *is* the row. Also, because a file can be downloaded, visitors have different options available to them when browsing document libraries than the options they have with lists.

Because document libraries and lists have so much in common, throughout this book you will see many instructions that are valid to both. In those cases the text makes it clear that the instructions are for either one. For example, "Add a Column to a List or Document Library" in Chapter 7 covers both document libraries and lists because the principle of how to create them is the same.

What Is a Form Library?

A *form library* is much like a document library, but it is supposed to host only Microsoft InfoPath forms. Microsoft InfoPath is electronic form creation software that integrates with SharePoint. Forms created with InfoPath can be published to SharePoint form libraries, and users can then fill out these forms.

If your company uses InfoPath to create forms, you might need to learn how to use form libraries, which are explained in Chapter 3, "Solutions Regarding Files, Documents, List Items, and Forms."

What Is a Picture Library?

A *picture library* is much like a document library, but it is supposed to host only images. A picture library has special views (see "What Is a View?," next) that show the images as thumbnails or as a slide show (film strip).

What Is a View?

Views allow the list manager to create different ways for you to see the information in a list or library. Different views may show different columns and have different sorting, filtering, grouping, and style.

In SharePoint, views can be either public or private. The public views are created by the list's or library's managers, and are available for anyone to use. The private views are created by users, and are used only by the users who created them. You might have the permissions to create a private view and customize it to show the information that you usually need to find the items or files that you usually work with.

Chapter 8, "Creating List Views," covers creating views in more detail, and Chapter 3 covers how to switch between views.

There are several types of views in SharePoint. Most of the views that you will see are the standard tabular views that resemble printed worksheets; they have column headers and values in rows but do not allow you to edit the data directly. However, some special view styles show the information in the list in different ways, including a datasheet view, which allows you to directly edit the data, or a calendar view, which shows the items as part of a calendar.

A calendar view shows the items in the list based on dates that are set on the items. Other types of views include the Gantt view and the datasheet view. The Gantt view is similar to the calendar view (it shows information based on dates in the list items' properties), and the datasheet view is a Microsoft Excel–like view that allows copying and pasting data into the list or library. These types of views are covered in detail in Chapter 8.

Consider this example of a possible difference between two views: One view for an announcement list might show the title of the announcement and the date that the announcement was changed, whereas a different view of the same list might show the body of the announcement and the date on which it will expire.

Figures 1.8 and 1.9 show the two different views.

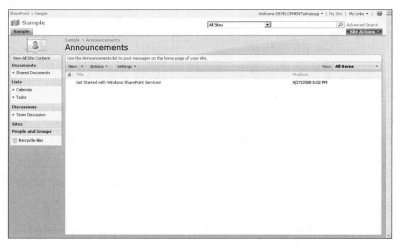

FIGURE 1.8
An announcement list, with a view that shows the Title and Modified Date columns.

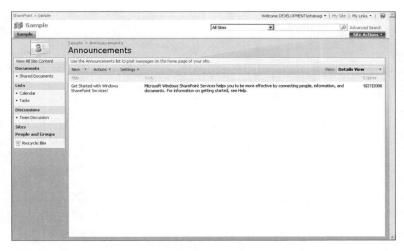

FIGURE 1.9
An announcement list, with a view that shows the Title, Body, and Expires columns.

Additionally, if you have multiple announcements, different views may sort the announcements differently. One might sort by the title of the announcement (see Figure 1.10), whereas another sorts by the modification date of the announcement (see Figure 1.11).

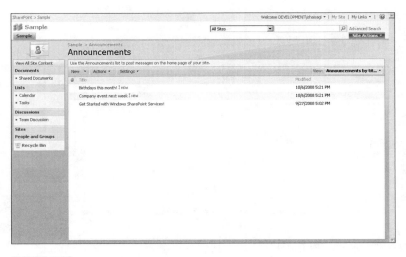

FIGURE 1.10
The announcement list, with a view that sorts by title.

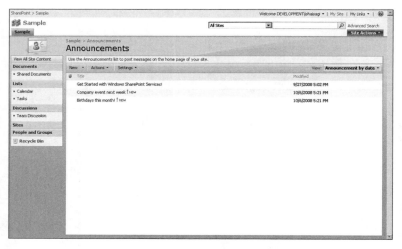

FIGURE 1.11
The announcement list, with a view that sorts by the creation date (new announcements last).

Some views change the style with which the items are displayed. For example, Figure 1.12 shows the announcement list with a different style, called *boxed style*.

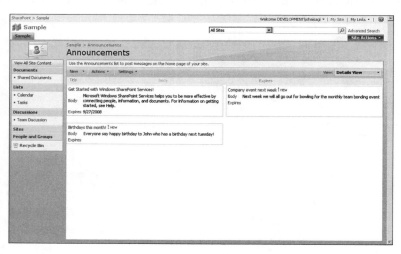

FIGURE 1.12
The announcement list with the boxed style.

A common view for announcements lists has a filter applied to it—to show only items that have not expired. Other views can be configured not to have that filter. So if you are viewing a list and the item you're looking for is not showing, consider the possibility that the current view is configured to filter that item.

Finally, some views might display the data grouped by one column. This display enables you to view the groups and expand the group you are interested in to see the items within that group. For example, in a contacts list, a view might be set up to group the contacts by their company name; this way, you can expand the view for a specific company (see Figure 1.13).

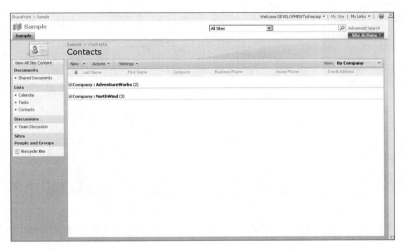

FIGURE 1.13
A contacts list, grouped by company.

To see the items in a group, click the plus (+) sign next to the group name or on the group field's name that shows up as a link (in this example, it is the Company link). This expands the group, showing you the items that belong to that group (see Figure 1.14).

FIGURE 1.14
A contacts list, grouped by company with the AdventureWorks company expanded.

SharePoint supports up to two grouping levels; for example, by country and then by company (see Figure 1.15).

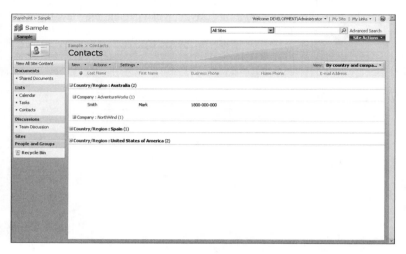

FIGURE 1.15
A contacts list, grouped by country and then by company with Australia and AdventureWorks expanded.

Picture libraries have their own special views that show the pictures that are in the library as either thumbnails (small representations of the picture) or a "film strip" of the pictures.

Some views support *paging*. Paging is a common way to show large amounts of data in websites without overloading the page. Using paging, the data in the list or library is split into pages, each page showing only a certain number of the items (see Figures 1.16 and 1.17). The user can then navigate back and forth between the pages. If you have a document library with a thousand documents, for example, showing all the documents to the users at once can cause the page loading time to be quite slow, and it can be hard for the users to find the document they are looking for.

The numbers indicate what documents are shown; in this case, it is the first 100 documents.
Use the page control to navigate between pages.
Shared Documents
1 - 100
without folders

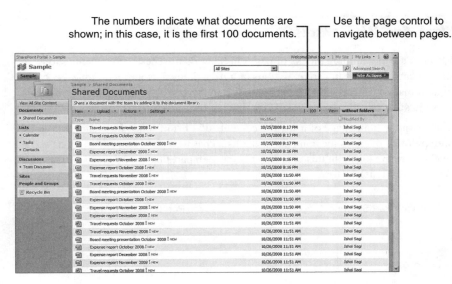

FIGURE 1.16
The first page view of a document library with a lot of documents, showing the first 100 documents.

This page shows the documents from 101 to 200.
Shared Documents
101 - 200
without folders
You can use the control to navigate to the next or previous page.

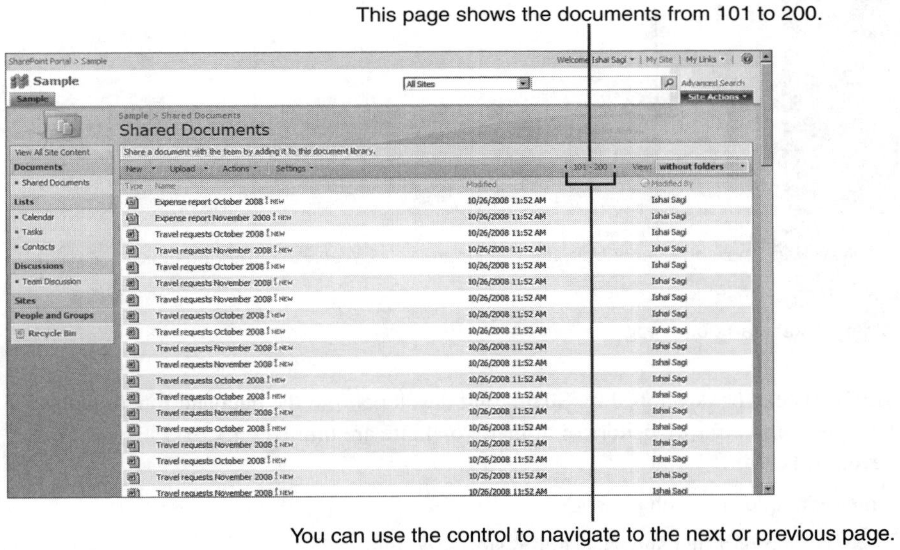

FIGURE 1.17
The second page of the view shows the next 100 documents.

What Are Web Parts?

Web parts are the building blocks of pages in SharePoint. These components show data and can be placed in certain regions of a page, known as *web part zones*. A page can hold many web parts, in different zones or in the same zone; they may be one under the other in some zones or side by side in other zones.

To show on the home page of a site the contents of a list of links, for example, you use a web part that displays the contents of the list. That web part is one that you have already seen previously in this chapter: it is the web part that shows views of lists and libraries (see Figure 1.18).

A Web Part Showing Announcements   A Web Part Showing a Picture

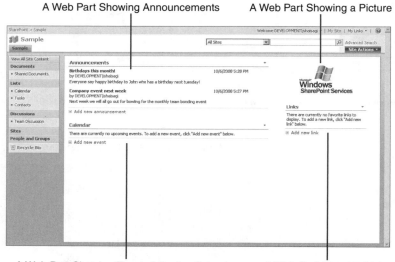

A Web Part Showing Events from the Calendar   A Web Part Showing Links

FIGURE 1.18
Different web parts on a page.

Web parts can be developed by SharePoint developers, so the data and functionality that web parts offer to visitors of a SharePoint site are limited only by what can be developed.

Other examples for web parts are

- ► A web part that shows search results (see Figure 1.19)
- ► A web part that shows a picture
- ► A web part that shows the users of a site
- ► A web part that shows the content of a site (see Figure 1.20)

A Web Part Showing Statistics on the Search Results

A Web Part Showing Actions on the Search Results

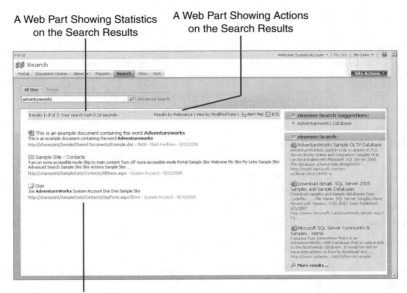

A Search Results Web Part

FIGURE 1.19
Search-related web parts.

The table of contents web part shows the content of the current site.

FIGURE 1.20
Content-related web parts.

It is important to remember that although web parts are a part of SharePoint, they can show information that is from outside SharePoint. For example, a special web part may be developed to show information from a corporate application for timesheets or project management. The web part might even offer interaction with the data, allowing users to modify data in the corporate application, but the data itself is not in SharePoint. However, such web parts usually must be developed, and most of the web parts that come with SharePoint out of the box are used to display data that is stored in SharePoint.

Although web parts may be important building blocks for a SharePoint page, as mentioned previously, other components make the pages what they are. Not everything you see on a SharePoint page is a web part, but identifying web parts is usually easy—especially if you have the permissions to edit a page, in which case the page editor shows you the web parts that are on the page, with the options to remove them or move them around, as well as add additional ones.

You learn to use web parts in Chapter 9, "Authoring Pages."

What Are Alerts?

Alerts notify users by email of changes in lists and libraries or even specific documents or list items.

SharePoint has a built-in alert mechanism that enables users to register for the different kinds of alerts. Basically, the users select the piece of content they want to be alerted on and request that SharePoint send them an email when that content changes.

A popular use of alerts is when a document library is supposed to have documents about a specific topic that you are interested in. You might want to know immediately when a new document has been added to that document library (see Figure 1.21). Another example is a policy document for which you want to know when changes occur because it is relevant to you (for example, the corporate travel policy is important to people who travel a lot). Alerts allow you to request to be notified when changes like that occur.

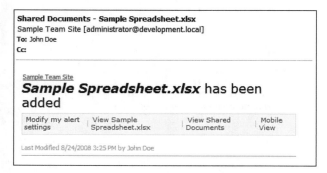

FIGURE 1.21
An alert email that is sent when a document has been added to a library.

What Is a Site Column?

A *site column* is a column for a list or document library that can be used in all lists or document libraries in the site in which it is created and in the subsites for that site.

This feature allows the site manager to define a specific column of data once and manage it from a central location instead of creating that column many times in many lists and libraries. Additionally, content types can use only site columns (unlike lists and libraries where columns can be created separately).

Using site columns is covered in Chapter 7, "Creating Lists and Document Libraries," and Chapter 13, "Customizing a SharePoint Site."

What Is a Content Type?

As mentioned earlier, lists and document libraries can store different kinds of content. These are known as *content types*, which the site manager can create and manage in a site. These content types are then available in that site and in all the sites under it. The different types of content may have different site columns and/or different settings, such as policies and workflows, associated with them.

Content types can use only site columns for column definitions. This means that to create a content type, you must choose what site columns should be included in that content type.

A simple example of a content type would be a contact list that stores two types of contacts: an *Internal Contact* and an *External Contact*. The Internal Contact content type is used for a contact inside the company—and as such does not need the Company property—because all internal contacts are from the same company. However, the External Contact content type does require the Company property because every contact might be from a different company. Hence, you have two different column requirements in the same list.

Another common example for the use of content types is in a document library, where you store many different types of documents (see Figure 1.22). Some documents are presentations and some are financial reports, whereas others are user guides and product whitepapers. The differences between these content types are possibly more than just different columns; the content types might also specify different templates that users should use when creating documents of these types. For example, when creating a presentation, a user should use a Microsoft PowerPoint template. When creating a financial report, a user gets a specific Microsoft Excel workbook as a template to start from. User guides might be from a certain Microsoft Word template, while product whitepapers are PDF documents.

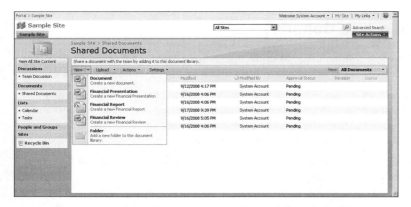

FIGURE 1.22
Choosing a content type when creating a new document in a document library.

Content types can be created in each site, and every subsite under that site can then use the content type. The subsites can either use the content type as it is defined in the parent site or create their own content types.

Content types are hierarchical, which means they can inherit from other content types. To use the example mentioned previously, the External Contact and Internal Contact content types can both inherit from the Contact content type. This way, if changes are made to the Contact content type (for example, if the property Birthdate is added), both child content types can get the update (depending on whether the person who applied the update to the Contact content type chose to apply the update to content types that inherit from that content type).

Because the content type of an item or file says a lot about what the item actually is, it is a very important piece of data that is associated with an item. This makes it very important that authors (people adding information to SharePoint) choose the right content type when creating data in SharePoint. However, sometimes content types are not used, and a list can just use the basic content type Item or a library will use the content type Document and add columns to the list itself, not impacting the content type itself. This means that all the columns are defined in the list or library and are added to all the items or files in it.

Content types use site columns to define the properties that the files or list items of that content type will have. Site columns are explained later in this chapter.

Chapter 7 shows how to add and remove a content type to a list or document library.

What Are Versions?

Document libraries and lists in SharePoint have an option to track versions. This option stores old versions of files or items each time a change is made. For example, if a user uploads a document, and then another user edits the document and saves it, SharePoint will save the original document as a version of the file. Later, users can look at the version history of the file and choose to open a specific version or restore it (make that version the current one).

SharePoint supports two types of versioning (see Figure 1.23). In one, each change is regarded as a major change, and the version numbers go from 1 (the first time a document was uploaded) to 2 (after the first change), and then 3 and 4 and so on. In the second type, each change is regarded as a minor change unless the user specifies that it is a major one. The version numbers go from 0.1 (the first time a document was uploaded) to 0.2 (the first change) and so on, until a user selects the option to perform a major change. Then the version number changes to 1.0, and subsequent changes will raise it to 1.1, 1.2, and so on.

For information about how to work with versions, see Chapters 3 and 7.

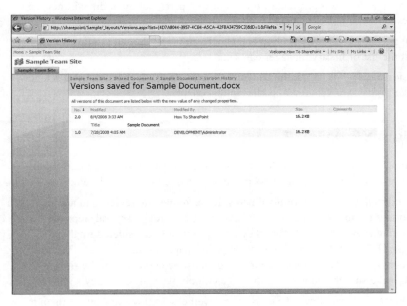

FIGURE 1.23
Viewing the lists of versions for a document.

What Does Check-In/Check-Out Mean?

Check-in and *check-out* are common terms in many document management systems, including SharePoint. The purpose is to prevent conflicts in an environment where multiple people might want to edit the same piece of content (in SharePoint, that is list items or files) at the same time. By checking out an item or a file, a user can prevent others from editing that content, and by checking in, the user can allow others to edit the content without the need to worry about overriding changes that others have made.

The term *check-in* describes the process of adding a new or modified item or file to a document library or a list to replace the previous version. The term *check-out* describes the process of getting a version of a document or list item in a list or library.

Usually when an item or a file is checked out to a user, that user can then work on that item or file, while other users cannot. Other users must wait for the user to check the item or file back in (perform a check-in) before they can edit that item or file. While the item or file is checked out, other users usually can see only the last version that was checked in—not seeing the changes made to the file by the user who has it currently checked out.

It is important to know that pages in SharePoint can also be in document libraries (and often are). This means that they too can be checked out and in, allowing page editors to change a page (for example, add or remove a web part), but the users will not see the changes until that editor is happy with the changes and checks the page in.

SharePoint does not require a check in and check out on all lists and libraries; that is a setting that the list or library manager can set.

When versioning is activated on the document library or list, a check-in creates a new version. See "What Are Versions?" earlier in this chapter.

What Is a Workflow?

In SharePoint a *workflow* is a series of steps—some automatic, some manual—that must be performed as part of a business process for a document or list item.

The most common workflows for documents, for example, are review and approval. Some important documents, such as contracts, must go through several steps of approval from different people before they can be officially considered final and published (see Figure 1.24). Another example is for pages in the site itself. In some SharePoint environments, each change to a page must be approved by the site's manager to make sure the contents of the page comply with the company's policies.

The SharePoint platform allows developers to develop workflows and attach them to documents or list items. As an end user, you might be expected to interact with the workflow—either approving documents or items, or to trigger a workflow to start it, or sometimes to stop it.

Chapter 11, "Workflows," covers the common tasks that you should know about workflows.

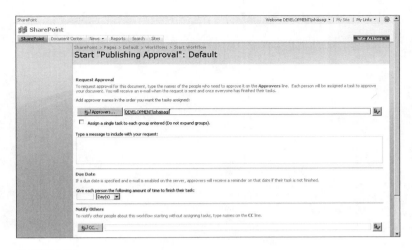

FIGURE 1.24
Starting an approval workflow to publish a page.

CHAPTER 2

Finding Your Way Around a SharePoint Site

This chapter shows you how to get around a SharePoint site, with some common tasks that you might want to do in every SharePoint site that you use. It explains the different navigation options in SharePoint sites and how to log on to a SharePoint site in the first place.

Get to a SharePoint Site

Scenario/Problem: You want to get to a SharePoint site and open it.

Solution: Getting to a SharePoint site depends on the location of that site. Most often, your system administrator gives you the location. Your company might have several sites, and the administrators should supply you with links to the sites you should be aware of.

Possible examples of such links are http://portal or http://home or http://*companyname*. This book uses http://sharepoint as the sample link.

NOTE SharePoint sites can have subsites, so if there is a subsite called "sample," the path to the site would be http://sharepoint/sample.

To get to the site itself, just open the link supplied to you in an Internet browser such as Internet Explorer, Firefox, or other browsers.

Depending on the setup of the site itself or the settings in your browser, you might or might not be prompted for a password. Because SharePoint is often configured to automatically identify you, it is very likely that you will not be prompted, and SharePoint will log you on with the username and password you used when you logged on to your computer. If you are prompted, fill in the username and password that your administrator advised you to use (see Figure 2.1).

FIGURE 2.1
Prompt for credentials when connecting to SharePoint.

If, for some reason, you do not have permissions to the SharePoint site you are trying to open, SharePoint displays an Access Denied page, telling you that you don't have permissions (see Figure 2.2). This page also enables you to sign in as a different user. By clicking that link, you are prompted for a username and password, which is used to log you on to the site again.

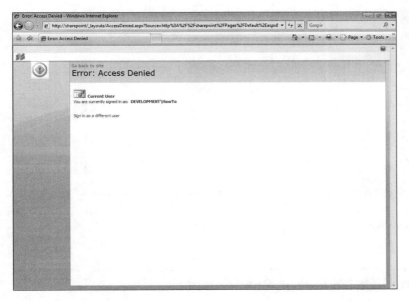

FIGURE 2.2
The Access Denied screen.

When you are logged on, the SharePoint site opens. Different SharePoint sites look different from one another, depending on the way the site manager set up the site. Figure 2.3 shows how such a site might look.

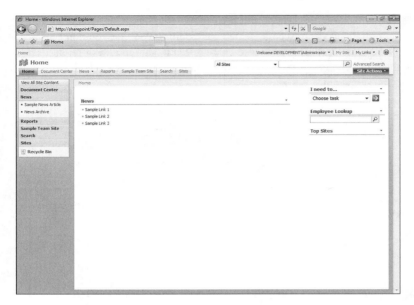

FIGURE 2.3
A sample SharePoint site.

Log On with Different Credentials

Scenario/Problem: Sometimes when you are viewing a SharePoint site, you want to log on as a different user. This might be required if you are logged on to the computer with one account but want to browse the SharePoint site as a different user.

Solution: After you have logged on to a SharePoint site, you might want to switch to a different user. You do so by clicking the Welcome [*your name*] link at the top of the page to open a drop-down menu and selecting Sign In as a Different User from the options (see Figure 2.4). After clicking that option, you are prompted for your username and password, as if you have not logged on to SharePoint before.

If you change your mind and want to log on again with the username and password that you used to log on to your machine, you can either type in the username and password or close the browser and open the site again.

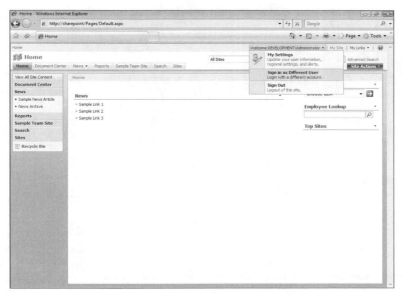

FIGURE 2.4
Signing in as a different user.

Change My Regional Settings

Scenario/Problem: While working in an environment that has sites from all over the world, you want to define in a specific site that you want the date formatting to appear in the way you are used to (have the month before or after the day in a date, for example) and to show time data in your time zone, and not in the time zone for which the site manager set it. For example, when viewing a list of events, you might see an event scheduled to start at 9:00 in the morning, but if the site was created by someone in Japan and you are in America, you need to know if that time is based on the time zone in Japan or in your time zone.

Solution: To set the date formatting, set your regional settings for the site. Depending on the configuration of the site, you might be able to define in that site your own regional settings, which would change how the site is presented to you without affecting anyone else who is viewing the site.

Changing the regional settings lets you define the way you want dates and number formats shown to you, the default sort order used for you in the site when you are viewing lists, the calendar format you want to see, and the way you define your workweek days.

Figures 2.5 and 2.6 show a calendar list of events with two different regional settings. Australian settings are shown in Figure 2.5.

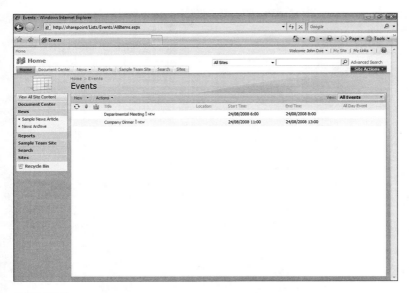

FIGURE 2.5
A list viewed using the Australian regional settings. Notice how the start and end time show the day before the month.

Figure 2.6 shows the American settings.

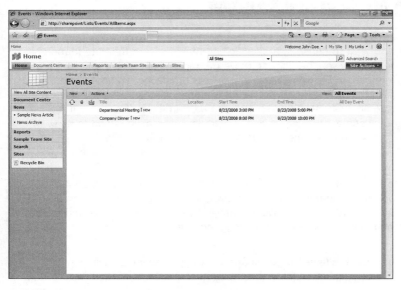

FIGURE 2.6
A list viewed using the American regional settings. Notice how the start and end time show the month before the day and how the times are different because of a different time zone setting.

To achieve this, click the Welcome [*your name*] link at the top of the page to open a drop-down menu and select My Settings, as shown in Figure 2.7.

FIGURE 2.7
Selecting your own settings.

Selecting this option opens a page showing your details as they are saved in the system. Click My Regional Settings, as shown in Figure 2.8.

Selecting this option opens the Regional Settings configuration screen (see Figure 2.9). In this screen you can choose to customize the regional settings for you by clearing the Always Follow Web Settings check box. This means that the content of the site will be displayed using different settings from the ones that are defined for the site by the site manager. If you select this option, the page will allow you to define the following settings:

▶ **Locale:** Sets the formats of dates, numbers, and sorting order.

▶ **Time Zone:** Sets your time zone so that times (for example, time for a meeting) will be displayed to you in your time zone.

▶ **Set Your Calendar:** Allows you to select a different calendar format (for example, the Jewish or Arabic calendars) to be displayed instead of the default one.

▶ **Alternate Calendar:** Allows you to select an alternative calendar format that will be displayed in addition to the default one.

▶ **Define Your Work Week:** Allows you to select your work week and working hours (which will change how calendars are displayed to you).

▶ **Time Format:** Allows you to select whether the time format should be 12-hour format (01:00 PM) or 24-hour format (13:00).

FIGURE 2.8
Changing the regional settings.

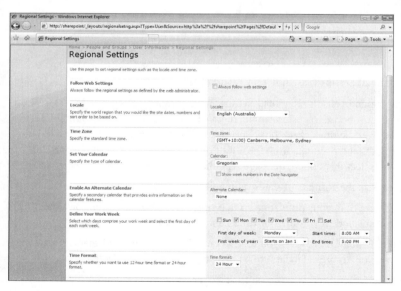

FIGURE 2.9
Changing settings on the Regional Settings screen.

Navigate Through a SharePoint Site

Scenario/Problem: You want to find what information is available in a SharePoint site.

Solution: The following section explains the different mechanisms that help you navigate through a site. A standard SharePoint site has two navigational aids that help you find your way in the site. These navigation bars are usually at the top and left sides of the screen. The site manager can change them to show different links to different parts of the site, and they should be your primary source of information to what you can view in the site.

Figure 2.10 shows a sample site with both navigation bars configured to show the same information.

The Top Navigation Bar

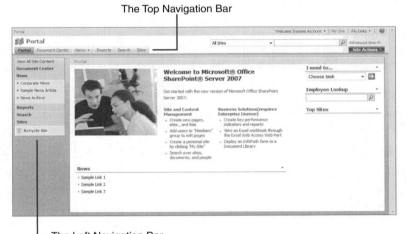

The Left Navigation Bar

FIGURE 2.10
A sample site with two navigation bars.

As you can see in the image, both navigation bars show links to subsites that exist under the current site and some of the actual content in one of those sites (the News site has two news items in it: Sample News Article and News Archive, which are pages in the News site). The top navigation bar exposes those articles as flyouts that show only when you hover the mouse cursor over the News menu item (see Figure 2.11).

FIGURE 2.11
Accessing fly-out menus in the top navigation bar.

To navigate to a subsite, you can click the links to that subsite in either navigation bar. Most likely (depending on how your administrator set up the navigation), the subsites show the same top navigation bar but a different left navigation bar, as shown in Figure 2.12.

The Document Center tab is highlighted because that is the current subsite you are watching.

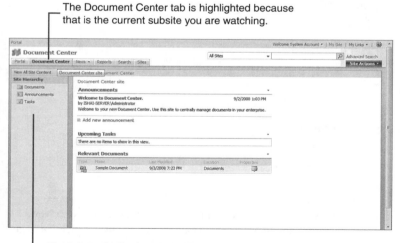

The left navigation bar shows items in the current site.

FIGURE 2.12
The left navigation bar might show different navigation links than the top navigation bar.

However, the administrator can choose that a subsite will display the same left navigation bar as the top site. This setup makes it look as if you are still in the same site, except for the fact that the top navigation bar highlights the current site you are on, as shown in Figure 2.13.

In the News subsite, the navigation menus are the same as in the root site but highlight that you are currently in the News site.

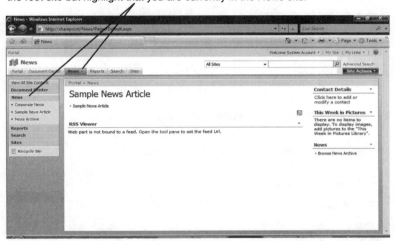

FIGURE 2.13
The left and top navigation bars might show the same navigation links.

Use the Left Navigation Bar

The quick launch left navigation bar, also known as *Current navigation*, is usually used to show content that exists in the current site and sometimes content from subsites, sites that exist under the current site (see Figure 2.14). The content is usually (but not always) lists and libraries, and is (usually) grouped so that document libraries are shown under a Documents header, lists under a Lists header, discussions under a Discussions header, and so on.

The left navigation bar highlights where you are in the navigation, but only when you are on a page that is shown in the navigation (see Figure 2.15).

This navigation bar is meant to be used as a "quick launch" bar—a useful list of links in the current site and sometimes the sites under it. It might even contain links to content that isn't in SharePoint—for example, an Internet site.

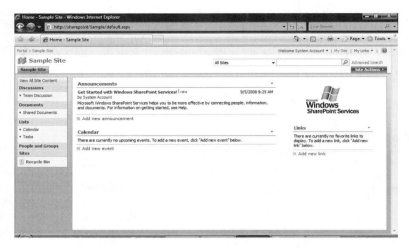

FIGURE 2.14
A site with a left navigation bar showing links to content in the current site.

The parent of the current site is highlighted on the top navigation bar.

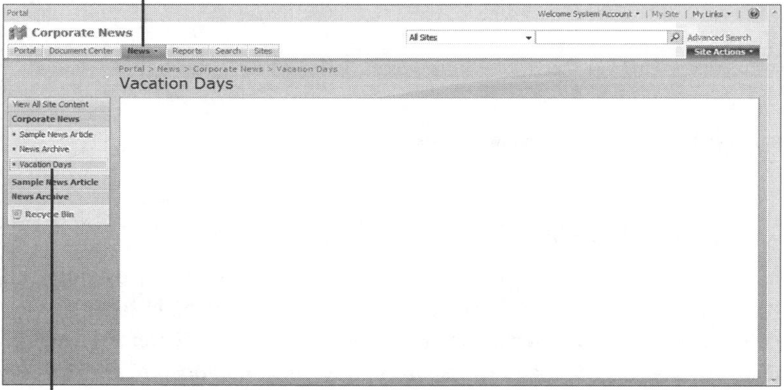

The current page is highlighted in the left navigation bar.

FIGURE 2.15
A site with a left navigation bar highlighting the current page.

TIP Some sites do not have a left navigation bar. If that is the case, you must rely on the information on the page to find your way in the site.

Use the Top Navigation Bar

The top navigation bar, also known as *Global navigation*, is usually used to show links to sites that are at the top level of the site hierarchy. This feature enables you to quickly see what important sites are available globally that the site administrator wants you to see.

This menu bar can support *flyout* menus. These menus become visible when you hover the mouse cursor over the parent menu items. You can usually know when a menu has flyout menus as children: it is marked with a triangle pointing to the direction in which the flyout menu will open.

In Figure 2.16, you can see a two-level flyout menu. The first level shows that under the News site, there is another site called Corporate News and also two articles. The second level (on the right of the first level) shows that there are three articles under the Corporate News site.

The arrow pointing down signifies that there is a flyout menu that will open down from the News link.

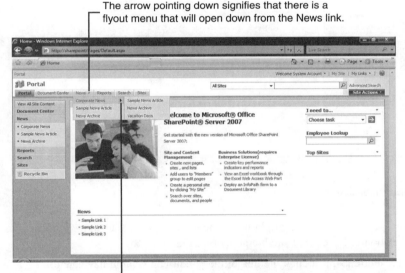

The arrow pointing right signifies that if you hover the mouse cursor on Corporate News, you will see a flyout menu to the right.

FIGURE 2.16
Opening the flyout menus using the top navigation bar.

TIP You can customize the top navigation bar to show many levels of sites and sometimes other links. If you see the small triangles or arrows, hover the mouse cursor over them to find out what navigation item is under them.

Use the Breadcrumbs

Breadcrumbs are a common mechanism to navigate in any website. They show you where you are in the site and what parents this site has so that you can go up the hierarchy to any of the parents easily and quickly.

In SharePoint, there are two built-in breadcrumbs in each page: global and local. The global breadcrumbs are usually at the top left of the screen and track where you are when switching between sites that do not share the same navigation bars (see Figure 2.17).

┌─ The global breadcrumbs show that Sample Site is under Portal.

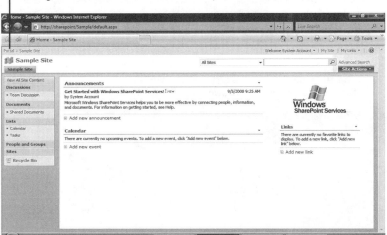

FIGURE 2.17
Using the global breadcrumbs.

The local breadcrumbs are usually right under the top navigation and show you where you are in relation to the current site hierarchy (see Figure 2.18).

To use the breadcrumbs, just click the link of the parent you want to navigate to.

> **TIP** When you are in a document library that has folders, using breadcrumbs is the best way to go back to the parent folder of the one where you are currently working.

The local breadcrumbs show that you are in the article Vacation Days,
which is under Corporate News, under News, under Portal.

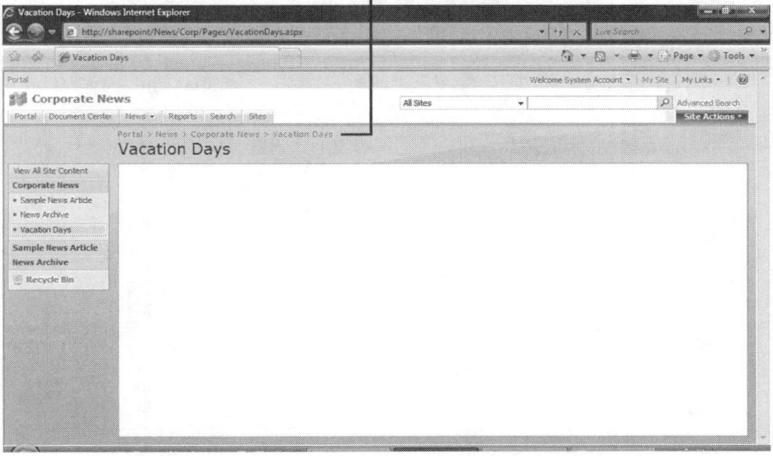

FIGURE 2.18
Using the local breadcrumbs.

Determine Whether a Site Is WSS or MOSS

There is no way to actually know whether a site is hosted on a server that has
Microsoft Office SharePoint Server (MOSS) installed by just looking at it. As you
learned in the explanation of Windows SharePoint Services (WSS) and MOSS, the
differences are mostly behind the scenes and are not visible to users. Customizations
that your company might have developed may cause a WSS site to look as if it has
some extensions that come with MOSS or might cause a MOSS site to look simpler—
by removing the MOSS-specific links that would help you identify a site as MOSS.

There are two things you can look for in any SharePoint site and be fairly sure that
your site is MOSS or WSS. The first is to look for the My Site link at the top of the
screen. If you have that link, it means you are viewing a site that is running on a server
with MOSS (see Figure 2.19). Not having the link does not necessarily mean that the
site does not have MOSS because the administrator can choose to disable that functionality.

The second way you can tell is by looking for the Advanced Search link. WSS sites
(unless customized) do not have that link, so having that link means you probably are
viewing a site that is running on a server with MOSS (see Figure 2.20). Another
related way to test this is to open the search screen (perform a search) and see whether
you have the option from that screen to switch to advanced search.

The My Site link appears only on sites that have MOSS installed.

FIGURE 2.19
Viewing a MOSS site with the My Site link.

The Advanced Search option appears only on MOSS sites.
The My Site link appears only on MOSS sites.

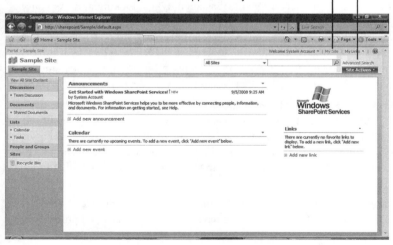

FIGURE 2.20
Viewing a MOSS site with the Advanced Search link.

CHAPTER 3

Solutions Regarding Files, Documents, List Items, and Forms

SharePoint is most commonly used to store information in the form of either list items or files, which can be documents, forms, or any other type of file.

This chapter explains how to perform common tasks in SharePoint; for example, it explains how to create and view list items, files, and their properties, as well as set up alerts that let you know when there are new files or list items or when specific files or list items have been modified. Most importantly, this chapter covers how to switch between list views, which allow you to see the content in a list in various ways, thus enabling you to find the content you are looking for more easily.

If you are looking for more author-oriented tasks, such as uploading files or creating new list items, skip to Chapter 6, "Creating and Managing Files, List Items, and Forms in SharePoint," which covers these topics.

See What Lists and Document Libraries Are in a Site

Scenario/Problem: When in a SharePoint site, you often want to see what is beyond the home page of the site—what document libraries are there to store information, what lists and surveys.

Solution: There are several ways to see the lists and document libraries available in a site. The following sections demonstrate how you can use these various ways to view the content in the site.

Direct Links in the Left Navigation Bar

Site managers can use the left navigation bar to show various links in different categories. Document libraries are usually shown under the Documents header, and lists are usually under the Lists header, as shown in Figure 3.1.

View All Lists and Libraries

Not all the document libraries and lists are shown in the navigation bar. Whether they are shown depends on how the site administrator set it up.

To see all the libraries and lists available, use the View All Site Content link in the navigation bar. This link directs you to a page with all the content in the site. The document libraries are displayed under the Document Libraries header, and the lists are displayed below the Lists header, as shown in Figure 3.2.

A Link to a Library of Documents in the Navigation
A Link to a List of Events in the Navigation

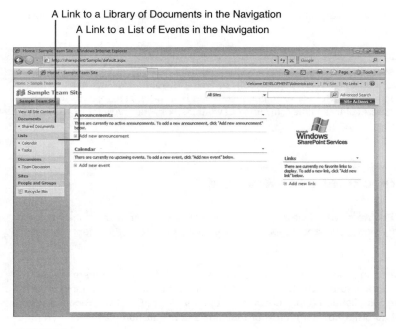

FIGURE 3.1
The left navigation bar with document libraries and lists.

Document libraries appear here as links.

Lists appear here as links.

FIGURE 3.2
The page shows all the contents of the site.

Click the link to the document library to view the documents in it or the link to a list to see the list items in it.

> **TIP** If the site has been customized and the View All Site Content link isn't on the page, you can get to the same page directly by typing **_layouts/viewlsts.aspx** at the end of the path to the site. For example, if your site is at http://sharepoint/sample, type **http://sharepoint/sample/_layouts/viewlsts.aspx** in your browser to get to the all content page.

Open a Document for Reading

> **Scenario/Problem:** When viewing a document library, either in the home page or in a library view, you want to open a certain document to see its contents.

Solution: When in a document library, just click the link to the document you are interested in (see Figure 3.3). The document opens either in a new window or in the associated application (Word documents open in Word, Excel workbooks open in Excel, and so on), depending on your machine's configuration.

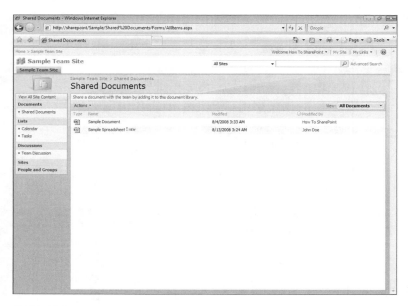

FIGURE 3.3
Opening a document in the document library.

Also, depending on the installed applications on your machine and on the level of permissions you have, you might be prompted with a choice of how to open the file (see Figure 3.4). To read, choose Read Only and click OK.

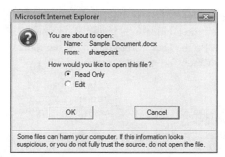

FIGURE 3.4
Selecting how to open the file.

View Properties of a Document

Scenario/Problem: When viewing a document library in either a web part on the home page or in one of the list views of that library, you want to see more details about a document before choosing what to do with it. These details might include who wrote the document, its subject, and maybe additional pieces of metadata describing the document—for example, the client it was written for or the date it expires.

Solution: To view the metadata of a particular file, move your mouse cursor over the link to the document. An option to open a drop-down appears (see Figure 3.5).

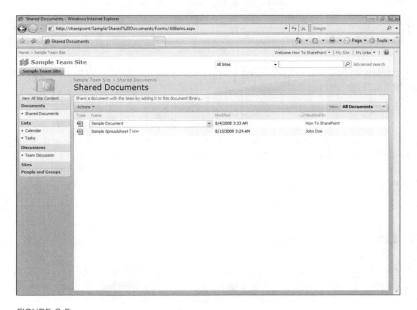

FIGURE 3.5
A drop-down menu becomes available when you move the mouse over the filename.

If you click the drop-down arrow, a menu opens. The choices in the menu are different based on the permissions you have on the file, on the applications installed on your computer, and the applications installed in SharePoint. Therefore, you might see more or fewer options than the ones in Figure 3.6, and each file may present you with a different menu.

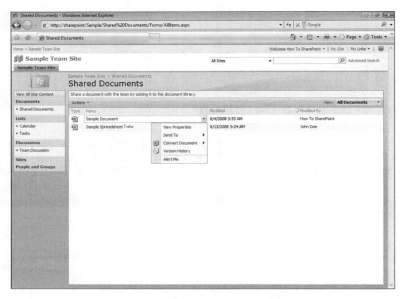

FIGURE 3.6
Opening the drop-down menu.

Click View Properties to open the properties page. You then see all the properties that the document has.

TIP When you set properties on a file, the properties are copied into the file itself. And when you upload a file with properties to a document library that has properties with the same names, they are copied back. This means that if you download a file and then upload it to a different document library with the same properties, the data of the properties is retained.

Send a Link to a File by Email

Scenario/Problem: When viewing a document library, you want to select a single file in that library and send a link to it to one of your colleagues via email.

Solution: Similar to the first step in "View Properties of a Document," open the drop-down menu. Select Send To, E-mail a Link (see Figure 3.7).

FIGURE 3.7
Selecting the options to send a link via email.

Your default email application should open with a new message containing a link to the document.

View Past Versions of Documents

Scenario/Problem: Some document libraries support versioning, which means that every time a file in the library changes, the old version is stored. Sometimes you want to view an old version of a document without restoring it to the current version.

Solution: To view the past versions of a specific document, open the drop-down menu on the document and pick Version History from the options (see Figure 3.8).

The version history list opens, showing past versions of the document (see Figure 3.9).

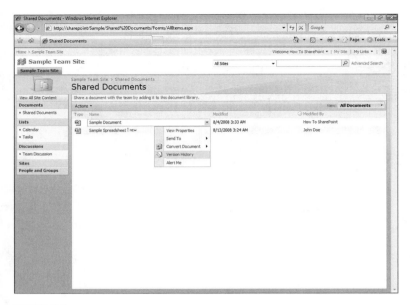

FIGURE 3.8
Selecting to view the list of past versions of a document.

The Second (and Final) Version of the Document

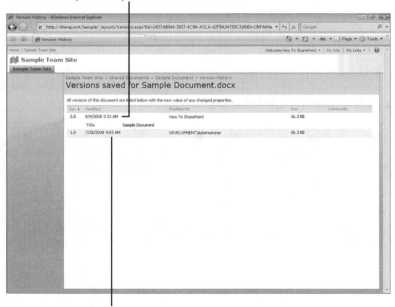

The First Version of the Document

FIGURE 3.9
Viewing the different versions of a document.

The documents are shown as dates, representing the date the version was created. Hovering the mouse cursor over one of these dates allows you to open a menu for the document; from this menu, you can choose to view the version.

View Properties of a List Item

Scenario/Problem: When viewing a list in either a web part on the home page or in one of the list views of that list, you want to see more details about a list item because the web parts or the list views do not show all the columns defined in the list. For example, a web part or a list view showing a contact list item might show only the contact's first and last names, and you want to see more details about the contact, such as the address, phone number, and more.

Solution: When viewing in a web part or list view, you either click the title of the list item to see its details, or open the drop-down menu and choose View Item (similar to viewing a document's properties), as shown in Figure 3.10.

FIGURE 3.10
The drop-down menu for a list item showing actions you can perform, including View Item.

Selecting this option opens a page with the metadata of the list item—all its properties.

View a Microsoft InfoPath Form

Scenario/Problem: As explained in Chapter 1, "About Microsoft SharePoint 2007," form libraries are used to host Microsoft InfoPath forms. In many cases you want to open one of the forms in a form library to view its contents.

Solution: The form libraries behave much the same as document libraries, and viewing a Microsoft InfoPath form that is in a form library is very much like opening a document for reading: Just click the link that is the form name (see Figure 3.11).

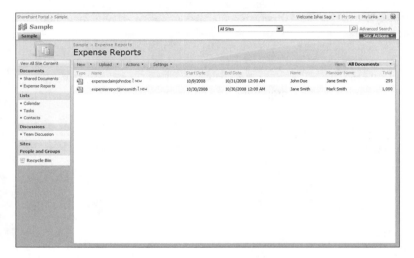

FIGURE 3.11
A form library with two forms. Click the name of the form to open it.

TIP Some forms are configured to allow the data in the form to be displayed as a column in the form library. This configuration enables you to preview the data in the form without opening it and can also help you find the specific form you are after more easily. In Figure 3.11, you can see that certain data from the form is displayed, such as the total of the expense claim, as well as the start and end dates for the expense claims.

If the site you are using has Microsoft Office SharePoint Server (MOSS) installed, or if the form or form library has not been configured to make forms open in the browser, clicking a form opens it using Microsoft InfoPath on your computer.

If the site uses MOSS, and the form and form library are both configured to show the form in the browser, clicking the form opens it using the browser interface.

To close the form and go back to the form library, either close the Microsoft InfoPath application (if the form was opened with the application) or click the Close link on the top of the form if it was opened in the browser.

Change Sorting and Filtering in a List or Library

Scenario/Problem: When you're working in a large document library or list, finding the piece of information you are looking for can be tricky. To help you find what you are after, you want to sort a specific column differently from its default sorting order or filter a column on a specific value. For example, in a document library, you want to sort the documents based on the date they were changed to see the last one that was changed, or in a contacts list, you want to filter the last name column to display only people with the last name Doe.

Solution: When you're viewing a list or document library, there are several ways to change the view to find the specific item or document you are after.

TIP The changes you make are not permanent; only you will see them. When you close the browser and navigate to the list again, the default sort order and filters that the list manager has defined are applied again.

To learn how to save a sort order or filter, see Chapter 8, "Creating List Views."

Sort

To sort a list view on a specific field, click the heading for that field. Clicking that field header causes the list to be sorted based on that field, either in an ascending or descending order. A small arrow appears to signify the sort order. Using this mechanism, you can sort based on only one field at a time.

Another way to define the sort order is to open the column's drop-down menu and click the sort order you want (see Figure 3.12).

Filter

To filter on a column, move your mouse cursor over the heading for that column, which causes a drop-down menu to appear. Click the drop-down menu and choose the filter value from the list (see Figure 3.13).

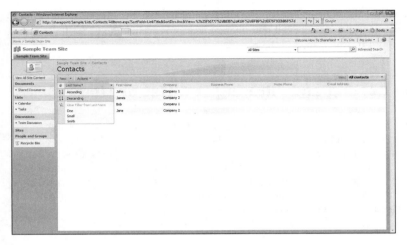

FIGURE 3.12
Choosing the sort order from the drop-down menu.

FIGURE 3.13
Choosing the filter value from the drop-down menu.

Switch List Views in Lists and Libraries

Scenario/Problem: Most lists and libraries have different list views showing different columns and applying different sort orders, filters, and styles. You want to switch to a different list view to find information more easily in the list or library.

Solution: To switch views, use the View menu on the top-right corner of the list. This menu shows the names of all the views available for you in the list (see Figure 3.14).

FIGURE 3.14
Selecting the list view from the drop-down menu.

These views are either public views (that everyone sees on that list) or a private view that you have created for yourself. For more information on list views, see Chapters 1 and 8.

To switch to the view that you want, click the view name, and the view changes.

> **TIP** Investigate the different views; they may be more efficient and helpful for you to quickly find data. Beyond filtering and sorting, other views can offer grouping on certain columns, show the information in different styles, and impose different item limits.

Some special instances of views have *subviews*. The subviews offer other ways to see the same view. For example, in calendar views you can switch between the daily subview, weekly subview, and monthly subview. These subviews show the information defined in the view itself (filtering the items, ordering the items) but in a different manner.

To switch between the subviews of a calendar view, use the Day, Week, and Month links at the top of the view (see Figure 3.15).

Use the links to switch between subviews.

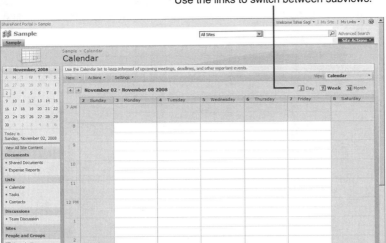

FIGURE 3.15
The weekly subview of a calendar.

Similarly, in image libraries each view has three subviews—Details, Thumbnails, and Filmstrip—that show the same data in different ways (see Figure 3.16).

FIGURE 3.16
Picture libraries offer subviews for each view.

Switch to a Datasheet View

As explained in Chapter 1, the Datasheet view is a special type of view that looks like a spreadsheet. This view allows you to copy information from the list to spreadsheet applications or do some calculations on data in the list.

To switch to the Datasheet view, open the Actions menu and choose Edit in Datasheet (see Figure 3.17).

FIGURE 3.17
Open the Actions menu in a standard view to get the option to switch to the Datasheet view.

The Datasheet view displays all the columns that were on the standard view (see Figure 3.18).

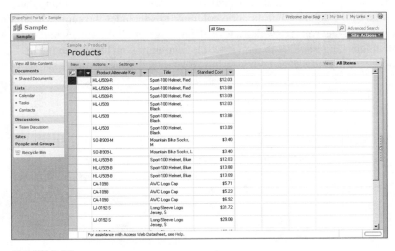

FIGURE 3.18
Viewing the columns in the Datasheet view.

Add Totals Calculations to the Datasheet View

If you want to calculate data that is in the Datasheet view, you can add totals to the view by opening the Actions menu and selecting Totals (see Figure 3.19). Selecting this option adds a totals row to the view, with options to perform mathematical calculations on the items in the view.

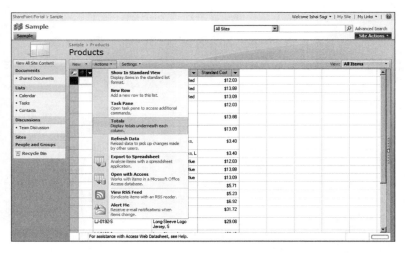

FIGURE 3.19
Open the Actions menu in a Datasheet view to get the option to add totals to the view.

After the totals row is added, any numeric column is automatically calculated with a sum so that the sum of the values in that column is displayed in the totals row (see Figure 3.20).

You can choose the type of mathematical calculation for each column by clicking the cell at the bottom of the column. For numeric columns, this includes the sum (which is displayed by default), the average (which shows the average of all the values in the view), the maximum (largest value in the view), the minimum (smallest value in the view), and more (see Figure 3.21).

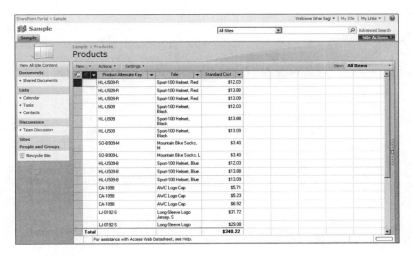

FIGURE 3.20
By default, only numeric columns have totals.

FIGURE 3.21
Numeric columns can do many different calculations.

For nonnumeric columns, you can choose the Count calculation (see Figure 3.22). This calculation shows how many values there are (see Figure 3.22). If you have 20 list items in the view, the count shows 20 as the total.

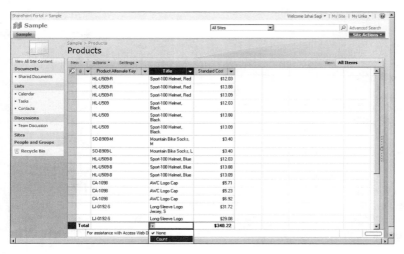

FIGURE 3.22
Nonnumeric columns can have only the Count total.

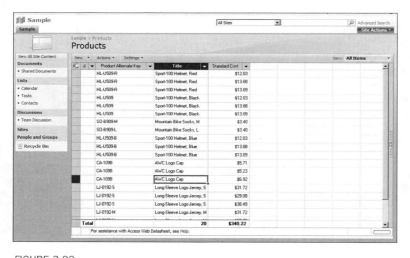

FIGURE 3.23
The Count total shows how many items there are.

Use Alerts

Scenario/Problem: Information in sites keeps changing; lists and libraries are updated with new items or files, and existing items and files are updated or deleted. Often, you need to know whenever something important to you is changed or updated. For example, if a document containing a policy that heavily impacts your work is updated, you want to know immediately. Or if a new list item is entered into a contacts list used to track potential customers, you want to know about it so that you can call the customer.

Solution: Alerts are useful mechanisms that notify you when some changes are made in SharePoint document libraries or lists or on single items. When you create an alert, you are asking the system to send you an email when a specific change occurs. The following sections explain how you can create alerts on different kinds of data and how to manage your alerts.

Create an Alert on a File or List Item

Setting up an alert on a document or list item makes SharePoint email you when changes are made to that document or item. To create the alert, open the drop-down menu of that document or list item and select Alert Me from the menu (see Figure 3.24).

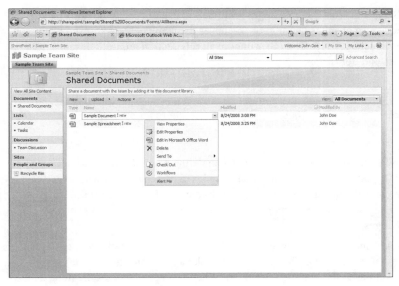

FIGURE 3.24
Selecting the option to set up an alert on a file or list item.

Selecting this option opens a screen where you can define what sort of alert you want to get on the item (see Figure 3.25).

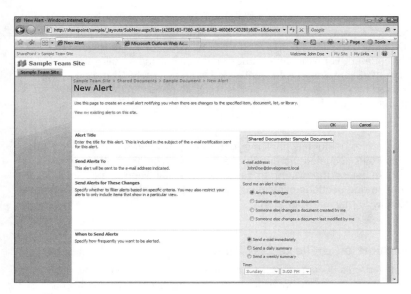

FIGURE 3.25
Selecting the settings for your alert.

Under the Send Alert for These Changes section, you can choose to be notified just when someone else changes the item or whenever the item is changed (even when you are the one who changed it). The other options in this section are not relevant for alerts on documents and items.

> **NOTE** If you are a site manager, you will also see a box allowing you to enter the email address for the alert. Thus, you can configure alerts for other users.

Under the When to Send Alerts section, you can define when the email for a change will be sent. If you choose immediately, an email will be sent to you whenever someone changes the document—one email per change. However, selecting a daily or weekly summary will reduce the number of emails and will send you a summary email of all the changes.

After you select the options you want, a confirmation email is sent to you, telling you that the alert has been set up. This process may take a few minutes, and the email should look similar to the one in Figure 3.26. When someone changes the item, an alert email is sent to you.

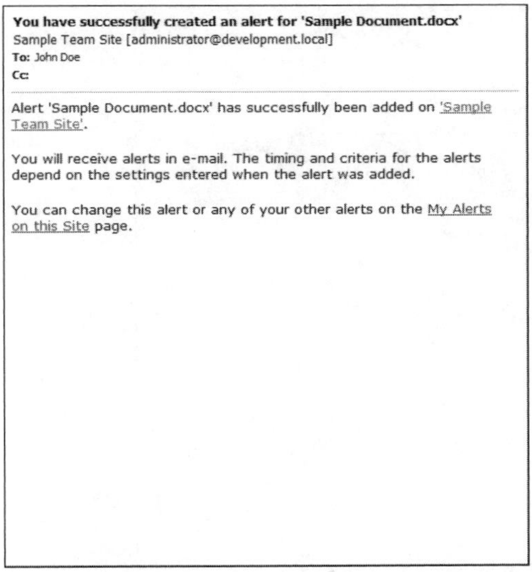

You have successfully created an alert for 'Sample Document.docx'
Sample Team Site [administrator@development.local]
To: John Doe
Cc:

Alert 'Sample Document.docx' has successfully been added on 'Sample Team Site'.

You will receive alerts in e-mail. The timing and criteria for the alerts depend on the settings entered when the alert was added.

You can change this alert or any of your other alerts on the My Alerts on this Site page.

FIGURE 3.26
An email confirming that your alert has been set up.

Create an Alert on a List or a Library

Setting up an alert on a list or library makes SharePoint email you when changes are made (when items are added, removed, or changed).

To create the alert, click the Actions menu of the list or library and select Alert Me from the drop-down options (see Figure 3.27).

Selecting this option opens the settings screen for the alert (refer to Figure 3.25). Here, you can specify what you want to be alerted on.

Under the Change Type section, you can choose what kind of change you want to be alerted on. For example, you can select to be alerted only when new items are added, only when items are deleted, or when anything happens (all changes).

Similar to setting up an alert on a list item, you can choose when the alert will be sent (either immediately or as a daily or weekly summary).

After you create the alert, a confirmation email is sent to you. Alert emails for lists look exactly the same as alerts on list items.

> **CAUTION** Don't forget that alerts can be annoying if you get too many emails. Creating an alert on a busy document library and setting it to email you immediately on every change can overload your mailbox. Consider the daily or weekly email options unless you really need to know about new documents or changes in existing ones.

FIGURE 3.27
Selecting the option to set up an alert on a list or library.

Modify or Remove an Alert

To modify or remove an alert, click the Modify My Alert Settings link that was sent to you by that alert. Doing so opens the site where that alert was created, in the alert management screen.

On this screen, shown in Figure 3.28, you can either click an alert to change its settings (such as when it should send the email or what changes it should alert on) or select the alert and delete it using the Delete Selected Alerts button.

Manage My Alerts in a Site

To see what alerts you have in a site and manage them, open the site and click the Welcome [*your name*] button at the top. Select the My Settings option from the drop-down menu (see Figure 3.29).

Selecting this option shows you your user information. Click My Alerts in the toolbar to open the alert management screen for that site, where you can modify or delete alerts.

FIGURE 3.28
Managing your alerts in a site

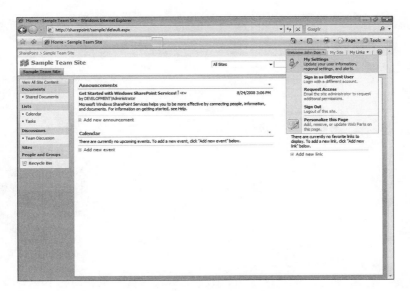

FIGURE 3.29
Selecting the My Settings option to manage your alerts.

TIP A quick way to get to the manage alerts page is to add _layouts/mysubs.aspx to the path to the site where the alerts are set. For example, if the site containing your alert is http://sharepoint/sample, type **http://sharepoint/sample/_layouts/mysubs.aspx** to get to the alerts page.

CHAPTER 4

Searching in SharePoint

SharePoint has a built-in search engine that enables you to search for files or pages in SharePoint or even in other sites or file storage applications. However, the different versions of SharePoint—Microsoft Office SharePoint Server (MOSS) and Windows SharePoint Services (WSS)—have different ways of searching and displaying the search results. This chapter explains how to search using SharePoint's different interfaces.

Search for Documents and List Items

Scenario/Problem: Sometimes you want to find a piece of content that may exist in your corporate network, but you are not sure where in the network it is. This content may be a document stored in SharePoint or in a file share or list item in SharePoint or in an application database, for example.

Solution: SharePoint has a built-in search facility that enables you to find content in it (and, sometimes, also content that is not in SharePoint, depending on the way the search administrator configured it). The search user interface can be customized, so the search screen in your SharePoint site might look different, but usually the main ways to get to search are the same.

It is important to note that WSS search is different from MOSS search. Indeed, that is one of the main reasons for corporations to buy and install MOSS, because the search options that come with MOSS are a lot more flexible for the administrator to configure and for the end user to use.

The basic search in both configurations is the same: you type the search keywords in the search box and click the search icon (usually a looking glass). However, MOSS has an additional option for Advanced Search that enables you to search all the SharePoint sites (unlike WSS search, which allows you to search only the site you are currently working on), as well as search content that exists outside SharePoint.

To search for anything, you usually just type in the search box a keyword that represents the item you want to search for and click the search icon. The location of the search box can vary, and if you are using MOSS, you might have other search options available, including Advanced Search and dedicated Search Pages. These options are covered later in this chapter.

The simplest form of searching in SharePoint, as described previously, is known as the *keyword search*. This keyword can be a word that appears in the document (part of the document's contents) or in the document's or list item's properties (see Figure 4.1). For example, it can be a document name or a contact's company name—anything that the search administrator decided should be included and searchable.

FIGURE 4.1
Searching for the word *AdventureWorks* shows results that include a document with the word in its contents, a contact, and a list view with the same word.

> **TIP** Because search results can sometimes be documents and sometimes list items and sometimes web pages or list views, what you get when you click a search result will be very different.
>
> When opening search results, you might want to open the result in a new window (or a new tab in some browsers) instead of losing the search results page that you are viewing. To do so, right-click the link and choose Open in New Window, or Shift-click the link to open in a new window (Ctrl-click opens in a new tab in some browsers).

You can search for more than one word; the search results contain everything that has any of those words.

> **TIP** Searching for the words *mountain bikes* results in all the documents that have either the word *mountain* or the word *bikes*, as well as *mountains* and *bike* and other forms of the two words. However, if you want to search for an exact match for a phrase, use quotation marks like this: **"mountain bikes"**. Alternatively, you can use the advanced search (see later in this chapter) to accomplish the same effect.

By default, the search results are sorted by relevance; the document that you are most likely looking for should be the first in the list. SharePoint calculates the relevance of the documents based on many factors, but basically, a document with more instances of the word you searched for should be higher in the list when it is sorted by relevance.

Another option that you can choose is to sort by modified date. To do that, click the View by Modified Date link, and the search results are reordered.

Finally, the search results screen offers two ways to be notified when a new search result for your search is added in the future: the Alert Me and RSS options. For example, if you search for *AdventureWorks* and you want to know whenever new documents or list items are created in the future, you can use those options.

The Alert Me option is similar to the alert functionality for other objects in SharePoint (such as documents or lists, for example; see Chapter 3, "Solutions Regarding Files, Documents, List Items, and Forms," for more information). However, it has fewer options, as you can see in Figure 4.2.

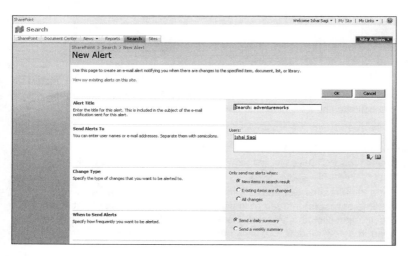

FIGURE 4.2
Selecting the alert options.

In the Change Type section, just select whether you want to be alerted only on new items, changed items, or both, and in the When to Send Alerts section, select whether you want daily alerts or immediate alerts when there is something to be alerted on.

Note, however, that alerts from search are never immediate. An email is sent to you only when the change has been picked up by the search engine, and depending on the search configuration set up by the administrator, that can take awhile.

Search in WSS

Scenario/Problem: When you are using a SharePoint site that is hosted on a server that has only WSS installed (and not MOSS; see "Determine the Difference Between WSS and MOSS " in Chapter 1, "About Microsoft SharePoint 2007," for more information), the search options are different.

Solution: This section details the search options available in WSS-only sites. Searching in WSS is simple and doesn't have many options; every site (usually) has a search box that enables you to search on documents and list items in that site.

Next to the search box is a scopes drop-down that enables you to choose from scopes if any are configured. By default, you only have the choice of searching the site itself (see Figure 4.3).

The Site Search Box

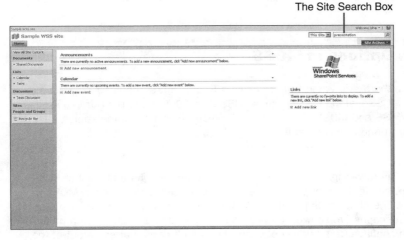

FIGURE 4.3
The search box in a WSS site enables you to search within the site.

When you are viewing a document library, the search box has an additional option in the scopes drop-down (see Figure 4.4). This option enables you to search only within the document library, excluding other document libraries.

The Search Scope Drop-Down

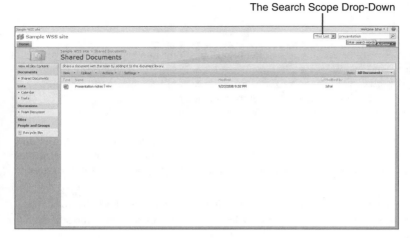

FIGURE 4.4
The search box in a document library enables you to search only in that document library.

Search Options in MOSS

Scenario/Problem: When you are using a SharePoint site hosted on a server that has MOSS installed (and not just WSS; see "Determine the Difference Between WSS and MOSS" in Chapter 1 for more information), the search options are different and more versatile.

Solution: The following sections explain the different options that exist in MOSS sites for executing different types of search queries. You can search in MOSS in many ways. The simplest is just like in WSS: Using a search box at the top of a page with a scopes drop-down, you pick what you want to search. Search administrators can configure and add scopes, but the default ones that come out of the box are All Sites, People, and in each site a This Site scope (see Figure 4.5).

By default, the All Sites scope searches on everything, excluding people, although the results may include people's personal sites if you search for a person's name. This also means that search results can come from sites outside SharePoint. MOSS can search on other sources of data outside SharePoint, and the All Sites scope, by default, searches on that content.

FIGURE 4.5
You can choose the scope for your search.

> **NOTE** Depending on the scope you choose, you might be directed to a different search results page, also depending on how the search administrator set up the search.

Use the Search Center

Another option is to use the *search center*. This site is dedicated to searching and is usually designed to give you a better searching experience.

To get to the search center, you can either find it on the navigation bar (if it has a link there, usually under the name Search) or just perform a simple search from any site. By default, in MOSS you are directed to a search center when you do that.

The search center has an option to display several search tabs or search pages (see Figure 4.6). Each of these tabs can be configured to display search results from different sources of content.

Other tabs can be created by the search administrator and can be configured to show different search results.

To switch between tabs, just click the tab name. If you have searched on a term before, the term for which you have searched is automatically transfered to the new tab, and a search is performed on it.

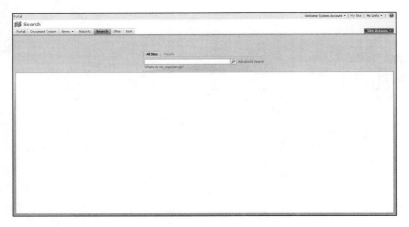

FIGURE 4.6
The default search center has a search page for people and a search page for other content.

Use Federated Search

Federated search is a new capability of the MOSS search that was added to the product after it was released, so it might or might not be utilized by the site you are using. The idea of a federated search is that the search displays results from more than just what SharePoint is indexing; for example, you also can search the Internet. This way, if you are researching a certain term—say *bicycle*—and would like to see everything related to bicycles from the SharePoint site, but also from an MSN search or Google, the federated search allows that.

> **TIP** If the federated search results come from the Internet, you might want to open them in a new window or a separate tab so that you don't lose the search results page (see Figure 4.7).

The search administrator can configure the federated search to show results from many sources outside SharePoint.

> **TIP** Remember that the federated search results might be results from the Internet and from sites that have unreliable data.

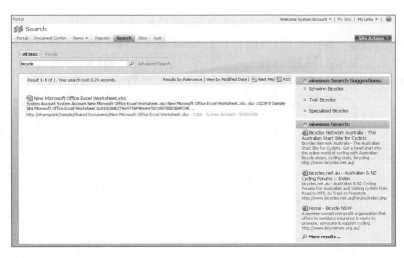

FIGURE 4.7
The federated search results from the Internet are shown on the right of the page.

Use the Advanced Search (Available Only in MOSS)

Scenario/Problem: Sometimes you want to search for a document or a list item based on the metadata of the document or list item (the information stored about the document or list item in the columns of the list or library). For example, if you want to search for documents written by John Doe, performing a simple search for the words *John Doe* returns documents that were not written by that person; instead, the search returns any document that has the words *John Doe* in the body of the document, as well as in other columns, such as who modified the document last.

Solution: The advanced search feature enables you to search for documents or list items in a more organized manner than just typing keywords. It lets you focus your search on a particular property of the documents or list items. For example, you can search for documents that person *X* wrote or documents that were created after 1/1/2008 or list items that have the word *Adventureworks* in the company property (and not in other properties).

To get to the Advanced Search page, either click the Advanced Search link next to the simple search box at the top of every page (see Figure 4.8), or go to the search center and click the Advanced Search link there.

The Advanced Search Link

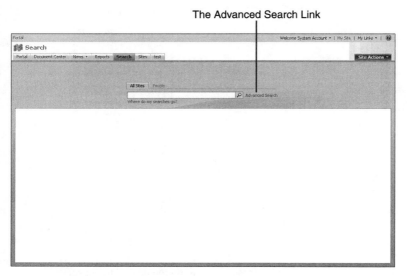

FIGURE 4.8
The advanced search link is usually next to the simple search box.

The Advanced Search page enables you to search more specifically and in a more exact manner on parts of the document or list item (see Figure 4.11).

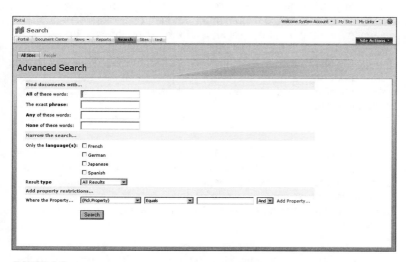

FIGURE 4.9
The Advanced Search page.

On this page you can specify that you want to look for words exactly like the simple search option: just by typing in the Any of These Words box. The All of These Words search results only in documents or list items that have all the words that you type, but not necessarily in the same order. You also can use the other options, such as The Exact Phrase, which lets you type a few words, and items are returned in the results only if the exact phrase appears in the document or list item. And you can specify words that you don't want in the documents by using the None of These Words box.

To narrow the search, specify a language (this option is usually used for web pages and for Microsoft Office documents, but not for other types of files unless those files have a property called Language).

In addition, you can specify the result type, selecting whether you want to search only for Microsoft Word documents, Microsoft Excel documents, or Microsoft PowerPoint documents (see Figure 4.10). Or you can just select Documents to make sure your search results only in documents and not list items. The search administrator may customize this box to have more types.

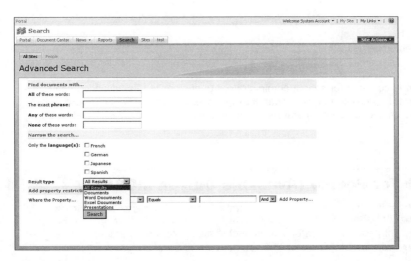

FIGURE 4.10
Selecting the result type.

Finally, you can specify a search on specific properties that the search administrator configured for you to search on. You can add up to five conditions consisting of "property X equals/does not equal to Y," as shown in Figure 4.11.

As you can see in Figure 4.11, you can chain a few conditions together and choose whether they should be chained using an Or or an And operator. For example, if you specify "Author equals John and Title equals Example," the only results are the ones whose author is *John* and the title is exactly *Example*. But if you search for "Author equals John *or* title equals Example," the results include documents that have been authored by *John* and documents whose title is *Example,* not just the ones where both conditions are true.

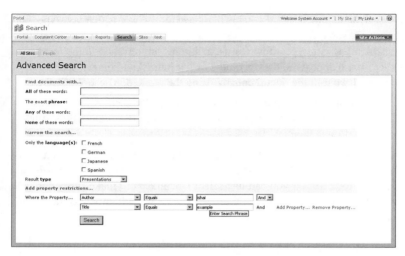

FIGURE 4.11
Searching on properties.

> **NOTE** It is common for search administrators to customize this advanced search interface. It is possible that your search experience here will be very different, allowing you to choose different operators (such as Contains, for example) if that was done.

Search for People (Available Only in MOSS)

> **Scenario/Problem:** Sometimes you want to find the contact details of people who work with you in the organization, including their phone number, the department they work in, the name of their manager, and so on.

Solution: MOSS has a user profile database that stores information about users. For more information about this feature, see Chapter 5, "Personal Sites and Personal Details (Available Only in MOSS)." If that feature has been set up, you can search for people and view their details. Also, if they have created personal sites for themselves, you are able to view the public views of their personal sites (for more information about personal sites and how to create them, see Chapter 5).

You can perform a people search from most MOSS sites by selecting People from the scopes drop-down, or by navigating to the search center and choosing the People tab (see Figure 4.12). As with documents and list items, you can perform a people search either by using keywords or using the advanced search and searching on properties.

The advanced search for people behaves slightly differently than the advanced search for documents and list items. To view the advanced search options, click the Search Options link in the People search tab in the search center. This exposes more search options, allowing you to still search by keyword using the same box and at the same time specify values for specific people properties (see Figure 4.12).

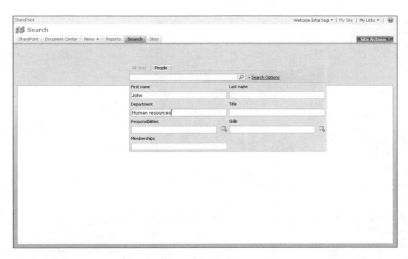

FIGURE 4.12
The advanced search options in the People search tab in the search center.

For example, you can specify that you want to look for someone whose first name is John who works in the Human Resources department. To do so, enter **John** in the First Name box and **Human Resources** in the Department box, as shown in Figure 4.12.

Some of the properties are choice properties—they enable you to select a value from a list of choices. These properties can be identified by the icon next to the text box. You can click that icon to open a dialog that enables you to select a choice. Figure 4.13 shows an example of the dialog that opens when you click on the icon next to the Responsibilities property. In the dialog, you can search for the term in the list of choices, and then select it by clicking on the term, and then OK. The dialog will close, and the value you picked will be automatically entered in the box for the property, enabling you to continue setting up the search query.

Finally, when you are ready, click the Search button. You get to the search results page, which shows you the people search results (see Figure 4.14).

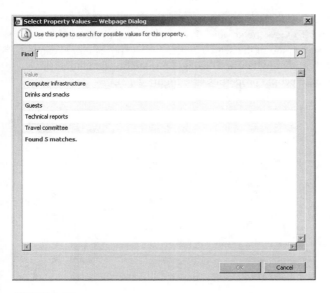

FIGURE 4.13
This dialog enables you to select a value to search for from a list of choices for the Responsibilities property.

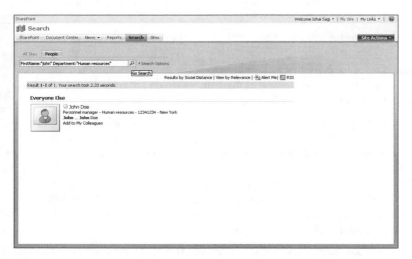

FIGURE 4.14
This page shows the results of your advanced people search.

Unlike the results for documents and list items, these results are ordered by social distance. This result is something special for the people search that shows you the people you work with first, people they work with second, and then anyone else.

SharePoint knows your coworkers only if you tell it by using the Colleagues mechanism. This mechanism enables you to specify whom you work with, either from the search results (use the Add to Colleagues link) or from your personal site (see Chapter 5 for more details). Some colleagues are automatically recognized by SharePoint, such as your manager, people you manage, and other people who have the same manager.

If you want to change the sort order, click the View by Relevance option on the results page.

People search results have another distinguishing feature that documents' and list items' search results do not have by default: the results are ordered in groups.

In Figure 4.14, you can see that John is in the Everyone Else group because John is not marked as someone who is important to the user who searched for him. However, if a user marks John as a Colleague, the group changes to My Colleagues, as shown in Figure 4.15.

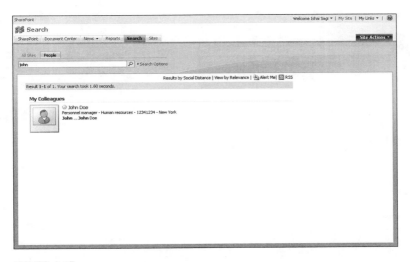

FIGURE 4.15
John is now identified as a colleague.

If your search returns more than one person, SharePoint will analyze the search results and try to find out ways to help you refine the search. For example, if the people returned by your search results have different job titles, a section will appear next to the search results with the list of the job titles (as shown in Figure 4.16), allowing you to click on one to refine the search.

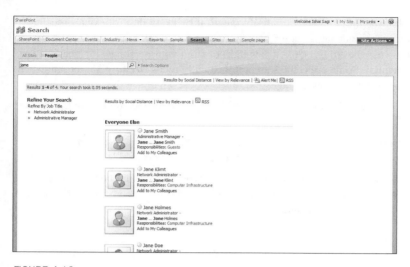

FIGURE 4.16
The refine your search section with different job titles.

CHAPTER 5

Personal Sites and Personal Details (Available Only in MOSS)

In some Microsoft Office SharePoint Server (MOSS) implementations, the option to create personal sites is enabled, allowing you to create a SharePoint site that is totally under your control. You can upload documents to be stored in the site instead of on your desktop and manage your private lists, such as lists of favorite links or lists of friends, and so on.

Additionally, with MOSS you get a user profile that stores information about you—for example, your phone number, email, and other details that would be useful for people in your organization who are looking for you. This chapter explains how you can view these personal details (of yourself or of others) and how you can edit your own details, as well as how to create and navigate around a personal site.

Create a Personal Site

Scenario/Problem: You want to store files and collaborate with your coworkers online, while keeping some information to yourself. Sometimes the SharePoint administrators have not created a specific site for the purpose you require, and you want to be able to work in the SharePoint environment but do not have the facility to do so.

Solution: My Site is a feature of MOSS through which every user can have his or her own personal site. The site can have private document libraries and lists that are shown and available only to the site owner (unless the owner chooses to share them with other people; see Chapter 10, "Managing Security," for more information) and public document libraries and lists where the user can collaborate with other users.

To create a personal site, click the My Site link at the top of the screen, as shown in Figure 5.1.

NOTE If the link to My Site does not appear it could be one of two reasons: Either you are working on a site that has WSS only (and not MOSS) or the site manager edited the format of the pages in the site and has removed the link. If the link is not shown and you are sure that the site is using MOSS, contact your administrator and ask for the link to My Site.

If you don't have a personal site, and the administrator allows personal sites to be created, a personal site is created for you.

The My Site Link

FIGURE 5.1
Clicking the My Site link enables you to create your own personal site.

After the site is created, a pop-up dialog might appear, asking you if you want to configure My Site for Microsoft Office (see Figure 5.2). This is a useful feature that adds a link to the personal site in Microsoft Office applications. This will make it easier for you to save documents to your personal site from Office. If you select not to configure it, a button will appear in the top of the site with the text Set as Default My Site that will enable you to configure it in the future.

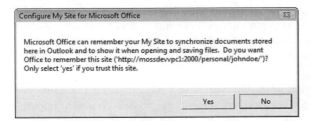

FIGURE 5.2
In this dialog, you can choose to create a link to your personal site in Microsoft Office applications.

Your personal site is then created and ready for you, like the one shown in Figure 5.3.

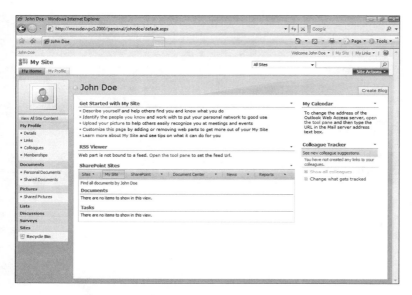

FIGURE 5.3
A personal site created for John Doe.

Get Started with Your Personal Site

Scenario/Problem: You have a personal site, and you want to customize it to show your personal data when you view it.

Solution: There are many things you can do with your personal site, including creating lists and libraries, modifying how the page looks, and changing the way the site looks. Some of these tasks are covered later in this chapter, and some are covered in other chapters; specifically, Chapter 7, "Creating Lists and Document Libraries," and Chapter 9, "Authoring Pages."

To start, it is recommended to follow the Get Started with My Site list that is usually displayed in new personal sites. This list offers some ideas and help on how to implement them and modify the site to your preferences. Among the tasks you can start right away are displaying your Outlook calendar, modifying the links shown under SharePoint Sites, and specifying your colleagues (see Figure 5.4).

Use this link to edit your details so
that other people can search for you.

Click here to set up the personal site
to show your Outlook calendar.

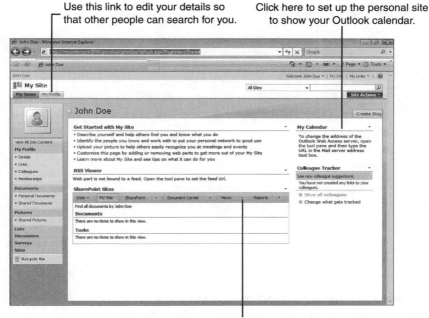

Use the drop-down menus to remove links from this section.

FIGURE 5.4
You can start to modify your preferences in this dialog.

Display Your Outlook Calendar in the Site

Click the Open the Tool Pane link in the My Calendar web part. This link opens a pane with settings that you need to fill for the web part to display your information (see Figure 5.5).

Fill in the link to your company's email server (ask your administrator if you are not sure what the link is) and click OK. The Outlook calendar appears, as shown in Figure 5.6.

Modify the Links in the SharePoint Sites Web Part

The useful SharePoint Sites web part shows you a list of the SharePoint sites of which you are a member. When you click on each of these sites you will be shown the documents and tasks you have been working on in them.

> **NOTE** The web part shows the sites that you are a member of. This means only sites that list you in their "site members" security group will be shown. However, you can add and remove links to sites if there are other sites that you want in this interface.

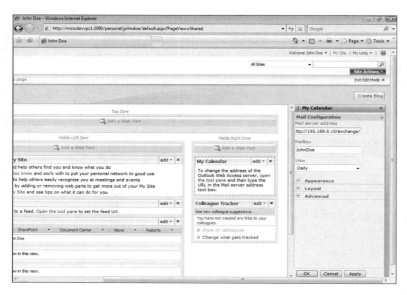

FIGURE 5.5
Select the Open the tool pane link to start changing settings.

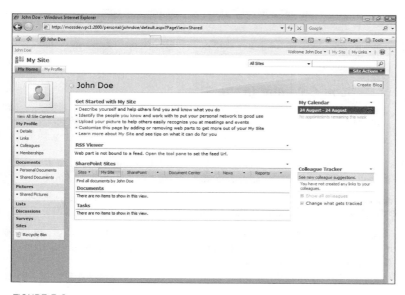

FIGURE 5.6
The Outlook calendar is now available in your personal site.

To add a link to a site that is not shown, click the Sites button on the left of the toolbar of the web part. This will show you an option to create a new site tab, as shown in Figure 5.7. Either point the new tab at any site you want by typing the link to the site, or choose from the list of sites to which you are a member to add that site if it was deleted from the list before.

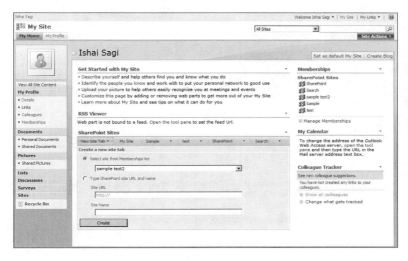

FIGURE 5.7
Adding a new site tab.

You can modify this list to hide or delete links to sites that you do not use often or in which you do not need to track documents and tasks.

To remove a link, simply open the drop-down of that SharePoint Sites web part link by clicking the small down arrow, and select either Hide or Delete from the menu (see Figure 5.8). Choosing one of these options does not delete the actual site, but just removes it from the list that the web part tracks.

Specify Your Colleagues

You might want to specify whom you are working with. This information helps SharePoint track for you what they are doing and helps you share information with them.

To specify your colleagues, click the Colleagues link in the left navigation bar. Selecting this link opens a screen on which you can add, modify, or remove your colleagues, as well as group them for your comfort (see Figure 5.9).

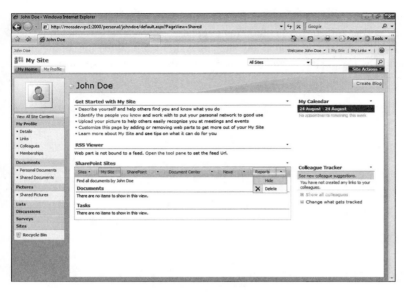

FIGURE 5.8
Choose to hide or delete links from the SharePoint Sites web part.

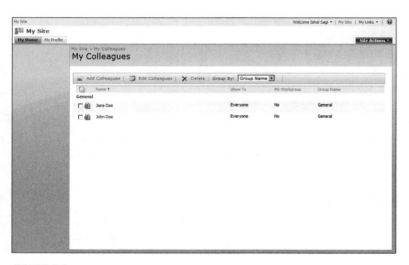

FIGURE 5.9
The My Colleagues page enables you to add, modify, or remove colleagues.

Clicking Add Colleagues may prompt you to allow SharePoint to check Outlook for people who might be your colleagues (see Figure 5.10).

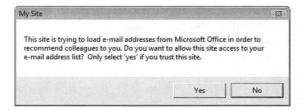

FIGURE 5.10
SharePoint asks whether you
want to access your Outlook
email list.

This feature can help you quickly add people with whom you are working. Regardless
of whether you choose to do so, you can then manually select people from the
company address book and mark them as colleagues in the Add Colleagues dialog (see
Figure 5.11).

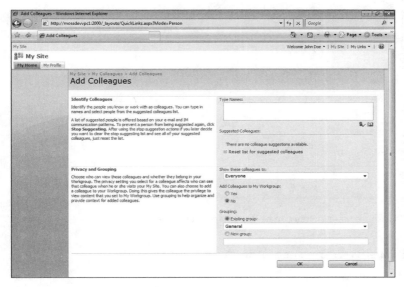

FIGURE 5.11
Add coworkers to your site using the Add Colleagues dialog.

Upload a Document to Your Personal Site

Scenario/Problem: When you are working in your personal site, you want to
upload a document to it.

Solution: To upload a document to your personal site, first open the personal site
by clicking the My Site link that appears in any SharePoint site.

When your site is open, you need to choose where to upload the document. Personal sites have two document libraries: a personal one, where only you can see the documents you upload, and a shared one, where documents you upload can be viewed by other users in your company. To select which document library you want to upload to, simply click the link to that document library in the left navigation bar (see Figure 5.12).

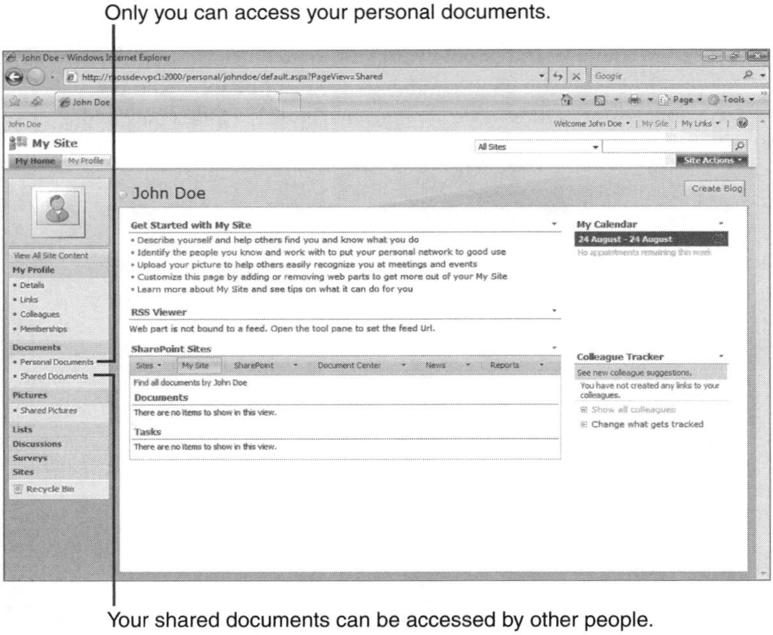

Only you can access your personal documents.

Your shared documents can be accessed by other people.

FIGURE 5.12
Use the left navigation bar to choose a location for uploaded documents.

Edit Your Details

Scenario/Problem: The details that other users see about you are no longer up to date, and you want to update them to reflect recent changes. For example, you might have been promoted and your job title changed, or maybe you have a new manager. Editing your details is very important because it allows other people in your company to find you quickly using the people search.

Solution: This section explains how you can change the details that appear to other users or are searched in the people search. The details that you can edit are different in every company, so you might see a different set of details to fill in when you open your details page.

To edit your details, click the Details link in the left navigation bar. Clicking this link forwards you to a page where you can edit your details. As mentioned previously, these details will be different depending on your company's configuration. In Figure 5.13, you can see how to enter text in an About Me section, upload a picture, and select your responsibilities and your skills.

FIGURE 5.13
The Edit Details page enables you to edit some details about yourself.

See What Tasks Are Assigned to You

Scenario/Problem: You want to see what tasks are assigned to you in multiple SharePoint sites from your personal site (My Site). This way, you are able to go to just one site (your personal My Site) and see all the tasks in one place.

Solution: The SharePoint Sites web part mentioned previously in this chapter enables you to see what tasks are assigned to you in the sites that that web part is configured to display.

To see what tasks you have in a specific site, click the link for that site in the web part's toolbar. Clicking this link does not transfer you to that site, but instead shows you the documents you were working on in that site and the tasks assigned to you in that site (see Figure 5.14).

FIGURE 5.14
The SharePoint Sites web part now lists documents and tasks assigned to you.

If a site of which you are a member does not appear in the toolbar, try looking for it under Sites in the SharePoint Sites web part. This button lists all the sites you have marked as hidden, as well as the ones that do not belong to the portal the web part was configured to display. For more information about how sites appear in this web part, refer to "Modify the Links in the SharePoint Sites Web Part," earlier in this chapter.

Use the My Links to Manage Your Links

Scenario/Problem: When using SharePoint, you are able to add links to a list of favorite links shown at the top of any SharePoint site (under the My Links button). Now you want to manage your links, grouping them in different groups, editing them, or deleting them when they are not required.

Solution: The My Links mechanism is a useful feature of the personal site. These links are stored in your personal site and are displayed to you in every SharePoint site, much like the Favorites mechanism in your browser.

To see the links in any SharePoint site, click the My Links link at the top of the screen (see Figure 5.15). Clicking this link opens a menu that shows the links, organized by groups.

FIGURE 5.15
Use the My Links link to see all your links organized by groups.

Add a Link

You can easily add a link to the My Links list. Click the My Links link at the top of the screen and select Add to My Links from the menu. Selecting this option opens an Add to My Links dialog, which is populated automatically with the details of the current site (see Figure 5.16). This dialog enables you to quickly create a link to the site you are currently viewing. If you want to create a link to another site, you can change the title and the address of the link in this dialog.

Also in this dialog, you can specify who can see the link (people who are looking at your personal site) and what group it should be categorized as. There is even an option to create a new group if you want to.

Edit a Link

To remove a link, click the My Links link at the top of the screen and select Manage Links. Selecting this option opens a page where you can manage your links (see Figure 5.17). To edit a specific one, select it using the check box and click the Edit Links button in the menu.

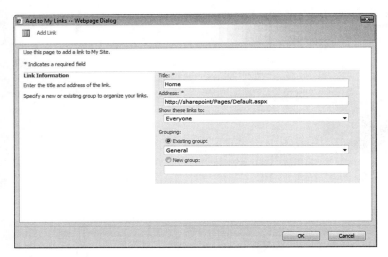

FIGURE 5.16
You can add links through the My Links link.

FIGURE 5.17
You can edit your links on this page.

Remove a Link

To remove a link, click the My Links link at the top of the screen and select Manage Links. Selecting this option opens a page where you can manage your links (refer to Figure 5.17). To delete a specific one, select it using the check box and click the Delete button in the menu bar.

Create Groups for Links

To create a new group for links, you can edit a link you want to belong to the new group, as shown previously. Alternatively, you can create a new link. In the dialog, select New Group under the Grouping section, and type the name of the group (see Figure 5.18). The link appears under the new group name in the My Links menu only if you have more than one group with links (see Figure 5.19).

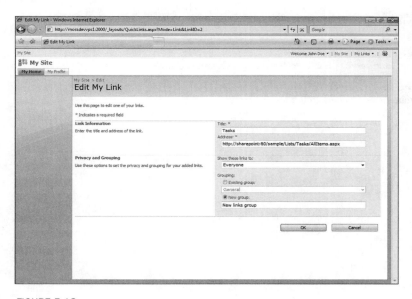

FIGURE 5.18
You can enter a name for a group in this dialog.

FIGURE 5.19
The new group name appears in the My Links menu.

PART II

Solutions for Authors and Content Managers

IN THIS PART

CHAPTER 6

Creating and Managing Files, List Items, and Forms in SharePoint

SharePoint is most commonly used to store files, list items, and forms. This chapter covers tasks for the authors of files or list items, such as how to upload a file, create a new list item, edit their properties, and publish the result to share it with other users.

Upload a File

Scenario/Problem: You want to upload a file to a document library in a SharePoint site.

Solution: Uploading a file to SharePoint is an easy process, but there are three ways to do so. If you are writing a document in a Microsoft Office application, an easy way is to upload the document straight from the application itself by saving it directly into SharePoint.

However, if the file you want to upload is not an Office file, or if you prefer to upload the file without opening it in an Office application, you can upload the file using the web interface with your Internet browser.

The third option, which is a bit more advanced, enables you to upload the file to a library as if that library was a folder on your computer. This method is known as *web folders* and requires some components to be installed on your machine, but when they are installed, it is easy and efficient to use.

Upload a File from the Web Interface

Using your web browser, browse to the library to which you want to upload the file, and go to the folder where you want to put the file. If you have the required permissions to add files to the folder, you see the Upload button on the menu bar (see Figure 6.1).

The Upload button can be used as a regular button (just click the button) or as a drop-down menu to show more options for uploading, namely the option to upload multiple files. This option, available only for users of Microsoft Internet Explorer, navigates you to a different page, which is explained at the end of this section.

Clicking the Upload button opens the upload file page, where you can pick a single file by using the Browse button.

If you are using a compatible browser and have the required components, you also have an option in this window to upload multiple files using the Upload Multiple Files link (see Figure 6.2). This link redirects you to the same page you would have opened if you had clicked Upload Multiple Documents from the Upload drop-down menu.

The Upload button appears only if you have
permission to upload a document to a folder.

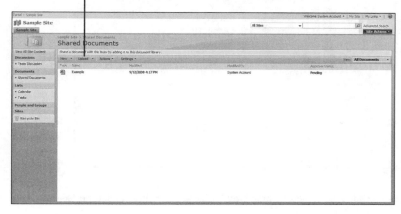

FIGURE 6.1
Using the Upload button on the menu bar.

The Upload Multiple Documents link appears
if you have the right documents installed.

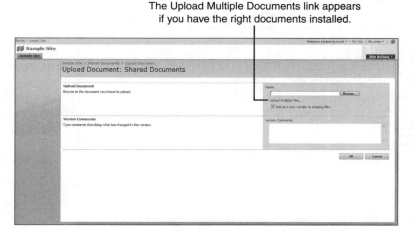

FIGURE 6.2
The File Upload page, with the Multiple Documents link that enables you to upload many files
at once if you have the right Microsoft Office components installed on your machine.

If you selected a single file, click OK to commit the upload. This process can take a
while depending on the speed of the network, size of the file, and load on the server.

When the upload is done, you might be prompted for metadata (properties) for the file
and see a Check In button, but that depends on the setup of the document library (see
Figure 6.3).

FIGURE 6.3
After the file is uploaded, you might be prompted for more information about the file.

Additionally, if the library supports multiple content types for files, you might have to select in this screen what content type this file belongs to, and that may change the metadata that you are asked for, as shown in Figure 6.4.

FIGURE 6.4
Metadata entry screen when the Presentation content type is selected.

If you selected to upload multiple files, you are presented with a page displaying documents on your computer, allowing you to select a folder on the left and then one or more files on the right using the check boxes (see Figure 6.5).

After selecting the files you want to upload, click OK. You see a prompt asking whether you are sure you want to upload all the files. Click Yes if the number of documents in the prompt matches the number of files you intended to select.

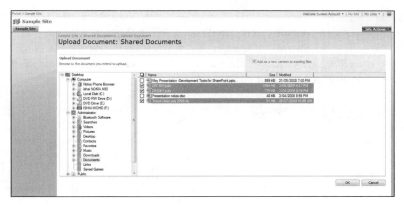

FIGURE 6.5
Selecting multiple documents to upload.

Now you see an Upload Progress screen (see Figure 6.6). The speed of the upload depends on many variables, such as network speed and load on the server, so this screen might be gone very fast—so fast that you might not even see it.

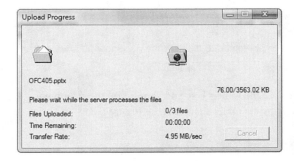

FIGURE 6.6
The Upload Progress screen shows your files being uploaded.

Using this method, you are not asked for metadata for the files, and they are all uploaded but not checked into the document library. You still need to check in each file that you uploaded and set the metadata for each one separately. Of course, if check-in is not required on the document library in question, you don't need to check in the files, but setting the metadata (like the titles for the files) might be a good idea.

See "Edit the Properties of a File or a List Item" and "Check In and Check Out a File or List Item" later in this chapter for more details on how to do this after you upload the files.

Upload a File from an Office Application

Office 2003 and later versions have a built-in functionality that enables you to save files straight into SharePoint. Different versions may present a different user interface for doing that, but the principle is the same.

To save a document from an Office application such as Word, PowerPoint, or Excel, use the Save or Save As functionality of the application. When the Save As dialog appears, type the path to the SharePoint site into which you want to save the file in the File Name box, and click Save or press Enter (see Figure 6.7). (This step does not save the document yet because you have not given it a name.)

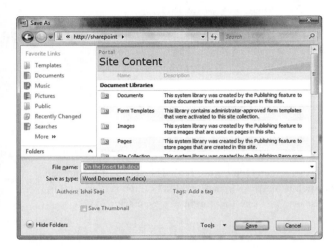

FIGURE 6.7
Clicking Save after typing the path to a SharePoint site displays the document libraries in the site inside the Save As dialog.

This action opens the site's structure in the dialog box and shows you the document libraries in that site, as well as the subsites under that site (see Figure 6.8).

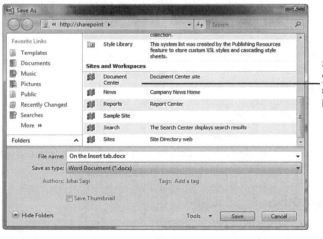

Subsites (under the site you selected); click the subsites to see the libraries in them.

FIGURE 6.8
To see the subsites, scroll down the window.

You can now navigate to the document library that you want by double-clicking its name (see Figure 6.9), or browse the subsites by double-clicking them and selecting a document library from there.

Double-click the document library to open it, or click it once to select it and then click Open.

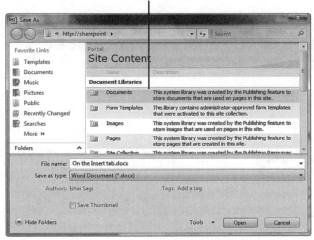

FIGURE 6.9
To open a document library and browse its folders, either double-click it or single click it to select it and click Open.

Alternatively, if you know the path to the document library or folder you want to save to, type that in the File Name box and click Save to open the folder directly. When you have browsed to the folder to which you want to save, give the file a name in the File Name box and click Save to save it to the folder.

Depending on the configuration of the document library, you might be presented with several different dialogs, which can look different if you are using Microsoft Office 2003 or Microsoft Office 2007. The following figures, for example, show the dialogs presented to Microsoft Office 2007 users.

In the first dialog you might be asked for the content type of the document (see Figure 6.10).

The next dialog might remind you that the document must be checked in before other people can see it. Then, a dialog might tell you about the offline editing options that are set in your computer and provide you with some assistance for changing those settings, as shown in Figure 6.11.

FIGURE 6.10
A dialog to ask for the content type of the document.

FIGURE 6.11
A dialog to let you know that the document is not checked in.

Finally, after all the dialogs have gone, your document is in SharePoint but still checked out. You can check it in from the web interface (see "Check In and Check Out a File or a List Item" later in this chapter) or from the Office application itself.

In the Office application, you have an option to check in the document in the menus. Again, depending on what version of Microsoft Office you are using, this option will appear in different places. In Microsoft Office 2003, it appears just under the File menu as a Check In menu option. In Microsoft Office 2007, it appears under the Microsoft Office button under the Server menu option (see Figure 6.12).

Selecting Check In prompts you to make sure you want to check in and prompts for check-in comments.

Upload a File Using Web Folders

Web folders is an interface into SharePoint that is usually installed as part of Microsoft Office but also can be distributed by other applications. This interface enables you to browse a SharePoint site as if it were a folder on the network. This capability can be useful for copying and pasting a large number of files to or from SharePoint and even deleting the files.

There are different ways to connect to a site using web folders. The first is to open the document library, open the Actions menu, and then select the Open with Windows Explorer option, as shown in Figure 6.13.

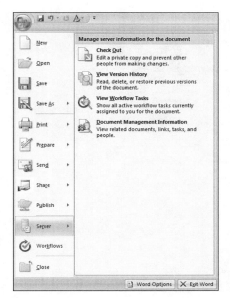

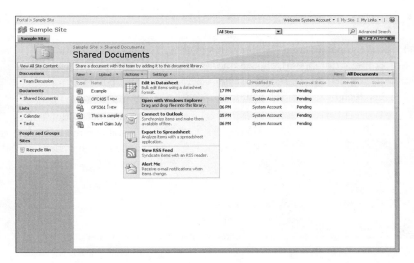

FIGURE 6.12
To check in (or perform other SharePoint-related tasks), use the Server menu under the Microsoft Office button.

FIGURE 6.13
Selecting the Open with Windows Explorer option from the Actions menu.

Selecting this option opens the document library, allowing you to copy and paste files into the library or one of the folders (see Figure 6.14).

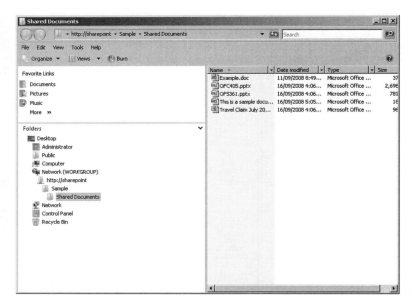

FIGURE 6.14
In this document library, you can copy or paste the files you want to use.

The second way is to open Internet Explorer (this method does not work with other browsers such as Firefox or Opera), choose File, and then choose Open (or press Ctrl+O). In the dialog that opens, shown in Figure 6.15, select the option Open as Web Folder, and in the Open box, enter the path to the website to which you want to upload a file.

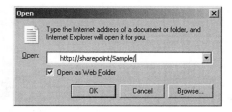

FIGURE 6.15
Enter the path for your file in the Open box.

Click OK when you are done to open the site as if it were a folder, allowing you to navigate to document libraries and folders, and to copy and paste files into the folders.

> **NOTE** Note that uploading files through web folders does not provide you with an interface for specifying the files' metadata, and you still need to edit the properties of the files through the web interface (see "Edit the Properties of a File or List Item" later in this chapter for information).

Upload a File Using the Explorer View

The last way to upload documents is using the explorer view in document libraries. This is also dependent on the same components as the web folders method, and is similar to it in that you can copy and paste files into the folders in the document library.

To get to the explorer view, open the document library in Microsoft Internet Explorer, and then open the view picker to choose the Explorer View from the list of views (see Figure 6.16).

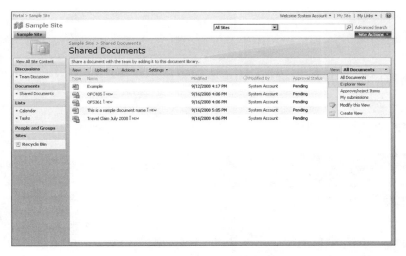

FIGURE 6.16
Choosing Explorer View from the view picker.

The explorer view shows the document library as a folder in a frame in the window (see Figure 6.17).

To upload files to the folder using this view, copy the files, and then right-click in the frame. This will cause a security prompt to appear and warn you that the system is trying to run code that is insecure. Select Yes to open the right-click menu that you get when you right-click in any folder in your machine. Then select Paste to upload the file using the regular Windows copying mechanism, as shown in Figure 6.18.

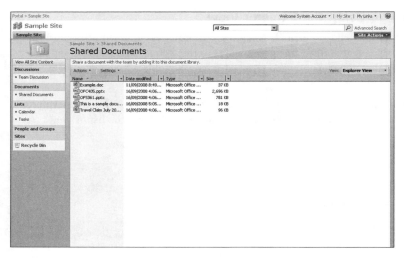

FIGURE 6.17
The document library in the explorer view.

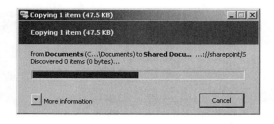

FIGURE 6.18
Uploading a file using the explorer view.

Create a New Document

Scenario/Problem: You want to create a new Microsoft Office document (for example, a Microsoft Word document or a Microsoft Excel workbook).

Solution: To create documents in document libraries, use the New menu in the toolbar. This opens the Office application and the template that was specified by the manager of that document library. For example, if the manager specified that the default template for a document library is a Microsoft Excel template, Excel opens and creates a new file out of that template.

When you are done authoring the document, click Save in the application, and it is automatically saved in the folder that you started from. For more information about saving files into SharePoint, see "Upload a File from an Office Application" earlier in this chapter.

The New button might offer more choices of templates if the manager configured additional content types for the document library. If that is the case, clicking the New button creates a new document based on the *default* content type's template, but using the drop-down menu for the New button (see Figure 6.19) enables you to select other content types that may use different templates and different applications.

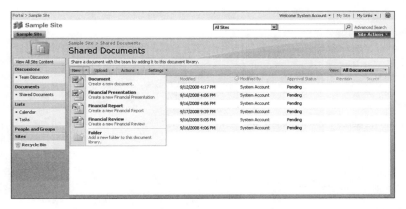

FIGURE 6.19
Using the New drop-down menu to select a content type for the new file.

For example, the content type Financial Presentation might use a Microsoft PowerPoint template, and the content type Financial Report may use a Microsoft Excel template, whereas Financial Review may use a Microsoft Word template.

Create a New List Item

Scenario/Problem: You want to create a new list item (for example, add a contact to a Contacts list or a new event to a calendar list).

Solution: When you're working in a list, you create a new list item by using the New menu in the toolbar. However, unlike with documents, using this menu does not open another application, but rather redirects you to a page that allows you to fill in the metadata (properties or columns) for the new list item (see Figure 6.20).

Because each list can have different properties (columns) in a different order, the screen can look totally different in each list. For example, the announcements list has metadata such as Title and Body (see Figure 6.21), whereas the contacts list has metadata such as First Name, Last Name, and Phone Number (see Figure 6.22).

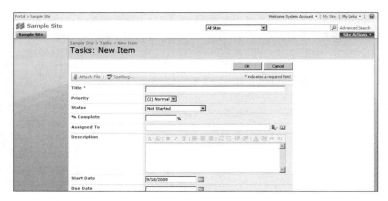

FIGURE 6.20
A sample metadata screen for creating a new task.

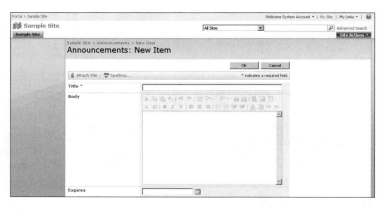

FIGURE 6.21
A sample metadata screen for creating a new announcement.

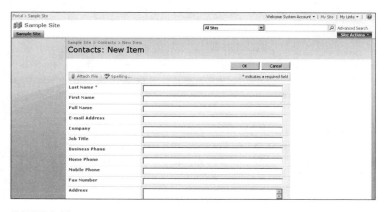

FIGURE 6.22
A sample metadata screen for creating a new contact.

Similar to document libraries, lists can also support multiple content types. This means that the New button might also offer a drop-down of options for you to pick what sort of list item you want to create (see Figure 6.23). Depending on the content type you select, the metadata fields may change.

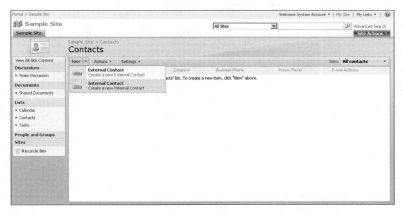

FIGURE 6.23
Choosing content types for creating different types of contacts.

For example, a contacts list might give you the option of creating an item of type External Contact, which should be used for contacts outside the company. This content type asks you to fill in the property for Company (see Figure 6.24). An item of type Internal Contact, on the other hand, does not ask for that property because it assumes that the contact belongs to your company. Instead, it has the property Department (see Figure 6.25).

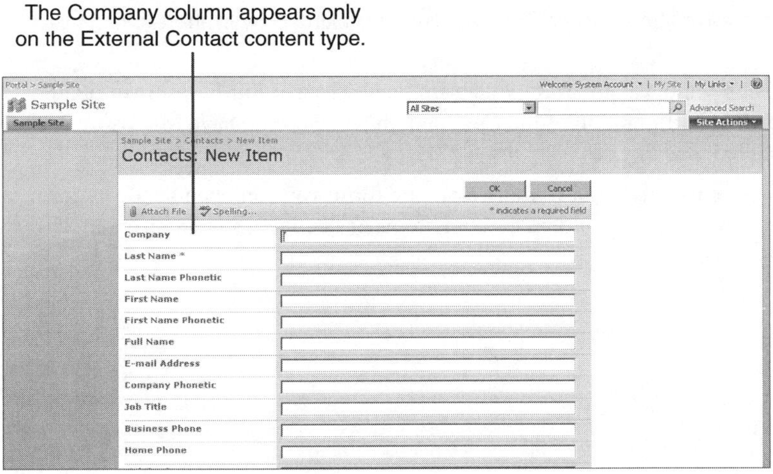

The Company column appears only
on the External Contact content type.

FIGURE 6.24
A sample metadata screen for creating a new external contact.

The Department column appears only
on the Internal Contact content type.

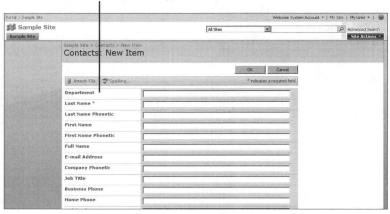

FIGURE 6.25
A sample metadata screen for creating a new internal contact.

Another way to create new list items is to use the datasheet view. This is described
later in this chapter under "Use the Datasheet View to Add, Edit, or Delete Items and
Files."

Fill a Form

Scenario/Problem: You want to fill a form in SharePoint form library.

Solution: In a form library, you can fill a form by clicking New in the toolbar.

Selecting this option opens the form, either in the browser or in Microsoft InfoPath,
depending on the configuration of the form and on whether you have Microsoft
InfoPath installed (see Figures 6.26 and 6.27).

If the library is configured to have more than one form, you can open the drop-down
menu for the new form, the same as creating items or documents from different
content types.

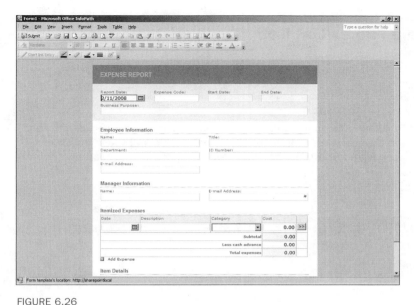

FIGURE 6.26
A form open in Microsoft InfoPath.

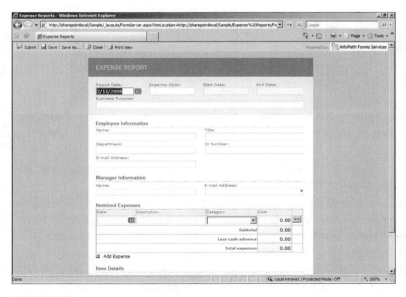

FIGURE 6.27
A form open in the browser.

Delete a File or List Item

Scenario/Problem: You want to delete an existing file in a document library or list item in a list.

Solution: To delete a file or a list item, hover your mouse cursor over the title, and then open the drop-down menu that appears. From the menu, choose the Delete menu item (see Figure 6.28). You are prompted to confirm the deletion.

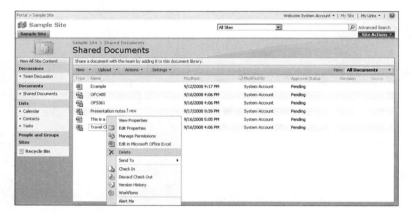

FIGURE 6.28
Selecting Delete from the drop-down menu.

Deleting files requires a different set of permissions than editing, so you might not see the Delete option in the menu. In that case, ask the manager of that list to delete the item.

When an item is deleted, it is stored in the site's Recycle Bin for 30 days, and you can restore it. See "Recover a Deleted File or List Item," next in this chapter.

To delete multiple files or list items, use the datasheet view. This way, you can select many list items or files and delete them in one action. For more information, see "Use the Datasheet View to Add, Edit, or Delete Items and Files" later in this chapter.

To delete multiple files in document libraries you can also use the explorer view. To do this, switch to the explorer view and select the files you want to delete, and either press the Delete key on the keyboard or right-click the files and choose Delete from the context menu.

Recover a Deleted File or List Item

Scenario/Problem: You have accidentally deleted a file or a list item that you need.

Solution: SharePoint has a built-in Recycle Bin functionality that allows you to retract deletions that you might have mistakenly made.

Files and items that were deleted are kept in this Recycle Bin for 30 days, after which they are moved to the administrator Recycle Bin. So if you don't see the file or list item that you have deleted in the past, ask your administrator to recover it for you.

To restore a file, click the Recycle Bin link in the left navigation bar. Clicking this link opens the Recycle Bin page, which shows all the files and list items you have deleted in that specific site (see Figure 6.29).

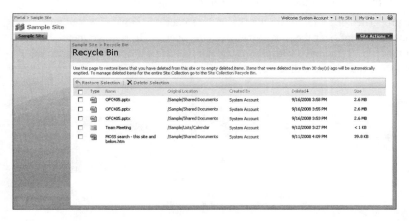

FIGURE 6.29
The Recycle Bin page.

In the deleted items table, you can see the name of the deleted item or file, the original location (site and document library or list and folder), and other data on the file or item, such as who created it in the first place, when it was deleted, and (for files) what size it was.

To restore one or more files and items, select the check box next to the items you want to restore and click Restore Selection. The item or file is restored with all its versions and properties.

You can also delete the item or file from the Recycle Bin by selecting Delete Selection.

Edit the Properties of a File or a List Item

> **Scenario/Problem:** You want to change some of the values that have been entered into the columns for a specific file or list item. For example, you want to change the details for an event in a calendar list or want to change the name or title of a document in a document library.

Solution: Lists and document libraries in SharePoint might be configured to ask you for metadata about files and list items. This data appears when you view the properties of a file or list item (see Chapter 3, "Solutions Regarding Files, Documents, List Items, and Forms") or as columns when you view the document libraries or lists, and may be also shown when you search for documents using the advanced search (see Chapter 4, "Searching in SharePoint").

This information is useful when you are looking for a file or a list item; you might be able to search for it based on the value that is set in its properties.

To edit the properties of a file, locate the file in the folder where it was saved and hover the mouse cursor over the link to the file. This opens a drop-down menu of actions for that file. If you have permissions to edit that file's properties, you see the option to do so in that menu, called Edit Properties (see Figure 6.30).

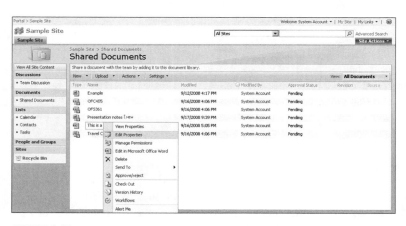

FIGURE 6.30
The Edit Properties menu option appears when you have permissions to edit a document or a list item's properties.

With list items, the procedure is slightly easier. Although you can do the same as for files (as described in the preceding paragraph), you can also simply click the title of the list item to view the properties and then choose Edit Item from the menu bar. Choosing this option opens a page where you can modify the current properties of the file or list item.

Properties that are mandatory are marked with a red asterisk (*) next to them, and you must fill in those properties to be able to save your changes (see Figure 6.31). If you don't fill in those properties, SharePoint does not let you click OK and tells you what properties are not filled in.

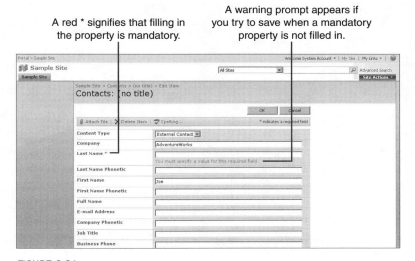

A red * signifies that filling in the property is mandatory.

A warning prompt appears if you try to save when a mandatory property is not filled in.

FIGURE 6.31
When you do not fill in a required property, SharePoint prompts you for it when you try to save.

File and list item properties can be of different types, and each type has a different way of capturing data (see Figure 6.32). For example, a text property displays a text box for you to enter data. A date property can appear as a text box (for the date) with a button next to it that looks like a calendar that will allow you to pick a date, and it might even have two drop-downs for selecting a time. A yes/no field appears as a check box.

SharePoint also validates the properties based on the types. This means, for example, that you cannot write text in a date field or in a numeric property. If you do so, SharePoint shows you a red error message under that field and prevents you from saving the properties until you fix the problem.

Additionally, the document library or list manager may choose to impose additional conditions on some of the properties—for example, stating that the title of a file should be up to 40 characters long. SharePoint also alerts you if you try to save the properties when one of those conditions is not met, and tells you what field is not set correctly and what limitations are configured for that field.

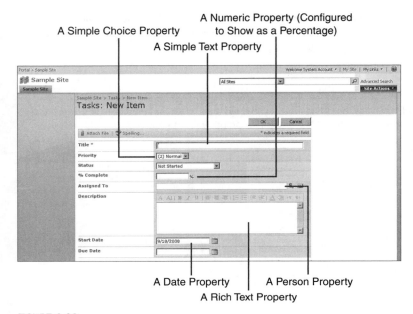

FIGURE 6.32
Different property types have different ways to enter or select data. In this task form, you can see six different types.

An important action when creating a new file in some document libraries is choosing the content type for the file. Different content types require different properties, so it is recommended that before you enter the other properties, you select the content type first. This should not be a problem because the content type property is always the first one to appear in the list of properties (if the document library was configured to use more than one content type), as you can see in Figure 6.33.

FIGURE 6.33
The content type selection is the first thing you need to choose when uploading a file.

Changing the content type causes the page to refresh and load the properties that are required for the selected content type. However, if the new content type has some of the same properties as the old, the values in those properties are not lost. You therefore can switch between content types without worrying about losing the information.

After you have filled in all the properties that you want, click OK at the bottom or the top of the page to save the changes.

If the document library is set up to require you to check in and check out files, you must check in the file after changing its properties. Read "Check In and Check Out a File or List Item" later in this chapter for more information on how to do so.

To edit the properties of multiple list items or files, you can also use the datasheet view. For more information on that, see the next section.

Use the Datasheet View to Add, Edit, or Delete Items and Files

Scenario/Problem: You want to add, edit, or delete multiple items to a list or library in an easy way, not having to click each one to edit or delete it separately, or not wanting to click the New button many times, especially because the details that you want to modify are similar.

Solution: The datasheet view, as explained earlier, is similar to a Microsoft Excel datasheet and allows copying and pasting data into the list or library (see Figure 6.34).

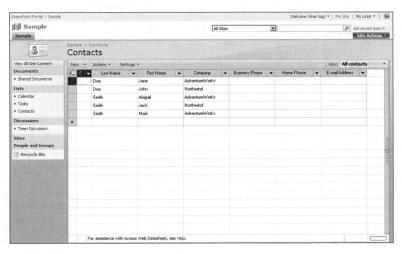

FIGURE 6.34
A datasheet view showing a contacts list.

This interface makes adding, editing, and deleting multiple list items or files a lot easier. You can create list items by copying data from Microsoft Excel or from other spreadsheet applications; you can edit the properties of many list items or files by copying cells, or delete many files in one action.

If you want to view a datasheet view, there are certain requirements for your computer. For one, the datasheet component must be installed on your machine. This component is part of the Microsoft Office installation for Microsoft Office Professional 2003 or 2007. Additionally, the browser you are using to view the site must be compatible with the datasheet view and allow showing ActiveX controls. If you are getting error messages, contact your administrator for assistance (see Figure 6.35).

FIGURE 6.35
An error message that appears when you're trying to switch to a datasheet view and Microsoft Office is not installed.

Switch to a Datasheet View

Some views are built to be datasheet views by default. In this case, just switching to the view displays the datasheet interface. For more information about how to switch between views, see "Switch List Views in Lists and Libraries" in Chapter 3.

However, you can also switch to a datasheet view version of any standard view, even if the view creator did not create it as a datasheet view. To switch to the datasheet view from a standard view, open the Actions menu for the list and choose the Edit in Datasheet option from the drop-down menu (see Figure 6.36).

To switch back to the standard view, open the Actions menu again and choose Show in Standard View.

> **NOTE** If you are trying to switch to a datasheet view with a browser that is not supported (for example, Mozilla Firefox), the option to switch to the datasheet view is not displayed.

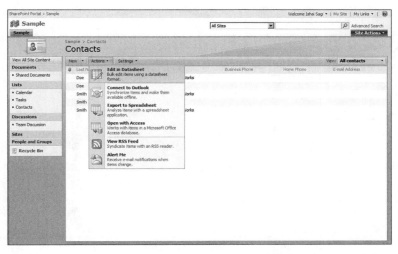

FIGURE 6.36
Switching to a datasheet view.

Add a List Item Using the Datasheet View

You can use the datasheet view to add list items. This approach does not work with document libraries because they require you to upload a file for each row, and the datasheet view does not have an interface to upload a file. Because list items are made strictly of data in columns, you can create new ones from the datasheet view.

> **NOTE** When some columns are mandatory and the view does not show these columns, the datasheet view does not let you create new items. To be able to create new list items in the datasheet view, you must use a view that displays all the mandatory columns.

To create a new list item in the datasheet view, just type values in the last row (the one marked with an asterisk) in the datasheet. The list item is created with the values you have typed in. To finish adding the list item, press Enter or click another row in the datasheet view. The datasheet creates the list item (see Figure 6.37).

If there are many rows in the datasheet and you want to avoid scrolling down to the bottom to add a new list item, a quick way to get to the last row is to open the Actions menu and choose New Row. Doing so scrolls down to the new row at the bottom.

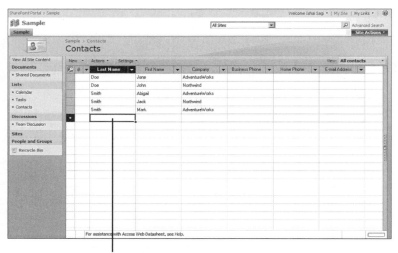

To create a new list item, type in the
values for the columns in the last row.

FIGURE 6.37
Creating a new list item using the datasheet view.

Add Multiple List Items from Microsoft Excel Using the Datasheet View

A useful way to use the datasheet view is to populate a list with the data from an existing spreadsheet. If you have a spreadsheet with many items, instead of typing them one by one using the method described in "Create a New List Item" earlier in this chapter, you can use the datasheet view to just paste in the values.

For example, if you have a Microsoft Excel spreadsheet with information about products, and you want to copy that information to a SharePoint list, you can use the datasheet view to copy the information to the list, even if the columns are not the same. To do that, open the spreadsheet and select the information you want to copy (see Figure 6.38).

Now switch to the SharePoint list to the datasheet view that shows the columns that you want to paste into. Remember, the view must have all mandatory columns for that list showing.

If the columns in the datasheet view are not in the same order as they were in the Microsoft Excel spreadsheet, you must reorder them in the datasheet view. To do that, simply drag and drop the column headers until the order is correct so that when you paste the information, the correct information goes in the right column. In the preceding example, the Product Alternate Key column should be first in the datasheet view because it was first in Excel, so it needs to be moved before the Title field in the view (see Figure 6.39).

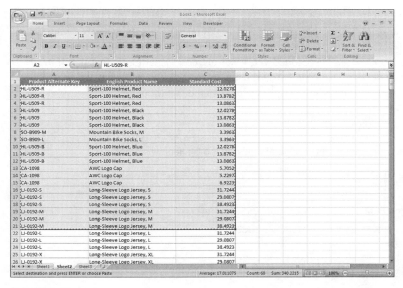

FIGURE 6.38
Select the information from Microsoft Excel that you want to copy to the SharePoint list, and copy it.

When the datasheet view is ready for the data, just right-click the first cell and choose Paste to paste the data from Microsoft Excel (see Figure 6.39).

FIGURE 6.39
Right-click the first cell in the first data column and choose Paste.

The information from the Microsoft Excel spreadsheet is pasted into the list. Because this can be a lot of information, SharePoint might take a while to actually create the list items. You can see the progress on the left side of the datasheet view (see Figure 6.40). If an item has not been added yet, it has an icon symbolizing that it still needs to be synchronized with SharePoint. You must wait until all the items have been synchronized before closing the window or navigating to a different page.

This icon symbolizes that the list item was not yet synchronized with SharePoint.

A row has synchronized with SharePoint, and the list item was created.

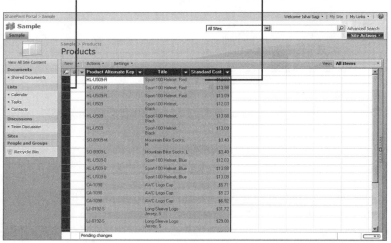

FIGURE 6.40
Adding multiple list items using the datasheet view.

Check In and Check Out a File or List Item

Scenario/Problem: Some document libraries and lists require you to check out a file or list item before changing it (changing includes changing the properties of a file or list item and editing a file's contents as well). You want to make changes to the file or list item and then share the changes with other people working on that site.

Solution: Checking in documents from the Office interface was mentioned earlier in this chapter under "Upload a File from an Office Application." You can use that method, and you can also use the same process to check out a document: Just open the document using the Microsoft Office application and select the Check Out option from the menus. If you choose Edit from the document's or list item's drop-down menu, usually the document or list item automatically checks itself out for you. However, check-out and check-in are also offered on the web interface because not all files are Microsoft Office documents, and sometimes you do not want to open a Microsoft Office application just to check out a document—for example, just to make sure no one else is modifying them. When you are done with your changes, you should check them back in if you want other people to see your changes.

To accomplish this, hover the mouse cursor over the title of the file or list item. This shows a drop-down menu for that item. Open that menu and choose the Check Out option to check out, as shown in Figure 6.41, or Check In to check in.

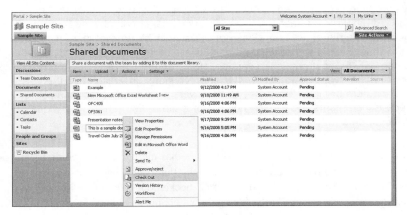

FIGURE 6.41
The Check Out option is in the file's or list item's drop-down menu.

When checking out files (as opposed to list items), if you are using a Microsoft Internet Explorer (other browsers may support this option in the future as well), you are asked whether you want to check out the file to a local drafts folder.

If you select OK, a copy of the file is placed in a special folder usually called SharePoint Drafts under your My Documents folder on your computer (this location can be changed from your Office applications). If you do not choose that option, the file is just marked as checked out to you, but no copy of the file is made. The SharePoint drafts folder allows you to work on the document on your machine, even when not connected to the SharePoint site. When you connect again, you can go back to the document library to check in the document; doing this uploads it from the SharePoint drafts folder.

Checking in a file increases the version number of the file. The amount of increase depends on the settings for the list or document library. The simplest setting means that every time you check in a file or list item, its version is increased by 1. However, settings can change that. See "Publish a File or List Item" next for more information on how different settings can affect the check-in process.

Publish a File or List Item

Scenario/Problem: A document library or list requires you to publish a file or list item that you have created or modified before it shows the new file or item to other users.

Solution: Some document libraries and lists require you to publish files and list items before other people can see them. This is similar to checking in a file or list item as described in "Check In and Check Out a File or List Item" earlier in this chapter. The big difference is that the list or library manager can choose to set it up so that checking in a file or list item does not make it visible to everyone. It will be visible just to other people with editing permissions on the library, and readers will be able to see only the last published version. However, the list or library manager may choose to allow everyone to see unpublished versions, in which case the publishing of an item or file is just a way to track version numbers; for example, a regular check-in increments the version number of a file or list item by 0.1, while publishing increments it by 1.

If the document library or list that you are working on has the publishing requirement, the drop-down menu for a list item or file includes the Publish a Major Version option, if the file is checked in but not published or if it is checked out to you (see Figure 6.42). Clicking that option checks in the file again but changes the version number of the item or file, and enables readers to view this version.

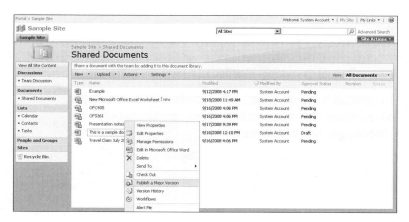

FIGURE 6.42
When publishing is required, you must choose Publish a Major Version.

If the list or library you are working on is set up to require approval, the file will not be published until someone with the appropriate permissions approves it (see Figure 6.43). This means that in spite of your publishing the file, readers may still see only the previously published version until someone approves your version. Of course, that, too, depends on the configuration.

A File That Has Been Checked In But Not Published

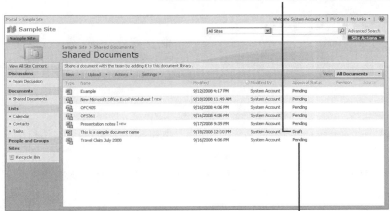

A File That Has Been Published But Not Approved

FIGURE 6.43
When publishing and approval are required, checked-in files are still considered to be drafts, and published documents that haven't been approved are considered to be pending approval.

To see how to approve a file that was published, see "Approve or Reject a File or List Item" later in this chapter.

See What Files or List Items Are Checked Out to You

Scenario/Problem: You have checked out some files or list items, and you want to find them to continue editing them, discard the check-out, or check them in again.

Solution: The option to see a report on all files or list items that are checked out to you in a site does not appear on all sites. Its inclusion depends on the features that the site manager enabled on the site you are using, or rather on the site collection you are using.

To access that report, you need to use the Site Actions menu that appears at the upper-right corner of the page (if you have the required permissions and if the site uses the right features), and from that menu, select View Reports. This exposes another flyout menu to the left with options for many reports (see Figure 6.44).

FIGURE 6.44
The reports for a site are under the Site Actions menu if the site has the reports configured.

Select the Checked Out To Me option from that menu, and you are directed to a page that shows all the files and list items from all the sites under the current site (see Figure 6.45).

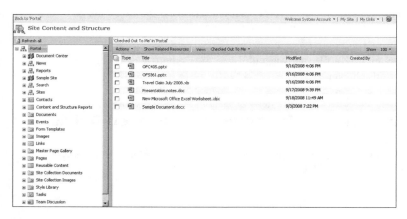

FIGURE 6.45
This page shows all the files and sites under the current site.

You can then use the drop-down menus for each of the files to check them in, or select multiple files with the check boxes and check them all in using the Actions menu at the top (see Figure 6.46).

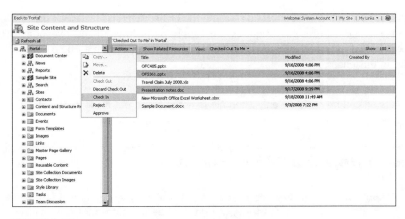

FIGURE 6.46
Selecting Check In from the Actions menu enables you to check in the files.

Restore a Past Version of a File or List Item

Scenario/Problem: You want to restore a file or list item to a past version and make it the current version.

Solution: Chapter 3 explained how to view the past versions of files and list items.

To restore one of those versions, hover the mouse cursor over the date and time for that version. This opens the drop-down menu. From the drop-down menu, select Restore from the options (see Figure 6.47).

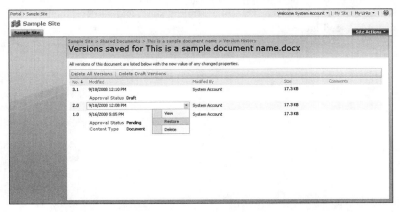

FIGURE 6.47
Selecting Restore brings back a past version of a file or list item.

Selecting this option creates a new version for the file or list item and increases the version number. If the list or library requires check-in or publishing, the new version still must be checked in after the restore. See "Check In and Check Out a File or List Item" earlier in this chapter.

> **NOTE** A version can be restored only if the file is not checked out by someone else.

Approve or Reject a File or List Item

> **Scenario/Problem:** You are the approver on a list or library, and you need to approve or reject a file or list item that another user has submitted for approval.

Solution: Some file libraries and lists require approval of files or lists. When this content approval setting is enabled, an item or file that has been checked in or published is not published automatically, but instead remains in a pending state until it is approved or rejected. This means that the file or item is still considered a draft and is given the Draft status.

To be able to approve or reject files or items, you need specific permissions on the library or list. When a file or item is approved, it is assigned an Approved status in the list or library, and it is displayed to anyone with permission to view the list or library.

When a file or item is rejected, it remains in a pending state and is visible only to the people with permission to view drafts (see Figure 6.48).

To approve or reject a file or an item, open the drop-down menu for that file or item and choose Approve/Reject from the menu options (see Figure 6.49).

Selecting this option directs you to the Approve/Reject screen, where you can choose to approve or reject or keep the file or item in a pending state, and add comments about your decision (see Figure 6.50).

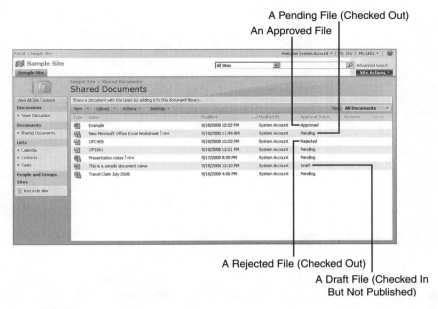

FIGURE 6.48
This page shows a file's status.

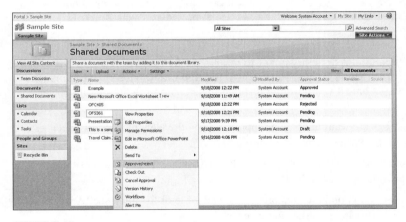

FIGURE 6.49
Selecting Approve/Reject from the context menu.

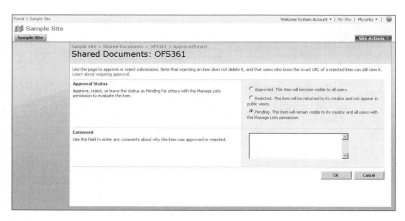

FIGURE 6.50
The screen enables you to change a file's or item's status.

See What Files or List Items Are Waiting for Your Approval

Scenario/Problem: You are the approver on a list or library, and you need to see what files or list items other users have submitted for your approval.

Solution: When a list or library is set to require content approval, views are added to the regular list views to help you manage the approval of files or list items. You see those views only if you have approval permissions on the list or library.

To see what files are waiting for your approval, open the view picker and select Approve/Reject Items as shown in Figure 6.51.

The view shows you all the items, grouped by their status. To see the ones that are waiting approval, look under the Pending group (see Figure 6.52).

For more information on how to approve or reject a file or list item, see "Approve or Reject a File or List Item" earlier in this chapter.

FIGURE 6.51
Selecting the Approve/Reject items view.

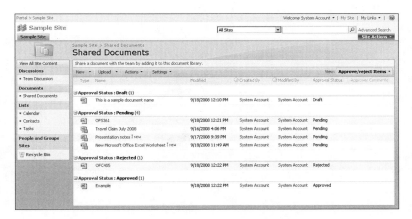

FIGURE 6.52
The Pending group shows files or items awaiting approval.

CHAPTER 7

Creating Lists and Document Libraries

IN THIS CHAPTER

- ▶ Open the Create Page for Lists and Libraries
- ▶ Create a New Document Library
- ▶ Create a New List
- ▶ Create a New Survey
- ▶ Add a Column to a List or Document Library
- ▶ Add a Site Column to a List or Document Library
- ▶ Choose a Default Value for a Column
- ▶ Choose a Column Type
- ▶ Change or Remove a Column in a List or Document Library
- ▶ Change the Order of Columns in a List or Document Library
- ▶ Branching in Surveys
- ▶ Add a Site Column to a List or Document Library
- ▶ Rename a List or Document Library or Change Its Description
- ▶ Change the Versioning Settings for a List or Document Library
- ▶ Change the Document Template for the New Button in a Document Library
- ▶ Add a Content Type to a List or Document Library
- ▶ Remove a Content Type from a List or Document Library
- ▶ Enable or Disable Folders in a List or Document Library

Lists and document libraries are used throughout SharePoint to store any information that users need. This chapter explains how to perform basic tasks around creating and customizing lists and document libraries, including creating columns (metadata), setting the document templates for document libraries, and more.

Open the Create Page for Lists and Libraries

Scenario/Problem: You want to create a list or a library.

Solution: There are different ways to get to the list or document/picture/form library creation page, and depending on the configuration of the site, the choices may be different.

The first step is to open the site where you want the document library to be created. In most sites, you can then open the Site Actions menu and choose the Create menu option to get to the Create page (see Figure 7.1).

FIGURE 7.1
Open the Site Actions menu and choose Create.

In sites that are configured to be publishing sites, the Create option is not in the menu—it is replaced by options such as Create Page, which is used to create pages in the site, and Create Site, which is used to create subsites under the current site. In sites where the option is missing from the menu you must use the View All Site Content option either on the Site Actions menu or the link in the left navigation bar (see Figure 7.2).

You can choose the View All Site Content option on the left navigation bar.   You can choose the View All Site Content option on the Site Actions menu.

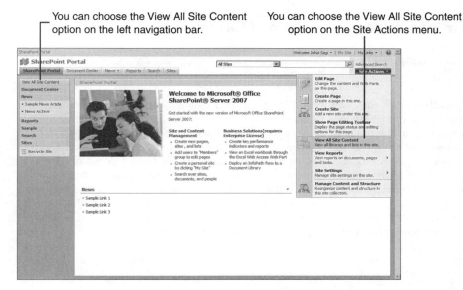

FIGURE 7.2
Use either option to get to the All Site Content page.

Selecting this option opens the All Site Content page, where you can then click the Create button to get to the Create page.

The page that allows you to create lists and libraries then opens, showing all the different kinds of lists and libraries that you can create in that site (see Figure 7.3). Different sites may show different kinds of list and library templates.

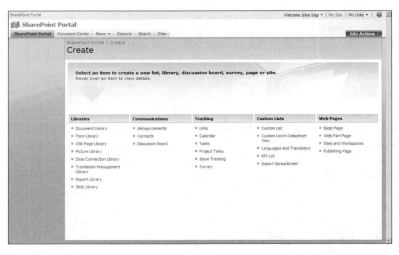

FIGURE 7.3
The list and library Create page.

Create a New Document Library

Scenario/Problem: You want to create a new document library.

Solution: After you open the Create page, as explained earlier in this chapter, click the Document Library link to create a new document library. The following page asks you for the required settings for the document library (see Figure 7.4). This page might show different options for the document library, depending on the server configuration. For example, some SharePoint servers can allow a document library to have an associated email address and receive emails sent to that library directly into the document library itself. If that option is enabled in the server, the settings page will ask you for additional information, such as the email address that should be associated with the document library. If the option is not enabled, the setting will not be displayed on the page, as can be seen in Figure 7.4.

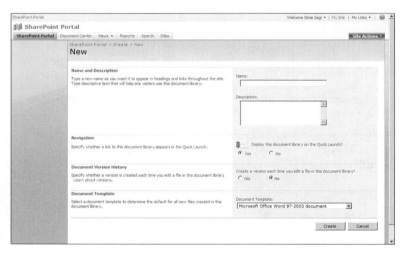

FIGURE 7.4
Settings for a new document library.

The first option is the name for the document library. This name determines not just the title that the users will see, but also the link that will be created for the document library. For example, if you call the document library Presentations, the link to the document library is the link to the site and then /Presentations. This point is important because although you can change the title of the document library later, you cannot change its link. You can also set the description for the library. This description is usually displayed to users in the All Site Content page next to the library's name, and in most cases it also appears in all the views for the library, just above the view. You can always change the description later in the library's settings.

For more information about how to change the title or description for a list or a document library, see "Rename a List or Document Library or Change Its Description" later in this chapter.

> **TIP**   If you want to avoid complicated links, choose a short name for the document library when you are creating it, and after that change the title for the document library. For example, if you want to create a document library for human resources policies, name it *HRP* when creating it, and then change the title to *Human Resources Policies* after it has been created. That way, the link is short and easy to type or view (when sending it in email, for example), and the title explains to all users what should be in that document library.
>
> This approach can also help you avoid unreadable links. For example, if your document library's name has spaces in it, the link to the document library will have the special character combination %20 instead of the spaces, which will make the link look long and complex. Using this tip you can create the document library with a short name without spaces, and then rename the title to have the spaces.

> **NOTE**   Although you can have two document libraries with the same title, you cannot have two document libraries with the same link. This means that the link to the document library must be unique, and in this initial screen, you choose the unique name. If that name is already in use, SharePoint prevents you from creating the document library and asks for another name. Remember that you can always change the title afterward.

The next option you can set is whether a link to the document library should be added to the quick launch navigation bar (the left navigation bar for the site). This option can be changed later also.

The next choice to make is whether SharePoint should manage versions for documents in the document library. If you choose YES then all changes in documents will create new versions of the documents. Although you can change this option later, if you choose NO, all changes made in documents until you change the setting will not be stored in separate versions. However, if your site has a size quota, and you are worried about consuming a lot of space, leaving this setting turned off can save quite a bit of space.

For more information about changing the versioning information for a list or document library, as well as setting some more advanced versioning options, see "Change the Versioning Settings for a List or Document Library" later in this chapter.

The last option, Document Template, enables you to pick the application or type of file that will be used when the user clicks the New button in the document library. For example, you can choose Microsoft Word to have SharePoint open an empty Microsoft Word document when the user clicks the New button, or you can choose any of the other Microsoft Office applications. For web pages, you can choose either Basic Page (an empty page that you can then type text on) or Web Part Page, which will create a page that allows the user to add web parts.

By default, the new document library has only the Document content type associated with it, so the New button does not show any options for different kinds of file types, but here you can set a specific file type that the users can use with the New button. This can be later changed also, as explained in "Change the Document Template for the New Button in a Document Library," later in this chapter.

When you are finished selecting the options, click Create to create the document library. A new, empty library is created with the settings you chose.

Create a New List

Scenario/Problem: You want to create a new list.

Solution: To create a list in a site, navigate to the site's list and library's Create page, and click the link for the type of list that you want to create. For example, you can create a list of events by choosing the Calendar type or a discussion board list by choosing Discussion Board. If you want a list that does not have any specific columns like those lists, choose the Custom List type; that creates a list that has only one column (Title), to which you can later add additional columns as explained in "Add a Column to a List or Document Library," later in this chapter.

Selecting one of these options opens the page that enables you to select the initial settings for the list. Some lists, such as the survey list, have special settings, which are covered later in this chapter, but most lists have exactly the same initial settings.

Similar to the initial settings for a document library, a list first requires you to choose a name. However, unlike with document libraries, the link to the list (or any other news) is the site link, then /Lists/, and then the name you choose for the list.

TIP As with document libraries, it is recommended that you choose a short name for the list when you are creating it and after that change the title.

NOTE As with document libraries, the name you choose here must be unique in the site. If you choose a name that is already in use in the site, SharePoint does not let you create the list and asks you for a different name. Remember that you can always change the title to anything you want after the list has been created.

You can also set the description for the list that will show up in the All Site Content page of the site next to the list's name and in the views of the list. This can be modified later in the list settings. For more information about how to modify the title or description of a list, see "Rename a List or Document Library or Change Its Description," later in this chapter.

Finally, you can choose whether a link to the list should be added to the quick launch (the left navigation bar) of the site. This, too, can be modified later, either through the list settings or through the site navigation settings (read more about changing the site navigation in Chapter 13, "Customizing a SharePoint Site").

When you are done selecting the options, click Create to create the list. A new, empty instance of the list type that you selected is created with the settings you chose.

Create a New Survey

Scenario/Problem: You want to create a new survey.

Solution: To create a survey, choose Survey in the list and library's Create page of the site. Selecting this option opens the survey initial settings page for the new survey you are creating.

Although most of the settings are exactly like the ones for a regular list, the survey list has two more settings that you need to set before creating the list. These options appear under the Survey Options section of the page.

The first option to configure—Show User Names in Survey Results?—enables you to decide whether the survey will be anonymous. Choosing No means that the person viewing the results of the survey will not be able to tell who answered what in the survey in any way. This setting is useful if you want to get honest feedback from people who might be concerned about revealing their true opinions—for example, using an employee satisfaction survey.

Choosing Yes tells SharePoint to show the name of the person who answered next to his or her answer in the reports. This setting is useful when you want to track who answered what—for example, a survey that collects data from employees about what hotel they like to stay in when they are traveling.

The next option is whether to allow multiple responses. By default, a survey allows each person to answer the survey only once—like a voting system. However, you might want to create surveys that allow people to respond multiple times—for example, a survey that asks employees for suggestions for improving the company, where every employee might want to answer several times, every time they think of a new suggestion.

After you finished setting the settings for the survey, click the Next button. Unlike with other list types, when creating a survey you will immediately be redirected to create questions for the survey.

The questions are almost identical to list columns, and creating them is almost the same as the process described in "Add a Column to a List or Document Library," later in this chapter. However, surveys also have additional options for column types that are not available in regular lists: the Rating Scale question type and a Page Separator. The task "Choose a Column Type" describes these options in more detail.

When you are finished configuring the first question of the survey, either click the Next Question button to create another question, or click the Finish button to finalize the survey. Questions can always be added, modified, or removed in the future (see "Change or Remove a Column in a List or a Document Library" later in this chapter).

When creating questions for surveys, the questions support another unique option called *branching*. This enables you to display different questions to users based on the answers they answered previously. For more information about branching, see "Branching in Surveys," later in this chapter.

Add a Column to a List or Document Library

Scenario/Problem: You want to create a new column and add it to an existing list or document library. For example, you might want to add a date column called Birthday for a contacts list or a choice or lookup column called Client to a document library so that the users can choose which client the document is about. (For more information about choice and lookup columns, see "Choose a Column Type," later in this chapter.)

Solution: To add a column to a list or document library, select the Create Column option from the Settings menu in any view of the list or document library, as shown in Figure 7.5.

TIP The Create Column option creates a new column in the list or library but does not let you select from the site columns that are already set up in the site. To learn how to add an existing site column to the list or library, see "Add a Site Column to a List or Document Library," later in this chapter.

Choosing the Create Column option opens the page where you can define the type of column you want to add, as well as set the settings on that column (see Figure 7.6).

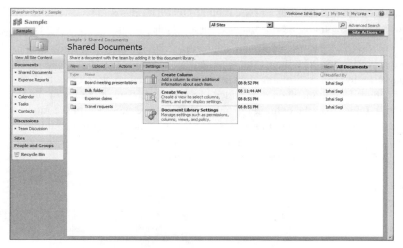

FIGURE 7.5
Open the Settings menu and choose the option to add a column to the list or library.

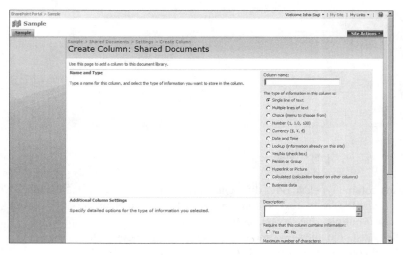

FIGURE 7.6
Creating a new column.

The first choice to make is the name of the column. Column names must be unique in the list (you cannot have two columns with the exact same name).

After choosing the name for the column, you must choose the type of the column, as shown in Figure 7.6. There are numerous types of columns, and developers may add to those types, so you might see more than the built-in types. Also, as mentioned earlier in "Create a New Survey," creating a new column in that list (also known as creating a new question) will show more options that are not available for standard list types.

All column types require you to choose a name for the column. They also allow you to specify the description for the column and whether the column is required (making the column mandatory in the list—forcing the user to fill it in when creating or editing an item), and whether the column should be added to the default view of the list or library (see Figure 7.7). Other than the column type all options can be modified in the future. Changing the column type for a column is possible but is limited to certain column types. For more information about modifying a column see "Change or Remove a Column in a List or Document Library," later in this chapter.

FIGURE 7.7
Defining the settings for a new column.

However, each column type can offer different configuration options for that column; for example, a Single Line of Text column type has a Maximum Number of Characters setting, whereas Multiple Lines of Text column type has a Configuration option for how many lines it should allow. For more information about choosing a column type and the different configuration options that each type may have, see "Choose a Column Type" later in this chapter.

Add a Site Column to a List or Document Library

Scenario/Problem: You want to add an existing site column that has been defined in the site to an existing list or document library.

Solution: As explained in Chapter 1, "About Microsoft SharePoint 2007," a site column is a column that is defined on the site level rather than on the list or library level. Reusing those columns in lists and libraries makes a lot of sense. If a change to the column setting is required in many lists and libraries, it is possible to change the column at the site level once, and that updates all the lists and libraries using that column.

If you want to use an existing site column instead of creating a new column, open the list's or library's settings page by opening the Settings menu in the toolbar for that list or library, and choose either List Settings or Document Library Settings (see Figure 7.8).

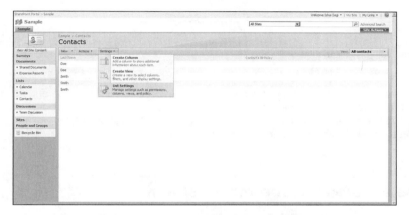

FIGURE 7.8
Getting to the list settings of a contacts list.

In the list's or library's settings page that opens, scroll down to the Columns section of the page. Here, you see the list of all the columns that have been added to the list or library. In this section, click the Add from Existing Site Columns link. This selection opens a page that enables you to pick one or more site columns to be added to the document library or list (see Figure 7.9).

To choose a column, locate it in the Available Site Columns box, select it, and click the Add button to add it to the Columns to Add box. If you regret your choice and want to undo it, select the column in the Columns to Add box and click the Remove button.

To more easily find a column, you can filter the columns that are in the Available Site Columns box by choosing the group for the column. Site columns are grouped in logical groups. For example, the Core Document Columns group holds columns that are commonly used by most documents: Author, Comments, Date Created, and so on. By default, you see the site columns from all groups available to you. To choose a different group, open the Select Site Columns From drop-down box and select a different group.

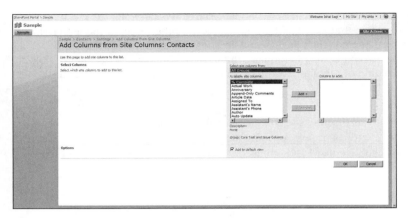

FIGURE 7.9
Choosing site columns for the list or library.

> **TIP** When adding a site column, you cannot specify any settings on it because any column settings are defined in the site level. However, after adding the column, you can modify it like any other column (see the instructions in "Change or Remove a Column in a List or Document Library," later in this chapter).

Choose a Default Value for a Column

Scenario/Problem: You want to define a default value for an existing or new column in a library or list. For example, in some instances you want date columns to default to the current day's date or text columns to default to the current user's name; or for choice columns, where the user can choose from multiple choices, you want to select one of the choices as the default.

Solution: Some types of columns can have default values. Default values appear in the column when a user is creating a new list item or is uploading a new file, but the user can then choose to change the value.

Some column types allow more advanced settings for default values than others, and the specifics for those column types are covered under "Choose a Column Type," next.

Choose a Column Type

Scenario/Problem: You are creating a new column in a library, list, or site, and you have to select a column type for the new column.

Solution: When you're creating a new column, the first thing you need to decide (apart from the name for the column) is its type. The type of the column defines what kind of data can go into it, and SharePoint has a lot of different built-in column types for you to choose from. The following sections explain each built-in column type and the different settings you can define for that type.

Single Line of Text

Use the Single Line of Text column type when you want the user to enter simple text, in a single line (no line breaks), as shown in Figure 7.10.

FIGURE 7.10
The First Name column in a contacts list is an example of a Single Line of Text column.

Aside from the regular settings, such as the description for the column and whether the column is mandatory, you can define the maximum number of characters allowed in the field (up to 255 characters) and the default value for the column (see Figure 7.11).

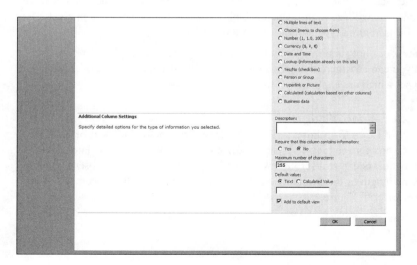

FIGURE 7.11
Defining the settings for a Single Line of Text column type.

The default value for a Single Line of Text column can be either a static piece of text that you type if you select the option Text, or a calculated value showing the current user's account name by using the token [Me]. For example, you might want to create a calculated default that will have a text (that the user can change) saying who purchased an item. The default will be the name of the current user filling the form, but the user might be filling the form for someone else, and the text might need to be changed. Figures 7.12 and 7.13 show how to configure this and how it will look to the users.

FIGURE 7.12

Defining a calculated default value.

Purchase Note	Purchased by:SHAREPOINT-TIPS\janedoe

FIGURE 7.13

The calculated default value when a user creates a new item.

Multiple Lines of Text

The Multiple Lines of Text column type allows users to enter text with more than one line (line breaks are allowed). It can be configured to allow different editing options for the user, as can be seen in Figure 7.14.

As shown in Figure 7.14 the column type can be configured to allow rich formatting of the text—you can make parts of the text bold; underlined; a different font or color; and even include pictures, tables, and links. This configuration is not available in document libraries, and you will see it only when adding a site column or a column in a list. The settings for this column type are shown in Figure 7.15.

This column does not support a default value, so there is no setting to configure one. However, you can configure the column with three settings that are special for this column type, which are explained in the following sections.

Number of Lines for Editing

The Number of Lines for Editing setting determines how many lines will be displayed in the editing box for the text. This can be any number from 1 (only one line will be displayed, but users can still scroll down or up in the box) to 1,000. This setting does not affect the length of the text that can go into the column, just the appearance of the editing box (refer to Figure 7.14).

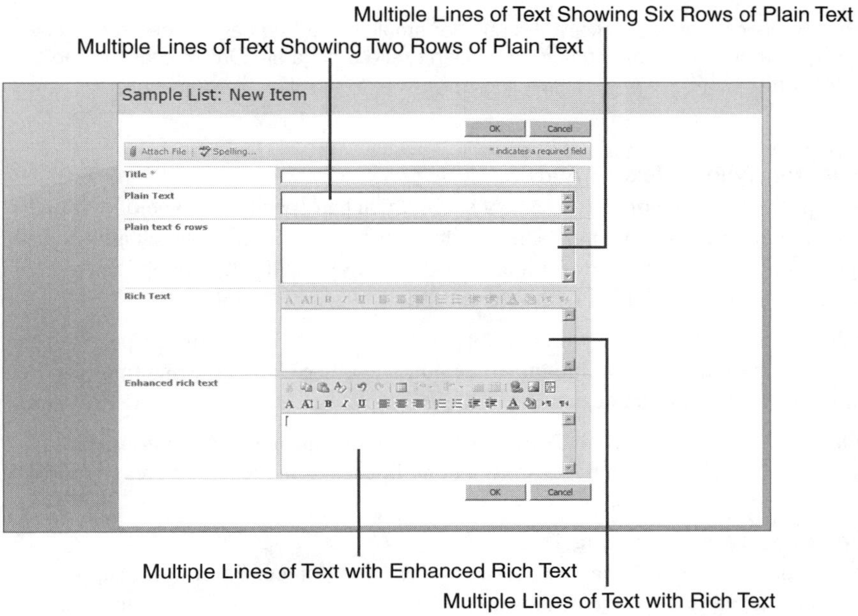

Multiple Lines of Text Showing Six Rows of Plain Text

Multiple Lines of Text Showing Two Rows of Plain Text

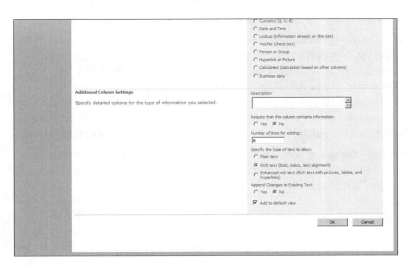

Multiple Lines of Text with Enhanced Rich Text

Multiple Lines of Text with Rich Text

FIGURE 7.14
Different configurations of the Multiple Lines of Text column.

FIGURE 7.15
Defining the settings for a Multiple Lines of Text column type.

> **TIP** It is recommended to keep the number small in the Number of Lines for Editing setting so that the column editing box doesn't take a huge amount of space in the editing form.

Specify the Type of Text to Allow

In the Specify the Type of Text to Allow setting, you can specify the type of text that can be entered in the editing box. The simplest option is Plain Text, which allows just simple, unformatted text (refer to Figure 7.14). The users will not have options to make any part of the text bold or a different font.

The next option is Rich Text, which enables the users to set formatting on parts of the text and set the font, font size, alignment, color, and other kinds of formatting that are common when writing rich text.

The last option, Enhanced Rich Text, allows even more special formatting, such as making parts of the text into hyperlinks, adding images to the text, and creating tables.

Append Changes to Existing Text

The last option, Append Changes to Existing Text, lets you configure what happens when someone edits the value of the column in a list item or a file. By default, the setting is No, which means that when someone edits the value, the value just changes to the new value. Users who then view the properties of the list item or file see the new value, not the old one. If they want to see the old one, they must open the list item's or file's version history, if versioning is configured in the document library.

However, choosing Yes here changes how the column is displayed when users view the properties of the list item or file. Instead of seeing just the current value, they also are shown the entire history of what the value was before, including who made the change and when. This option can be turned on only when versioning is enabled on the list or library because SharePoint must track the old versions of the value to show this information. For information about how to configure versioning on the list or library, see "Change the Versioning Settings for a List or Document Library," later in this chapter.

When the Append Changes option is enabled, the old entries and the current one appear under the editing box for the column. If there are no old entries, that is shown also, as shown in Figure 7.16.

FIGURE 7.16
The Address column shows there haven't been any old values.

When there are old entries, such as corrections to a value, they are shown to a user viewing the item as a list of values, complete with who wrote the value and when (see Figure 7.17).

FIGURE 7.17
The Address column shows the history of changes when viewing the properties of a list item.

When you are editing a list item of a file, the list of values appears below the editing box for the column, while the edit box itself does not have anything in it (see Figure 7.18).

FIGURE 7.18
The Address column shows the history of changes when editing the properties of a list item.

Choice (Menu to Choose From)

A choice column is often used when you want the users to choose from a list of options for the value of the column in different configurations; for example, a list of regions or countries, as shown in Figures 7.19 through 7.21, with different controls appearing to the user.

FIGURE 7.19
A choice column allowing users to select one or more choices from a list.

FIGURE 7.20
A choice column allowing users to select only one choice, using the drop-down menu configuration.

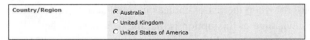

FIGURE 7.21
A choice column allowing users to select only one choice, using the radio buttons configuration.

Choice columns enable you to specify the values you want the users to choose from, and you can configure them to allow the users to either make a single selection or select multiple values from the list (see Figure 7.22).

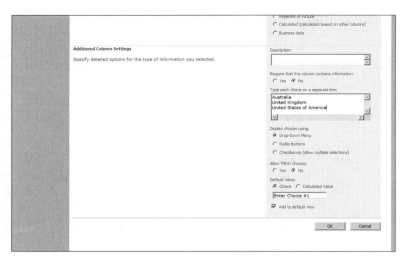

FIGURE 7.22
The configuration options for a choice column type.

Specify the Choices

To specify the choices that users will be able to choose from, simply type the choices in the box titled Type Each Choice on a Separate Line (refer to Figure 7.22). Use a line break to separate choices. For example, for a list of countries, type the countries in the box with a line break between each country name.

Choose How the Choices Will Be Displayed

The next configuration setting you can set is how the choices will be displayed to the user when making the choice. The first two options, Drop-Down Menu and Radio Buttons, enable the users to select only one option from the list of choices, whereas the last option, Checkboxes, allows multiple selections of values.

The Drop-Down Menu option is useful when you have a lot of choices and don't want to overwhelm the user who has to make the choice. The values appear in a drop-down menu, which opens to reveal the list of choices (refer to Figure 7.20).

The Radio Buttons option is useful when the list of choices is small and will not take a lot of space on the page. The advantage of this option is that the user sees all the options on the page without having to open a drop-down menu (refer to Figure 7.21).

The Checkboxes option is useful when you want the users to be able to choose more than one option (refer to Figure 7.19).

Allow Fill-in Choices

When you choose to allow fill-in choices, the column enables users to type a value if the value they are looking for does not exist in the list of choices you chose (see Figure 7.23). The values that users type are not added to the list.

FIGURE 7.23
When the Allow Fill-in Choices option is enabled, users can type the value manually.

Default Value

As in most other column types, you can type a default value that will be selected when the user creates a new item. If you want nothing to be selected by default, clear the Default Value box; otherwise, make sure you type in the Default Value box the exact text of one of the choices.

Number (1, 1.0, 100)

The Number field is useful when you want to capture a numeric value. With this column type the user will be asked to type a number in a text box. For example, you might ask for a 1 to 10 rating for a document or the number of products in stock, and so on. Figure 7.24 shows the settings for this column type.

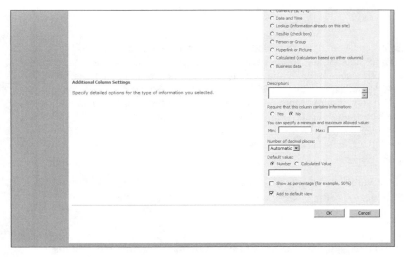

FIGURE 7.24
The configuration options for a Number column type.

Minimum and Maximum

The first option you can configure for a Number column is the minimum and maximum numbers that the user can choose in the value.

Number of Decimal Places

In the Number of Decimal Places option, configure how many decimal places the value can have. Choosing the value 0 does not allow fractions of numbers, and only integers are allowed. Choosing the value 1 enables users to specify numbers with one decimal place, such as 15.4, while choosing the value 2 allows a precision of two decimal places, and so on up to five decimal places. The default option for this setting is Automatic, which will display how many decimal points are in the entered number.

Show as Percentage

Choosing the Show as Percentage option causes the value entered in this column to be displayed as a percentage.

Default Value

Like other columns, this column supports a default value that you can enter as a static default value or as a calculated value. This column supports many mathematical formulas using standard arithmetic operators (such as +, -, * and /) to perform calculations. For example, you can have a calculated default value of =128+10, which results in a default value of 138. Another option is to use special functions in the calculation. Number columns support such functions as Pi(), which returns the number for Pi; AVERAGE(), which returns the average of the numbers you give it; and MAX, which returns the biggest number in the list of numbers you give it.

> **NOTE** As you can see, having calculated defaults for the number column is not extremely useful; essentially, you are typing in a static number. However, these formulas do work in this column type, and you might find a use for them. To take full advantage of these formulas, see the "Calculated (Calculation Based on Other Columns)" section later in this chapter. More information about the types of formulas and how to use them can be found at http://tinyurl.com/SPcalculated.

Currency ($, ¥, €)

The Currency column type is almost exactly the same as the Number column type. Figure 7.25 shows the settings section for this column type.

Currency Format

The only option that is different in the Currency column type from the Number column type is the Currency Format. This option determines what symbol will be used next to the value when displaying the value in the item's or file's properties. For example, choosing United States displays values with the dollar sign ($) next to the value, while choosing one of the European currencies displays the Euro sign (€) next to the value.

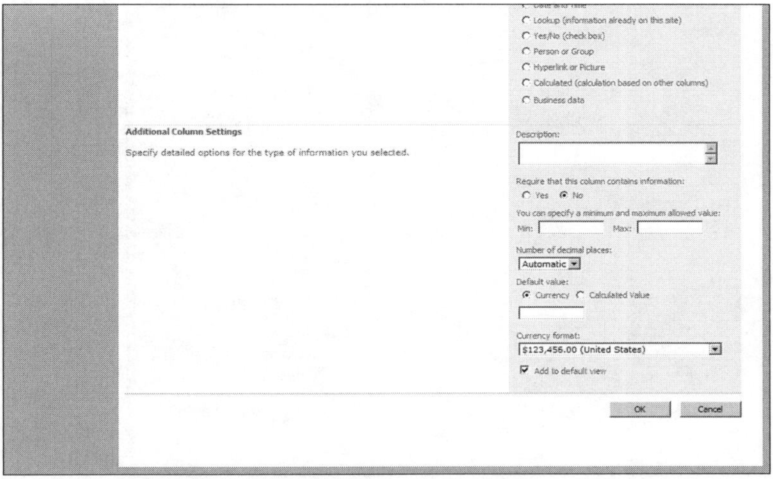

FIGURE 7.25
The configuration options for a Currency column type.

Date and Time

The Date and Time column type lets users specify a date or a date and time as the value for the column. For example, in a calendar list, users can specify the start date and time of a meeting. However, for a list of contacts, if you want a column with the birth date of a contact, for example, you need to configure the column to ask only for the date, not for the time. Figures 7.26 and 7.27 show the two modes for this column.

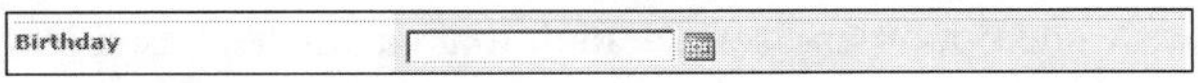

FIGURE 7.26
A date and time column showing only dates.

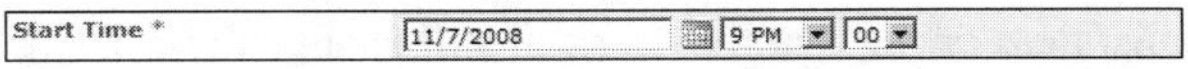

FIGURE 7.27
A date and time column showing date and time.

Figure 7.28 shows the configuration options for this column type.

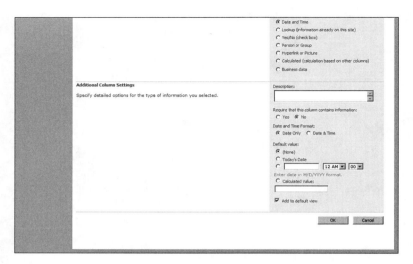

FIGURE 7.28
The configuration options for a Date and Time column type.

Date and Time Format

In the Date and Time Format configuration option, you can choose whether the users can choose just a date or a date and time. This choice changes what the date choosing control looks like.

Default Value

You also have the option to choose a specific date or make the current date the default. Also, you can use the Calculate Value option and set a default that calculates based on the current date using the [Today] token. For example, to set the default to be two weeks from the current date, type **[Today] +14** in the calculated value. This capability is useful when you want to use a column as an expiry date, for example, while allowing the users to change the expiry date. You can set the default value to be two weeks in the future from creating the list item or file, but the user can still change the date manually.

> **NOTE** It might be worthwhile to note that if a user just selects a time and not a date, SharePoint will not save anything in the column. To avoid this, setting a default date value for the column is very helpful.

Lookup (Information Already on This Site)

A Lookup is one of the most useful column types. It is similar to the Choice column type in that the users get to choose from a list of values (refer to Figure 7.20 earlier in this chapter for an example how this appears to users). However, unlike the Choice column type, the Lookup column type does not store the choices in the settings of the column. Instead, the choices are in another list or library.

For example, if you create a SharePoint list in the site and enter a list of countries in that list, you can use the Lookup column type to show values from that list. This feature is helpful when you want other users to be able to manage the list of choices. The other users do not need permissions to change settings on the current list; they just need the permissions to change items or files in the list of values (the remote list).

Unlike the Choice column type, though, in the Lookup column type the values that users pick show up as links to the list item or file that was selected. This can help create a complicated system of lists connected to one another—for example, a list of orders connected to a list of products. When users create a new order, they can choose a product (or products), and when they view an order, the product name appears as a link to the product list item.

Figure 7.29 shows the configuration options for this column type.

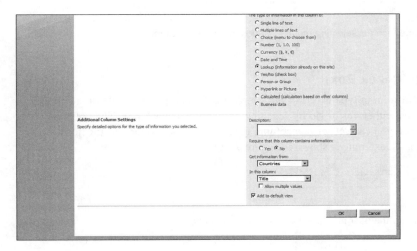

FIGURE 7.29
The configuration options for a Lookup column type.

Get Information From

In the Get Information From field, you specify which list has the information you want to display to the user to choose from. The choices here are the available lists in the current site. It is not possible to reference a list from another site.

In This Column

In the In This Column configuration option, you specify which column in the list to which you are connecting will be displayed to the user as the possible values. For example, the most common choice for this setting is the title column, which displays the titles of the list items or files as the options for the user to choose from.

Allow Multiple Values

As you can do with the choice column, you can have this column enable users to choose more than one value. When you select the Allow Multiple Values option, the user interface for selecting values changes, allowing the users to select multiple values, as shown in Figure 7.30.

FIGURE 7.30
The user interface for selecting multiple values in a lookup column type.

Yes/No (Check Box)

The Yes/No column type is one of the simplest column types available. It enables the user to select either Yes or No by selecting or clearing a check box. The only configuration option you can set for this column type is the default value for it: Choose either Yes or No. An example is shown in Figure 7.31.

FIGURE 7.31
An example for the user interface for a Yes/No column type.

Person or Group

The Person or Group column type enables users to pick a value from a list of users or groups (see Figure 7.32).

FIGURE 7.32
The user interface for entering data in the Person or Group column type.

An example of this column type can be found in the tasks list, where users who want to assign a task to other users choose from the list of users to whom they want to assign the task. The selected values appear as the names of the users picked when a user views a list item or a file's properties, with the name being a link to the chosen user's properties page. As you can do with lookup columns, you can configure whether this column type allows multiple selections. This can be seen in Figure 7.33.

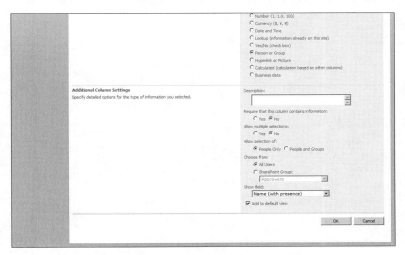

FIGURE 7.33
The configuration options for a Person or Group column type.

Allow Multiple Selections
The Allow Multiple Selections configuration option lets you define whether the column will allow users to pick more than one user in this column.

Allow Selection Of
The Allow Selection Of configuration option defines whether the user will be able to pick only people (other users) or also groups. If you want groups to be selectable, you must change this option.

Choose From
In the Choose From configuration option, you specify what users and groups will appear to the user to pick from. By default, this option is set to All Users, which enables the user to choose from the list of all the users that SharePoint recognizes, even users who do not have access to the current site or list. The second option is to limit the selection to users in a specific security group in the current site or site collection. This option is useful if you want to let users select from a restricted list of users, in which case you should create a security group and set the column to show only users from that group.

Show Field

In the Show Field configuration setting, you define what will be displayed as the selected value when a user views the list item or file properties (see Figure 7.34). The default is the name of the user who was selected, together with that user's presence information (whether that user is online or busy, and so on; this requires a special instant messaging software installed and configured on the user's machine to work). However, you can change this option to display other information about the selected user, as can be seen in Figure 7.34.

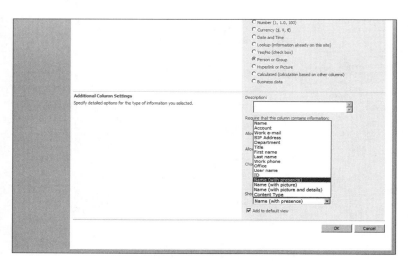

FIGURE 7.34
Choose what should be displayed for the user when viewing the selected value.

Hyperlink or Picture

The Hyperlink or Picture column type enables users to enter data that will be displayed as either a link or a picture when the value is viewed (see Figure 7.35). Choose this column type when you want the users to freely type a link to a web page (in SharePoint or otherwise) or to a picture.

FIGURE 7.35
The user interface for entering data into a Hyperlink or Picture column type.

Format URL As

The only setting to set on a Hyperlink or Picture column type, Format URL As determines how to format the link that the user types when he views the list item's or file's properties. The first option is to format it as a hyperlink, which will display the title that the user chose as a link to the page the user chose. The second option is to format as a picture, which will show the picture to which the user typed the link instead of showing the link itself.

Regardless of what settings you choose, the user interface looks the same: The user is asked to enter a URL path and a title (refer to Figure 7.35). However, when you're looking at list views and viewing the properties of a list item or file, the difference is apparent (see Figures 7.36 and 7.37).

FIGURE 7.36
A view showing a column configured to show the data the user typed as a picture.

Calculated (Calculation Based on Other Columns)

A Calculated column type does not allow the user to enter data in it; it is used only to show data based on a calculation of other columns. This column type does not have a user interface for entering data because the data in it is a calculation of other data. For example, if you want a Full Name column that displays information automatically based on the First Name and Last Name columns, you can create a calculated column that concatenates the values in those two columns.

Another example is in a list of orders that has a column for the number of products ordered and another column for the price for a single product; the calculated column can display the total revenue for the order by multiplying the numbers in the two columns.

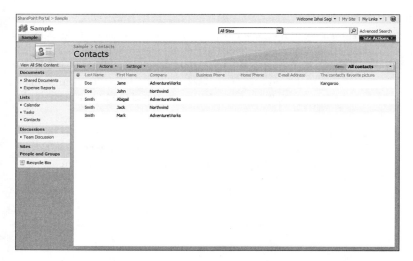

FIGURE 7.37
A view showing a column configured to show the data the user typed as a hyperlink.

The configuration options for this column type include a special "formula builder" control that enables you to specify the calculation required for the column, as can be seen in Figure 7.38.

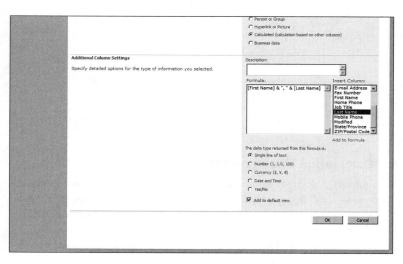

FIGURE 7.38
The configuration options for a Calculated column type. The formula in this figure is concatenating two columns and a piece of text.

Formula

In the Formula text box, you can define the calculation that will be performed (refer to Figure 7.38). You can select the columns on which you want to perform a calculation from the list on the right, and click Add to Formula to add a reference to that column in the formula.

For example, to concatenate two text columns, add the two columns from the list and use the ampersand (&) character to connect them. You can also add a piece of text in quotation marks. The value is automatically displayed everywhere, including in list views and when you're viewing the list item's or file's details.

For a complete list of formulas that you can use, see http://tinyurl.com/SPcalculated.

The Data Type

The second option you need to configure for the Calculated column type is the data type that will be used for the calculation. Select the appropriate data type that matches the data type of the columns for which you are performing an operation. It is possible to perform an operation on columns of different types. For example, you can multiply the value in a Number column by the value in a Currency column, but you must decide how the result of the operation will be displayed—either as a number or as currency.

Rating Scale

This column type is available only in surveys. It is used when you want the user to rate several items in a Likert scale control. It's like asking many questions in one column, where the answer for each question is a number. These questions are referred to as the subquestions of the column.

For example, you might want to gather input on user satisfaction on several aspects of a service, or you might want to know how much they agree with certain statements about different aspects of a book (see Figure 7.39).

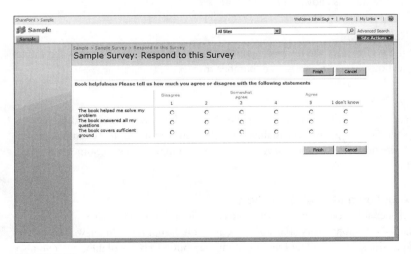

FIGURE 7.39
The rating scale column data entry user interface.

This column type is useful in surveys where you want to assess how users feel on multiple subjects—it gives the user an easy interface to answer many questions quickly. You can configure this column to specify what questions will be included, what ratings the user can choose, and what the values mean. The configuration page for this column type appears in Figure 7.40.

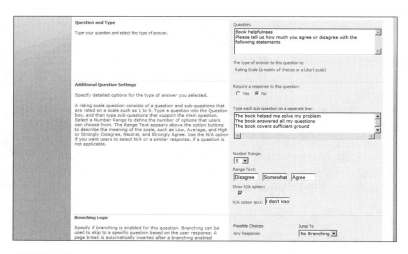

FIGURE 7.40
The configuration page for the rating scale column type.

Type Each Subquestion on a Separate Line
This is where you specify the subquestions that appear to the user to rate. Type each one in a separate line, as shown in Figure 7.40.

Number Range
In this setting you specify the range of numbers the users can choose from when rating your subquestions. You can choose any number from 3 to 20.

Range Text
Here you specify the text that will be displayed above the low, medium, and high rating options. This helps the user realize what the numbers mean. For example, in Figure 7.39 the number 1 means Disagree, while the number 3 means Somewhat Agree and number 5 is Agree.

Show N/A Option and N/A Option Text
These options enable you to specify whether you want to allow the user not to rate some of the subquestions. This is useful if the user might not have an answer for one of the subquestions. If you select that you want the option to be available, you can also

change the text shown for the option. For example, in Figure 7.40 the text was modified to "I don't know."

Page Separator

This column type is also unique to surveys. It enables you to add a page break between questions, so if you have a very long survey a user is not presented with a single page with all the questions on it, but instead with a subset of the questions and a Next button to go to the next page.

A page separator does not have any settings that you need to set. You can't even give it a name.

Business Data

The Business Data column type is available only when you have Microsoft Office SharePoint Server (MOSS) installed. It is used in a similar fashion to the Lookup column type, but instead of allowing the user to select a value from a list in the current site, it shows the user values from a business application that the administrator or developer has set up.

A common example for this is a company that has a database with information about customers. Instead of migrating that information into a SharePoint list, the administrator configures a business data application integration, after which you can create columns that will allow the users to pick from the list of customers that exist in that database. By default, no business application is configured, so this column type is used only after developers and administrators have configured it. Figure 7.41 shows the configuration options for this column type, when a business application and type are selected.

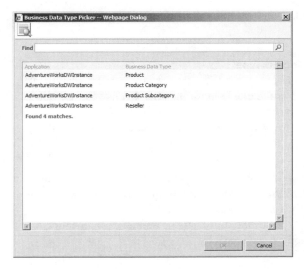

FIGURE 7.41

The configuration options for a Business Data column type, with a business application and type selected.

Type

In the Type selection box, select what the column will connect to. Click the address book icon and a dialog box appears showing you all the entities that you can select from and to what business application they belong. If no application is configured in your system, the dialog tells you so.

In the dialog you can search for the entity you want to allow the users to select (for example, Product) and select it. After you select an entity, more options you can set on the column become available (see Figure 7.42).

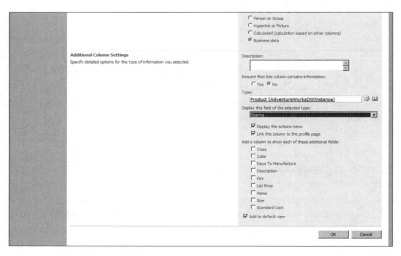

FIGURE 7.42
Displaying more than one column in a Business Data column.

Display This Field of the Selected Type

The Display This Field of the Selected Type option enables you to select what field from the database would be used as the title field for the selection that the user made. For example, in the Product entity, choosing the Product Name field makes a lot of sense. However, you might want to pick the Product Serial Number field instead.

Display the Actions Menu

The Display the Actions Menu option enables you to select whether an Actions menu should be displayed when a user moves the mouse cursor over a value in the column. Some entities can have actions that the developer has developed for them, such as Show Product or Delete Product. To see the list of actions available for an entity, select this option and then see what actions show up.

Link This Column to the Profile Page

The Link This Column to the Profile Page option determines whether the values appear as links. When this option is clicked, the user is redirected to a profile page for the entity. For example, when showing the name of a product, the name appears as a link that, when clicked, will open a page with more information about the product and actions to perform on the product.

Add a Column to Show Each of These Additional Fields

You might want to display more information than just the name of the selected entity when users are viewing the list item's or file's properties. The Add a Column to Show Each of These Additional Fields option enables you to select more properties of the entity that will be displayed as if they are separate columns when viewing the properties of the list item or file, even though, when editing the properties, the column is shown as only one (refer to Figure 7.42).

Change or Remove a Column in a List or Document Library

> **Scenario/Problem:** You want to modify the settings of a column in a list or library. For example, you want to change the default value for the column, change the column's title, or add or remove choices for a choice column.

Solution: To change a column's setting in a list or document library, go into the list or document library's Settings screen by opening the Settings menu in the toolbar for that list or library and choosing either List Settings or Document Library Settings (refer to Figure 7.8).

In the list or library settings page, scroll down to the Columns section of the page. Here, you see the list of all the columns that have been added to the list or library. Click the title of the column you want to modify or remove from the list or library. Doing so opens the settings page for that column (see Figure 7.43). In this page you can either modify the column (rename it, change its settings, or even change its type) or delete the column using the Delete button at the bottom of the page.

> **NOTE** Some columns cannot be deleted, and the Delete button is not displayed for those columns. These built-in columns are an integral part of SharePoint and cannot be removed from lists and libraries.

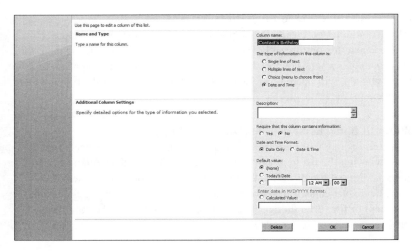

FIGURE 7.43
The settings page for the Contact's Birthday column.

> **CAUTION** Changing the type of a column can have significant repercussions. You can lose data if you move from one column type to another. For example, switching from any type of column to a choice column causes any value that doesn't exist in the choice list to be lost.

Change the Order of Columns in a List or Document Library

> **Scenario/Problem:** You want to change the order in which columns are displayed to the user when either entering the values for the columns or viewing the details for a list item or file. For example, in a contacts list you might want the users to enter the first name before entering the last name.

Solution: To change the order of columns in the data entry page for a list or library (but not in the views), go into the list's or document library's settings screen by opening the Settings menu in the toolbar for that list or library and choosing either List Settings or Document Library Settings (refer to Figure 7.8). (If you want to change the order of columns in a view, see "Specify the Order of the Columns in the View" in Chapter 8, "Creating List Views.")

In the list or library settings page, scroll down to the Columns section. Here, you see the list of all the columns that have been added to the list or library.

Click the Column Ordering link that is under the list of columns. Doing so opens the page that allows you to reorder the columns (see Figure 7.44).

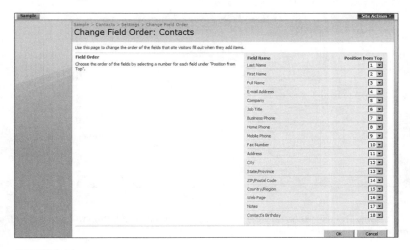

FIGURE 7.44
Reordering the columns in a list or library.

In this page you can specify for each column what should be its order by using the drop-down boxes to the right of the column names. If you change the order for one column—for example, change mobile phone to be the third column—the column automatically moves to the place you have selected, pushing the other columns down as necessary.

When you are finished ordering the columns to your liking, click OK at the bottom of the page.

Branching in Surveys

As mentioned earlier in "Create a New Survey," surveys have a special capability to redirect users to different questions based on the answers to previous questions. This is known as branching.

For example, if you create a survey with three questions: "Did you read the book?", "Do you plan to read the book?", and "Was the book good?" you can assign a branching on the first question so that if the users answered Yes they are redirected to the third question. If they answered No they are redirected to the second question. The second and third question will not be shown when the survey interface is first shown to the users, but after answering the first question, the users will have a Next button that allows them to continue to the next question in the branch. Figure 7.45 shows how branching looks to the user.

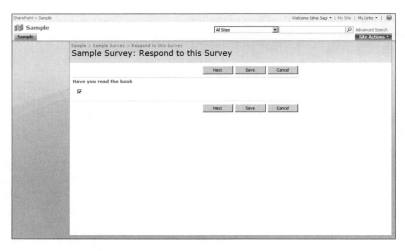

FIGURE 7.45
Branching in a survey. The user sees only the first question, with a Next button to go to the next question, depending on the answer.

To define the branching, first create all the questions, and then edit the columns you want to be conditional so that they have the branching. You don't need to add page separators unless you want to—the survey will automatically split the questions into different pages depending on the branching. Figure 7.46 shows how to define the branching on the first question to redirect the users based on the answer to different questions.

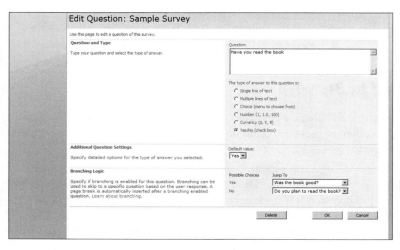

FIGURE 7.46
Defining branching in a survey.

Add a Site Column to a List or Document Library

As explained in Chapter 1, a site column is defined on the site level rather than on the list or library level. Reusing those columns in lists and libraries makes a lot of sense; if a change to the column setting is required in many lists and libraries, it is possible to change the column at the site level once, and that updates all the lists and libraries using that column.

If you want to use an existing site column instead of creating a new column, open the list's or library's settings page by opening the Settings menu in the toolbar for that list or library and choosing either List Settings or Document Library Settings (refer to Figure 7.8).

In the list or library settings page, scroll down to the Columns section. Here, you see the list of all the columns that have been added to the list or library. In this section, click the Add from Existing Site Columns link. This opens a page that enables you to pick one or more site columns to be added to the document library or list (refer to Figure 7.9).

To choose a column, locate it in the Available Site Columns box, select it, and click the Add button to add it to the Columns to Add box. If you regret your choice and want to undo it, select the column in the Columns to Add box and click the Remove button.

To more easily find a column, filter the columns that are in the Available Site Columns box by choosing the group for the column. Site columns are grouped in logical groups. For example, the Core Document Columns group holds columns that are commonly used by most documents: Author, Comments, Date Created, and so on. By default, you see the site columns from all groups available to you. To choose a different group, open the Select Site Columns From drop-down box and select a different group.

> **TIP** When adding a site column, you cannot specify any settings on it because any column settings are defined in the site level. However, after adding the column, you can modify it like any other column (see the instructions in "Change or Remove a Column in a List or Document Library," earlier in this chapter.)

Rename a List or Document Library or Change Its Description

> **Scenario/Problem:** You want to rename a list or document library, or you want to change the description shown for that list or library. For example, a library might have been created with the name Documents, and you want to modify it to a name that tells the user more about the types of documents that should be uploaded to that library—Management Presentations, for example.

Solution: If you want to change an existing list's or library's title or description, open the list's or library's settings page by opening the Settings menu in the toolbar for that list or library and choosing either List Settings or Document Library Settings (refer to Figure 7.8).

At the top of the page, under the General Settings section, click the Title, Description and Navigation link (see Figure 7.47).

The General Settings Link

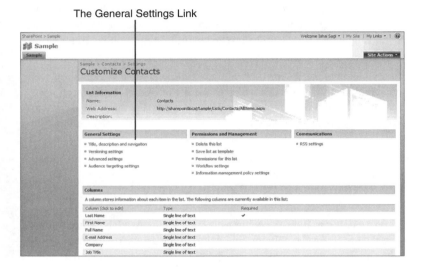

FIGURE 7.47
Click the Title, Description and Navigation link to get to the list's or library's General settings page.

On the page that opens, shown in Figure 7.48, you can set a new title to the list or library, change the description, and choose whether a link to the list or library should appear in the left navigation bar (the quick launch).

NOTE Changing the name of a list or library does not change the link to that list or library. The link stays the same, but the title that is displayed changes.

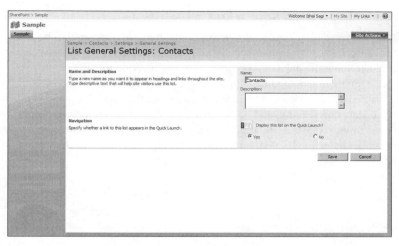

FIGURE 7.48
Changing the list or library name, description, and navigation options.

Change the Versioning Settings for a List or Document Library

Scenario/Problem: You want to change how a list or library deals with storing versions for the documents and list items. For example, a document library might have been created with versioning turned off, and you want to turn it on. Or a library was created and configured to have versioning but not to support automatic check-out of a document when a user opens a document for editing, and you want to change that.

Solution: If you want to change the versioning settings for a list or library, open the list's or library's settings page by opening the Settings menu in the toolbar for that list or library and choosing either List Settings or Document Library Settings (refer to Figure 7.8).

At the top of the page, under the General Settings section, click the Versioning Settings link (refer to Figure 7.47).

In the versioning settings page, you can define how the list or library will create versions for list items or files. This page is different for lists and libraries because documents and list items behave differently.

Set the Versioning Settings for a List

The first setting for versioning in a list is whether content approval is going to be required (see Figure 7.49). This option is not strictly about managing versions of the list item, but rather about the publishing process of a modification to a list item. If you select this option, every time a modification is made to a list item (or when one is created), the list item is not displayed to all users automatically. Instead, the list item gets an approval status of pending, and no one can see it except its author and people with permissions to view drafts in the list—until a person with the permissions to approve items in the list approves that item, thereby changing its status from Pending to Approved.

FIGURE 7.49
The Versioning settings page for a list.

The next section is Item Version History. Here, you can define whether versions will be tracked for the list and how many versions should be kept. This second option is optional, and you can leave it unlimited if you want to. Finally, if you set the Require Approval option, you can also limit the number of approved versions to keep.

The last option in this page, Draft Item Security, is also valid only if you chose to require approval. It lets you define who can see draft items that have not been approved yet. The options are any user who can read items in the list, only users who can edit items in the list (who might need to be able to see the drafts to edit them), or just the people who can approve items in the list (which is the minimum required because they must be able to view the drafts to approve them).

Set the Versioning Settings for a Document Library

The versioning options for a document library are almost identical to those of a list (see Figure 7.50). The only two differences are explained here.

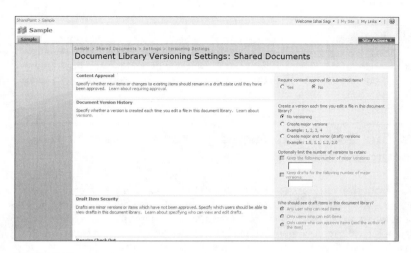

FIGURE 7.50
The Versioning settings page for a document library.

The first option that is different is that, instead of just selecting that the library should store versions, you can select how versions will be stored: either as major versions (which is how lists behave) or so that any change will result in a new version (changing the version number from 1 to 2 to 3, and so on).

This setting does not enable you to specify that a certain change is not major enough to warrant an increase of the version number for the document. For example, if you change a document by spell checking it and correcting the spelling, or updating the date it was last printed, this change might not be important enough. This is why you might want to choose the option for major and minor versions, which allows users to decide whether the change is major, thereby increasing the version number by 1, or minor, thereby increasing the number after the decimal point for the number.

The second option that you can configure for document libraries only is the Require Checkout option. Selecting this option can help reduce conflicts when several users want to work on the same file. This option forces the users to check out a file before editing it by automatically checking out the file for them, which prevents others from editing it. This prevents users from forgetting to check out the file but starting to work on it, not realizing that another user is also working on the same file.

> **CAUTION** It's important to remember that when the Require Checkout option is selected, uploading multiple documents will add those documents as checked out, and they will not be visible to other users until you check them in.

> **CAUTION** There is no automatic check-in of a file because SharePoint cannot know when the editing is done and the user is ready to check in the changes. Users therefore must be aware of this fact, and get used to checking in the files and not keeping them checked out forever, not sharing their changes with their colleagues.

Change the Document Template for the New Button in a Document Library

> **Scenario/Problem:** You want to change what kind of document is created when the user clicks the New button in a document library. For example, you want to make the New button create a Microsoft PowerPoint presentation out of a specific template in the document library that is specific for presentations, or you want a Microsoft Excel template for expense reports to open in the Expense Reports document library.

> **TIP** You might want to show several choices of templates to users as a menu under the New button. That is possible if you use content types. See "Add a Content Type to a List or Document Library," later in this chapter, as well as "Create a Content Type" in Chapter 13 for more information.

Solution: If you want to change the template or application used when a user clicks the New button in a document library, you can specify it in the document library settings. Do so by opening the Settings menu in the toolbar for that list or library and choosing Document Library Settings to get to the settings page for the document library (refer to Figure 7.8).

At the top of the page, under the General Settings section, click the Advanced Settings link (refer to Figure 7.47). On the page that appears, you can either edit the template that is used by clicking the Edit Template link on the right side, or link to a Microsoft Office Document that you have uploaded to SharePoint (see Figure 7.51). Make sure the link to the document that you entered works by clicking the Edit Template link after adding the link.

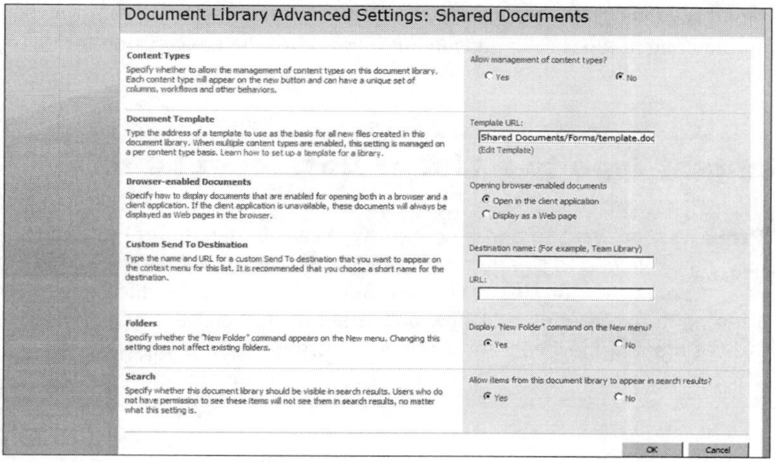

FIGURE 7.51
Change the link to the template for the new button by changing the Template URL.

It is recommended that you upload to the Forms folder that exists in any document library. That folder is hidden, and users do not see it in list views, which means they will not see your template as a file to be modified and managed. However, you can decide to put the template in another location, not in the current document library. Just remember that this location must be readable by all users, and not just you. Therefore, putting the document in another location can be problematic from a security point of view because you must be sure that all the users who are allowed to create documents in the document library are also allowed to read from the location of the template.

> **TIP** To get to the Forms folder, type the link to the document library, followed by /forms/. For example, if the link to your document library is http://sharepointlocal/ Sample/Shared Documents/, type the link **http://sharepointlocal/Sample/Shared Documents/Forms**. This link opens the Forms folder (which should look empty), to which you can upload a document to be used as a template.

Depending on the file type that you use as a template, the corresponding application will be used when the user clicks the New button. For example, if you choose a Microsoft Excel document as the template, the Microsoft Excel application will open when the user clicks the New button.

> **NOTE** Not all file types can be used as templates. You can use only file types from applications that are compatible with SharePoint, such as Microsoft Office applications.

If you want to add several options for templates under the New button, you must do so by adding multiple content types to the document library. See the next section for details.

Add a Content Type to a List or Document Library

Scenario/Problem: You want to add a content type that is defined in the site to a list or library. As explained in Chapter 1, content types provide a useful way to specify groups of properties for files or list items. Content types can also specify a document template for creation of a new document of that content type. For information about creating new content types, see "Create a Content Type" in Chapter 13.

Solution: To add a content type to a list or library, first enable management of content types in that list or library. To do so, go to the list or document library settings page by opening the Settings menu in the toolbar for that list or library and choosing List Settings or Document Library Settings (refer to Figure 7.8).

At the top of the page, under the General Settings section, click the Advanced Settings link (refer to Figure 7.47). On the advanced settings page, shown in Figure 7.52, select Yes under Allow Management of Content Types? and click OK at the bottom of the page.

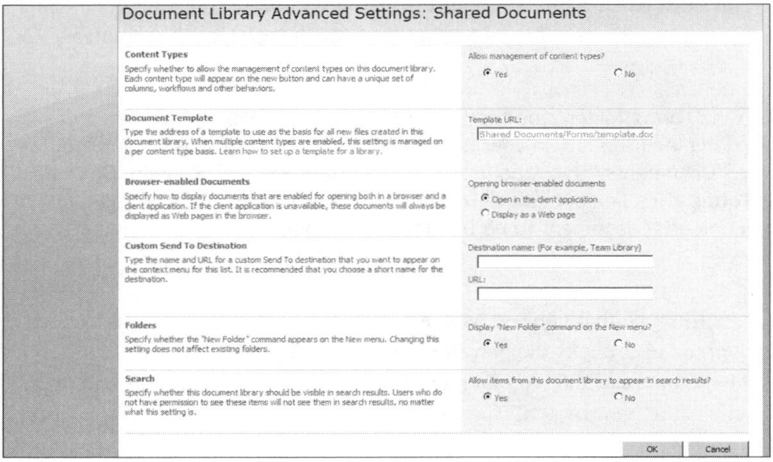

FIGURE 7.52
On the advanced settings page, select Yes to enable content types for the list or library.

You then return to the list or library setting page, which now has a section for content types (see Figure 7.53).

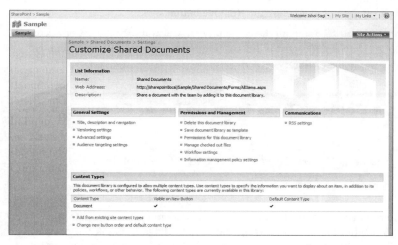

FIGURE 7.53
The Content Types section appears only if content types are enabled for the list or library.

To add a content type, click the Add from Existing Site Content Types link under the Content Types section. This link opens the content type selection page, which enables you to select one or more content types to add to the list (see Figure 7.54).

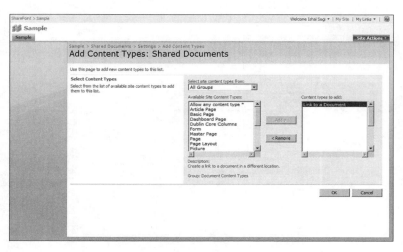

FIGURE 7.54
The Add Content Types page.

On this page the available content types appear in the box on the left. Select the one you want and click the Add button to move it to the box on the right (which shows the types you selected). If you want to remove a content type you added by mistake, select it from the box on the right and click the Remove button.

When you are finished selecting all the content types you want for the list or document library, click OK. The resulting list or library settings page shows the list of content types available in the list or library.

Remove a Content Type from a List or Document Library

Scenario/Problem: You want to remove a content type from the list or library so that it is not available for the users in that place.

Solution: To remove a content type from a list or document library, go to the settings page for that list or library by opening the Settings menu in the toolbar for that list or library and choosing List Settings or Document Library Settings (refer to Figure 7.8).

The settings page shows the list of content types available in the list or library (if content types are enabled), as you can see in Figure 7.55. To remove one, click the link to that content type.

FIGURE 7.55
To remove the Link to a Document content type, click the Link to a Document link under the Content Types section.

The configuration page that opens shows the content type for that specific list or library (see Figure 7.56). Changes that you make in that page affect only the list or document library but not other lists and libraries that use the same content type. You can tell that by the fact that the content type has a parent with the exact same name—something that is possible only when viewing the settings of a content type in a list or library, and not the settings for the content type that is defined in the site. As long as you see that, changing the content type affects only the list or library from which you started.

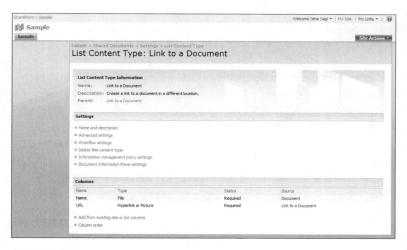

FIGURE 7.56
The content type settings page.

To remove the content type from the list or library, click the Delete This Content Type link. Doing so opens a prompt asking you to confirm you want to delete the content type. Click OK to remove the content type.

NOTE The Delete This Content Type link does not actually delete the content type; it just removes the content type from the list or library. An easy way to be sure that you are not deleting the content type from the site is to look in the breadcrumbs in the top of the page. If the breadcrumbs show that you are under the settings for the list or library, you are not deleting the content type but instead are just removing it. In any case, SharePoint does not let you delete a content type from a site if it is still in use by a list or library, so you can feel safe to click this link.

Enable or Disable Folders in a List or Document Library

Scenario/Problem: You want to enable or display folders in a list or library. For example you want to prevent users from creating subfolders in a document library, or you want users to create list items in a folder structure inside a list.

Solution: To enable or disable folders in lists and libraries, go to the list or library settings page by opening the Settings menu in the toolbar for that list or library and choosing Document Library Settings or List Settings (refer to Figure 7.8).

On the settings page, click the Advanced Settings link to get to the advanced settings page of the list or library (see Figure 7.57). On that page, choose Yes or No for the option that allows you to enable or disable folders. The Display New Folder Command on the New Menu? selection is located in the Folders section.

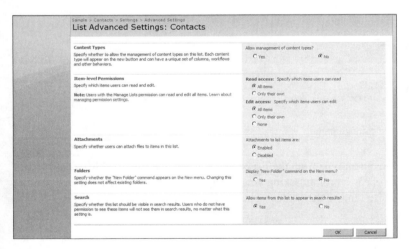

FIGURE 7.57
The Display New Folder option.

CHAPTER 8

Creating List Views

As explained in Chapter 3, "Solutions Regarding Files, Documents, List Items, and Forms," list views are important and help users find the content they are looking for more easily. If you are in charge of a document library or list and want to make it more accessible and more usable to users, you should consider creating list views for the users. Even if managing a particular list is not your responsibility, you will want to learn how to create a personal view that is visible only to you, where you can preset the view to display information that is relevant to you specifically and that you often need to find. You will find that this view saves you a lot of time.

This chapter covers how to create custom list views, either personal or public ones, and what settings can be set on them.

Create a Personal or Public View for a List or Library

Scenario/Problem: In some lists you might be given permissions to create new views—either personal views (that only you are able to see) or public ones (that everyone is able to view). You now want to create a view that will help you or other users find information in the list or library more easily.

Solution: To create new views (regardless of whether they are personal or public), choose Create View from the view picker drop-down menu (see Figure 8.1).

FIGURE 8.1
Select Create View from the view picker drop-down menu.

On the page that opens, choose from a list of available view types (see Figure 8.2). Different lists can have different types of views. For example, the events list has a special view type for recurring events; this list shows instances of each recurring event as if it were a single event.

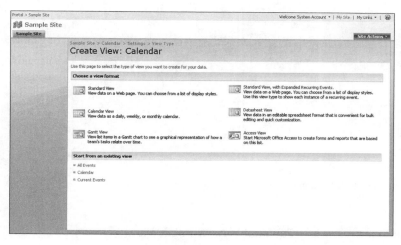

FIGURE 8.2
The view type selection page.

Also, depending on what applications you have installed on your computer, you might get additional view types, such as the Access View that is displayed only if you have Microsoft Access 2007 installed and configured on your machine.

Create a Standard View

If you want a standard list view, select the Standard View link. The next page enables you to name your view if it is going to be the default view for the list (see Figure 8.3). You also can select whether it is going to be a public or personal view and choose the actual settings of the view itself.

Select Whether a View Is a Default View

Making a view a default view causes SharePoint to display that view when users navigate to the list or document library. Because that setting affects all users, and not just you, this option is valid only for public views because personal views are visible only to you, and not to other users.

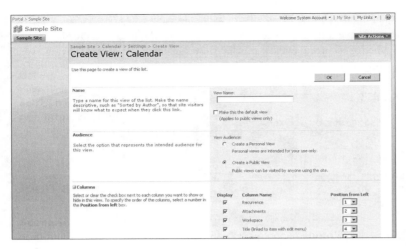

FIGURE 8.3
The view creation page for a standard view.

Select Whether a View Is a Personal View or Public View

The option to choose between a public or personal view is a very important one. If you have the permissions to create public views, consider carefully before creating the view as a public one. After all, creating too many views can confuse the other users of that list or library. If you are creating a view for your own use, it is better to keep the view private.

> **TIP** Naming the view is very important. You will want to know how the view is different when selecting the view from the view picker, and the only thing you will see is the view name. However, avoid long names because they are hard to read in the view picker.

If you do not have permissions to create public views, the option to create one is grayed out, and you are able to choose only to create a personal view.

After filling in the name for the view and selecting whether it is a personal or public one (and if it is public, whether it should be the default), save the view by clicking OK. The view is created, and you can select it from the view picker. However, you probably will want to change the view first. The other tasks in this chapter explain what you can change in a view.

Create a Calendar View

Calendar views show information from a list or document library as if they were events on a calendar. For this, there must be one date column to define as the start date column and one column to define as the end date—the time interval. It is enough to have one column to be both the start and end dates. For example, in a document library you can create a calendar view that shows the documents based on the day they were created (see Figure 8.4).

FIGURE 8.4
A document library with a calendar view based on the created date.

To create a calendar view, select the Calendar View type. The first two options in the view setting screen are similar to that of the standard view: naming the view and selecting whether it is going to be a default view and whether it is a personal or public view (see Figure 8.5).

The next setting is choosing the columns on which the time interval in the calendar will be based. For example, in a document library, to create a calendar view based on the modified date of the document, select the Modified column for both the beginning and end (see Figure 8.5).

As another example, for a tasks list you can choose the start date of the task as the start column and the due date as the end column to create a view that shows you the tasks in a calendar style view.

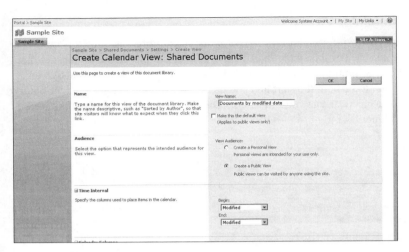

FIGURE 8.5
Configuring a calendar view based on the modified date for a document library.

Calendar views have three subviews: the day view, which shows each day separately (see Figure 8.6); the week view, which shows week by week (see Figure 8.7); and the monthly view, which shows the entire month (refer to Figure 8.4).

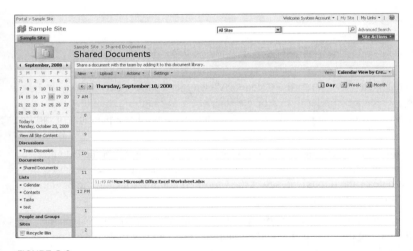

FIGURE 8.6
The daily view for a document library.

These subviews are part of the view itself and are all configured as part of creating the calendar view. For more information about configuring the subviews separately, see "Specify Columns for a Calendar View," later in this chapter.

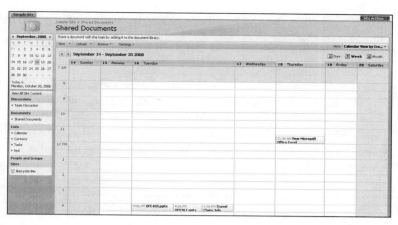

FIGURE 8.7
The weekly view for a document library.

Create a Gantt View

A Gantt view displays items based on date columns—very much like the calendar view. However, it shows the items in a Gantt chart where each item is displayed if it was a task in a project plan. A tabular version of the view appears under the chart, showing more details on the list items (see Figure 8.8).

The Gantt Chart

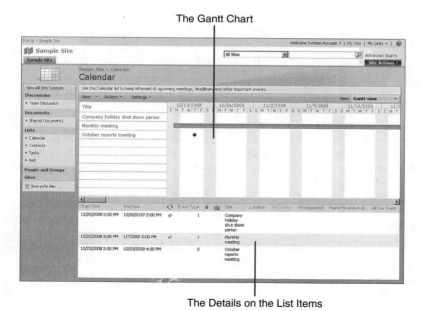

The Details on the List Items

FIGURE 8.8
The Gantt view for an events list.

Creating a Gantt view is similar to creating a standard view. Select the Gantt view type in the view type selection page, and you get the same options to name the view and select whether it should be the default view and whether it should be personal or public.

After configuring those options, scroll down to the Gantt Columns section of the page. In this section configure what columns will be used as the title column, starting date column, and due date column. Optionally, you can also specify a percentage column that will indicate in the Gantt chart how the item has progressed.

The column you select in the Title box is displayed in the Gantt chart as the title of the item (see Figure 8.9).

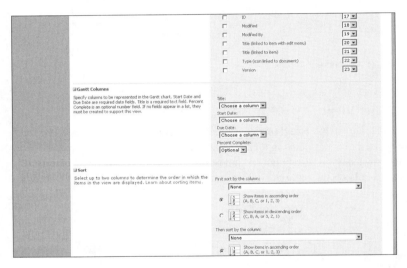

FIGURE 8.9
Creating a Gantt view.

> **TIP** The Percent Complete option shows only number columns. If you want such a column and the list doesn't have one, you must create one for the list. For more information, see Chapter 7, "Creating Lists and Document Libraries," or Chapter 13, "Customizing a SharePoint Site."

Create a Datasheet View

Creating a datasheet view is exactly like creating a standard view. Select the datasheet view type in the view type selection page, and you get the same options to name the view and select whether it should be the default view and whether it should be personal or public.

Specify Columns for the View to Display

Scenario/Problem: When creating or editing a view in a list or library, you want to specify different columns to be displayed to the users in the view. For example, in a contacts list you want to display the first and last name columns in the view, but not the company.

Solution: The following sections explain how in different types of views you can select which columns are displayed to the users.

Specify Columns for a Standard View or a Datasheet View

After filling in the name for the view and selecting whether it is a personal or public one (and if it is public, whether it should be the default), scroll down to see the list of columns (see Figure 8.10). Here, you can choose what columns will be displayed in the view and in what order they should appear. To select a column, select the check box next to the column name. To hide a column, remove the check from the check box.

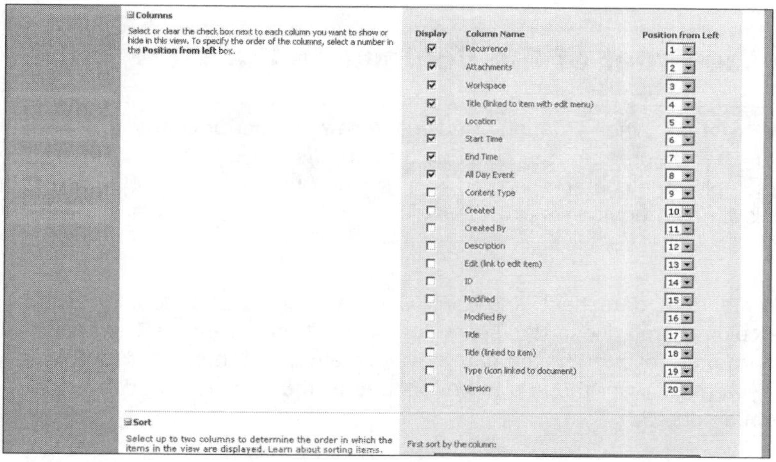

FIGURE 8.10
The list of columns available in a view.

TIP In document libraries the Title column is separate from the Name column. The Name holds the actual filename, while the title can be blank. When building views for document libraries, remember that the name of the document is more likely what the users are looking for, and that unlike in lists, it is the Name column that can be displayed as the link to the file, and not the title column.

Specify Columns for a Calendar View

In calendar views you can't choose multiple columns to display and order them in the same way that you do for standard views. The reason is that in a calendar the users see only one column as the heading for the item.

It is possible to set for each subview separately what column will be displayed as the link to the item or file. Normally, you would use the title column (for lists) or name column (for document libraries), but you can choose any column you want. That column will be displayed as the heading for the item or document in the view.

Both the daily and weekly subviews support a subheading column, which will be displayed beneath the heading. You can either choose a column to be used as a subheading or leave it not configured if you do not want a subheading.

Specify Columns for a Gantt View

In Gantt views, as explained earlier in this chapter, you must choose a column that will be used as the title in the Gantt chart, under the Gantt Columns section. However, unlike a calendar view, a Gantt view also shows a tabular view of the items below the chart, which means you can also modify which columns are displayed in that part of the view. To do so, use the Columns section of the page to select which columns will be displayed.

Specify the Order of the Columns in the View

Scenario/Problem: When creating or editing a view in a list or library, you want to specify a different order for the columns that are displayed to the user in the view. For example, in a contacts list you want the first name to be displayed before the last name or vice versa.

Solution: In standard, datasheet, and Gantt views, you can choose to change the order of the columns you chose to display. For example, you might want to show the title of the item first, followed by the date it was created, and then the date it was modified; or you might want the title to be followed by the modification date and then the creation date.

NOTE In calendar view you don't have the option to reorder columns because only one column appears (two in daily and weekly views).

To rearrange the order of the columns in the view, use the Position from Left drop-down boxes. These drop-down boxes contain numbers that you can choose for the column order. If you want a column to be displayed first, change the number in the drop-down box next to that column to 1. The next column will be 2, and so on. If you change a column that had a higher order number to a lower number (say, from 4 to 1), the other columns automatically arrange themselves. For example, changing the Position from Left for the Title column that had the value 4 to the value 1 automatically changes the three columns that are before it (Recurrence, Attachments, and Workspace) to be 2, 3, and 4.

> **NOTE** The Title (or Name in document libraries) column usually appears three times in this view creation page because there are three different ways to show the title for a list item. The simplest one is just Title, which displays the title of the list item or document as regular text. The second option is Title (linked to item), which displays the title as a link to the item. The last option is Title (linked to item with Edit menu), which displays the title as a link but will also allow a drop-down menu to open when the mouse cursor hovers over the title. This last one is the default in most views.

Specify How Items in a View Are Sorted

> **Scenario/Problem:** In a lot of cases you want to specify for a view how it should sort the items. For example, in a contacts list you want it to sort on the last name column in an ascending order so that Adams is before Brahms. Furthermore, if two people have the same last name, you want them sorted by their first names, so that Anne Adams appears before Brenda Adams.

Solution: SharePoint supports sorting based on up to two columns. To select the sort order, scroll down to the Sort section of the view creation page (see Figure 8.11).

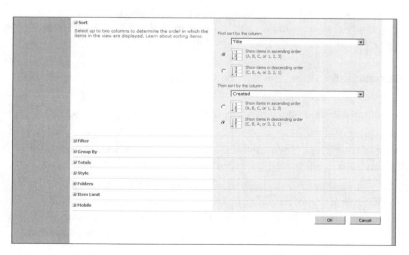

FIGURE 8.11
Changing how items are sorted in a view.

Under First Sort by the Column, choose the column by which the view will sort first and how that sorting should take place (ascending or descending). Then you can optionally select another column to further sort the items using the second column selection drop-down. This determines how items with the same value in the first column you selected will be sorted.

For example, you might want to sort an event list by Start Date first and Title second; that way, if two items have the same start date, the one scheduled to start first will appear first.

A different example would be to sort a document library using the Title column (ascending) and then the Created column (descending) as the second (refer to Figure 8.11). That way, if two files have the same title (not name) the one created later would appear before the older one.

> **NOTE** Some view types do not allow you to pick a sort order. For example, the Calendar view type does not have a sort order because calendars always display the events in them sorted by the starting date of the event.

Specify How Items in a View Are Filtered

Scenario/Problem: You want to limit the view so that it shows only items with certain values in certain columns. For example, a common requirement is to display announcements until a certain date, when they then expire.

Solution: Filters determine what items or files are displayed in a view, based on the data that is in the columns. A solution to this problem would be to create a column for the expiry date and add a filter to the view that will display only the announcements whose expiry dates are in the future.

To define filter criteria for a view, scroll in the view creation page to the Filter section (see Figure 8.12).

By default, no filter is applied on a new view, so the view displays all items.

To define a filter, use the column picker drop-down and select the column based on which you want to filter items. Then choose the operator that you want for the filter and the value you want to use for the comparison.

For example, if you want to filter the view to display only items that have a title (excluding the items that do not have a value in the Title column), pick the Title column in the column drop-down, select Is Not Equal To, and leave the value box empty (refer to Figure 8.12). This forms the condition Title Is Not Equal To Nothing.

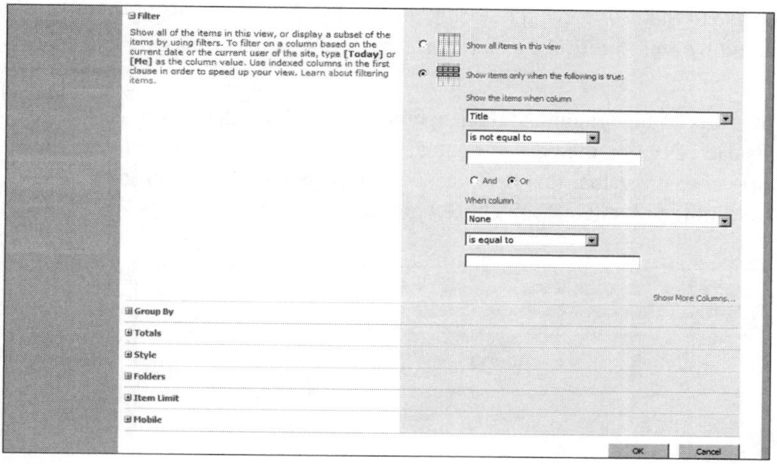

FIGURE 8.12
The Filter section in the view creation page.

NOTE Not all columns can be filtered. The column picker drop-down shows only columns that support filtering. For example, columns of type Hyperlink do not support filtering and are not shown in the column picker drop-down.

Another example for a filter you might want to create on a view would be items that you or another person created. The simplest way is to choose the Created By column in the column drop-down, select the Is Equal To operator, and then enter the name of the person you want (either you or anyone else) in the value box (see Figure 8.13).

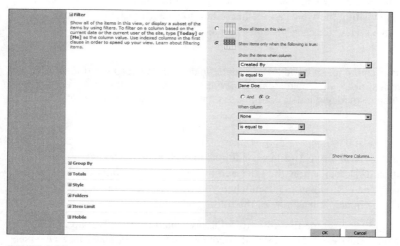

FIGURE 8.13
Setting a filter for the Created By column by typing the name of the person.

When you browse to the new view, the documents (or list items) are displayed only if they were created by a user with the exact name that you typed (in this example, Jane Doe).

If you want the filter to be dynamic and change based on whom the person is, you can use a token instead of typing the person's actual name. For example, you can use the [Me] token instead of the value; this is replaced with the name of the user viewing the view, and is not limited to a name you chose beforehand (see Figure 8.14).

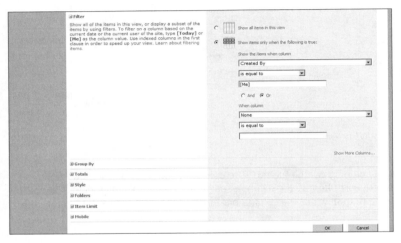

FIGURE 8.14
Setting a filter for a view that displays for every user his or her documents using the [Me] token.

This capability is useful when you want to set up a public view (for everyone to use) so that anyone visiting the view can see his or her documents or items without you having to create a view for each person separately.

TIP Another useful token is [Today]. For date fields, it is replaced with the current date. With this token, you could create a view that displays only the documents or items created or modified today, or in a tasks list show all the items that are due today.

You can add, or *chain*, up to 10 filter conditions in each view. To add an additional filter condition, first decide how the filter will be added—using either the AND or the OR operators. The OR operator is used when you want the items or files to be displayed if they match at least one of the filter conditions.

For example, you can set the first filter to column Created By Equals John Doe and use the OR operator to add the second filter column Created By Equals Jane Doe (see Figure 8.15). This condition sets the view to display only documents that were created by either John or Jane.

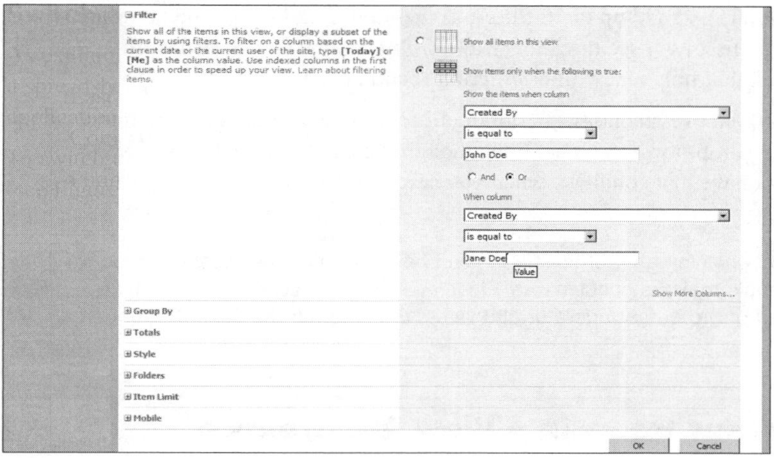

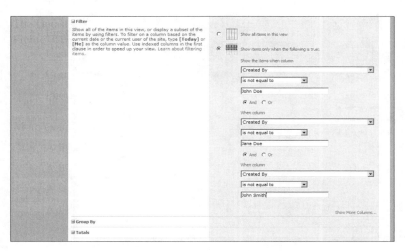

FIGURE 8.15
Setting up two filters using the OR chaining operator to show documents that were created by either John or Jane.

Using the AND chaining operator, you can create conditions such as column Created By Equals John Doe and column Created Equals Today. This operator restricts the view to display only documents that match both filters. Another example would be to create a filter on the column Created By Is Not Equal To John Doe and column Created By Is Not Equal To Jane Doe (see Figure 8.16). When viewing this view, the users see all files (or items) that have been created by users other than John or Jane.

FIGURE 8.16
Adding another filter criterion and joining the criterion with the AND chaining operator.

You can continue and add up to 10 filters, as mentioned earlier. To add additional filters after the first two, use the Show More Columns link below the last filter. Every time you click that link, a new filter criterion section appears.

If you want to remove a condition from the filter, just change the column in the column picker drop-down to None. Even though the condition section still shows, the filter does not have that condition when you save the view.

> **CAUTION** Chaining a lot of conditions can be confusing. The most common mistake people make is choosing AND instead of OR or vice versa. Make sure you selected not only the right operator and value, but also the right chaining operator.

Specify How Items in a View Are Grouped

> **Scenario/Problem:** In many instances you want to group the data shown in the view. Grouping is useful because it is easier to get to the content you are after if you know what group it belongs to.

Solution: SharePoint list views support a feature called *grouping* that enables you to define a grouping on a column in a list view. For example, grouping contacts by the company to which they belong is a common use of grouping. Grouping documents by the person who created them can be another good idea (see Figure 8.17).

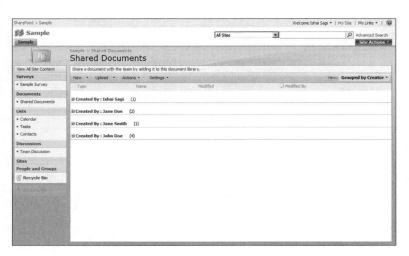

FIGURE 8.17
A view of a document library grouping files by the Created By column.

NOTE Grouping is available only for Standard and Gantt view types.

Grouping is done by selecting the column whose values you want to use as groups. If there are empty values in the selected column for some of the items or files in that view, they are placed under a group without a name (see Figure 8.18).

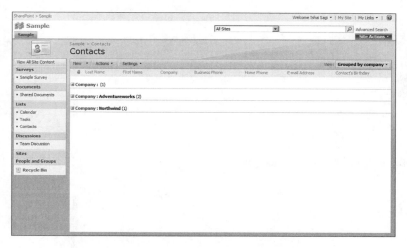

FIGURE 8.18
A view of a contacts list, grouped by the Company column, where one contact doesn't have a value in the Company column.

To define the grouping when creating a view, scroll down to the Group By section in the page and expand it by using the plus (+) sign next to the section title (see Figure 8.19).

Aside from choosing the column, you can also select the order in which the groups appear: either ascending or descending.

You can specify up to two columns for grouping. The second column groups appear under each group only if there are items in that group. For example, grouping contacts by company and then by country makes finding people easier if you know what company and what country they are from (see Figure 8.20).

TIP When grouping by a column, it's a good idea not to display that column as part of the view because the values appear as a group. For example, if you are grouping by country, remove the Country column from the list of columns displayed in the view.

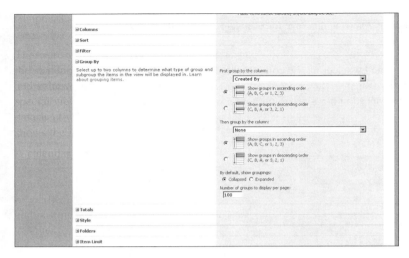

FIGURE 8.19
The Group By section in the view creation page.

FIGURE 8.20
Grouping by company and then by country.

Aside from specifying the columns for grouping and the order of the groups, you can also specify whether the groups show up expanded or collapsed by default. If you choose that columns should be collapsed by default, you can also pick how many groups to display per page. These settings affect both grouping columns.

If you choose that the groups should be expanded by default, the view displays the groups with the items shown as soon as users open the view (see Figure 8.21).

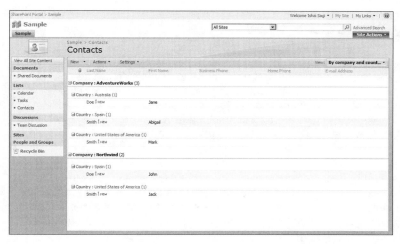

FIGURE 8.21
A view showing contacts grouped by company and then by country, with the groups expanded by default.

If you select that the groups should be collapsed by default, you can also select how many groups will appear per page. If you choose this option, views with a lot of groups still show the users a manageable list (see Figure 8.22).

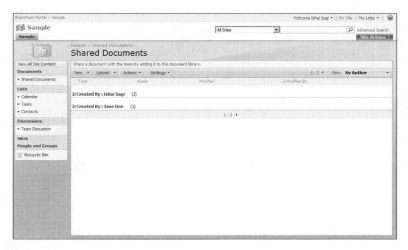

FIGURE 8.22
A view showing the items grouped, with a limit of two groups per page.

The paging mechanism enables the users to move back and forth between the pages using the arrow on the bottom of the view.

Specify Totals for a View

Scenario/Problem: You want to include a mathematical calculation on a column in the view. For example, you want the view to show an average of the numbers in a certain column or the total of another. For example, you have a number column called Number of Leave Days that is used to track how many leave days have been requested by a contact, and you want to create a view that will display the average leave requested by everyone in the list.

Solution: A total is a mathematical calculation that you can add to a view. The result of the calculation shows up at the top of the view, just under the header for the column being calculated. If you want to see some calculations of the values in a column, you can specify that under the Totals section of the view creation page.

Different column types can have different kinds of calculations. For example, a date column can show the count of unique date values in that column, then average of the date values, then the largest date or smallest one. A text column can show only the count of unique values because it is not possible to do mathematical calculations on pieces of text. A number column can have more functions, such as sum (the sum of all the values in that column), standard deviation, and variance.

For example, if you have a number column called Number of Leave Days that is used to track how many leave days have been requested by a contact, you can create a view that will display the average leave requested by everyone in the list. The average shows up at the top of the view, just under the header for the column (see Figure 8.23).

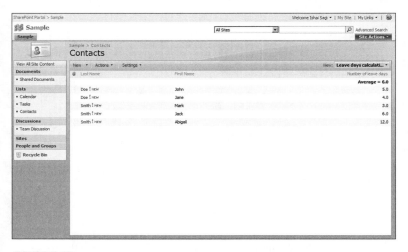

FIGURE 8.23
A view showing the average of a column.

Totals are also supported in the datasheet view type, and the totals appear as a row in the bottom of the view (see Figure 8.24).

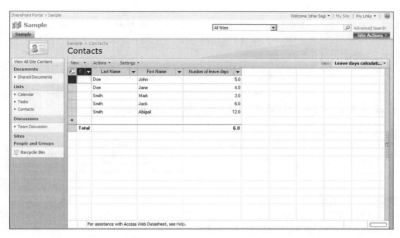

FIGURE 8.24
A datasheet view showing the average of a column.

To specify a total for one or more columns, scroll down to the Totals section in the view creation page and expand it using the plus sign next to the section title. You then see a list of all the columns selected under the Columns section (see Figure 8.25). For each one, you can open the drop-down and choose the calculation that will be done for it.

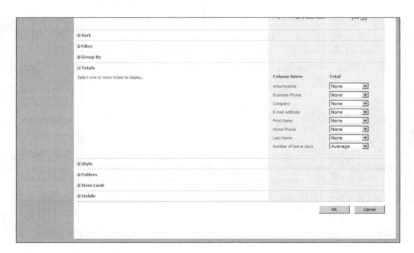

FIGURE 8.25
Creating a view with an average total on a column.

You can specify only one calculation per column. If you want to do different calculations, you must create separate views for each calculation.

TIP You can add a total to a column only if it appears in the view. If the column to which you want to add a total does not show up under the Totals section, make sure it is selected under the Columns section.

Specify a Different Item Style for a View

Scenario/Problem: You want to change how the view displays items, not showing them in the regular tabular way in which views normally present items.

Solution: Some view types support displaying items in different styles. This means that instead of showing items in a simple table, the items are displayed in different manners that may make the view easier to read.

A common example is the Shaded style, which shows every other row in the table with a different shade or background color (see Figure 8.26).

FIGURE 8.26
A view showing contacts with the Shaded style.

Another example is the Boxed style, which displays each item in a box (see Figure 8.27).

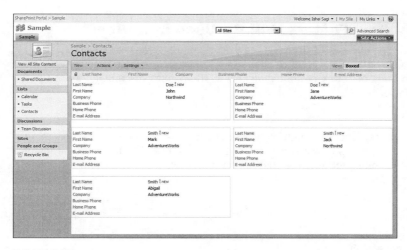

FIGURE 8.27
A view showing contacts with the Boxed style.

To specify the style for the items in your view, scroll to the Style section of the view creation page and expand it using the plus sign next to the section title. You see a list of the styles available for that view type (see Figure 8.28). Simply select the style that you want.

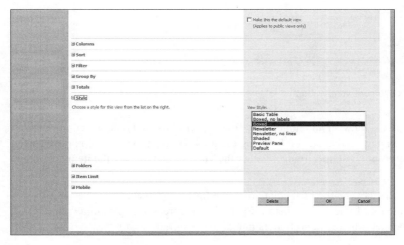

FIGURE 8.28
Specifying the boxed style for a view.

> **TIP** Try the different view styles. You might find that one of them is better suited for your purpose than the default one.

Specify How Folders Will Be Used in a View

Scenario/Problem: You want to choose whether a view should display the folders in a list or library or should display all the documents and list items without folders.

Solution: You can choose whether a view will show the contents of the document library or list in folders or will show all the items and files as if there are no folders. A view that is configured to show the items without folders is known as a *flat view* (see Figure 8.29).

FIGURE 8.29
A view of a document library showing folders.

To specify that a view should not display folders, scroll to the Folders section in the view creation page and expand it by using the plus sign next to the section title. You then have the option of specifying whether the view should display the items in folders (see Figure 8.30).

A flat view displays all the items that are in the list or document library, even if they are not in the root folder of that list or library (see Figure 8.31). Essentially, this view makes it look as if there are no folders in that list or library.

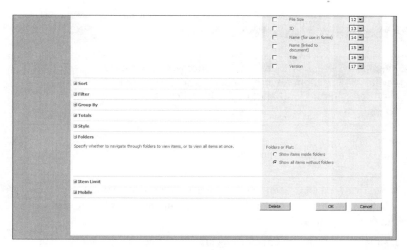

FIGURE 8.30
Configuring a flat view.

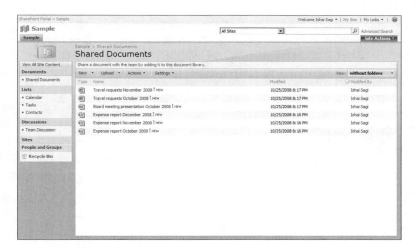

FIGURE 8.31
A flat view of the document library shows all documents from all folders.

CAUTION A flat view makes it hard for users who create or upload documents or list items because the flat view does not display the folders and the user cannot specify in which folder the document or list item should be created. It is recommended to create this kind of view only in addition to a view that does display the folders.

Specify the Item Limit for a View

Scenario/Problem: Because there are many items in a list or library, you do not want the view to display them all in one page. Displaying them all can cause the page to take a long time to load and makes it harder for the users to find what they are looking for.

Solution: You can specify an item limit on a view.

An item limit on a view enables you to either specify the maximum number of items that will be displayed in the view or specify the maximum number of items that will be displayed in each page in a view.

For example, suppose you have an announcements list that gets used a lot. With at least three announcements made every day, after a year the list will have more than 1,000 announcements. Displaying all the announcements in one page makes it very hard for the users to focus on the current announcements.

A common solution to this problem is creating a view with an item limit that displays only the last three announcements (see Figure 8.32). To do this, make sure the view sorts the announcements by their creation date (or modified date), and then set the item limit to three.

FIGURE 8.32
An announcement list showing only the last three announcements.

To specify the item limit for a view, scroll to the Item Limit section in the view creation page and expand it using the plus sign next to the section title. You then have the option of specifying how many items should be displayed, and whether the view should limit itself to that number or display the items in groups of that number (see Figure 8.33).

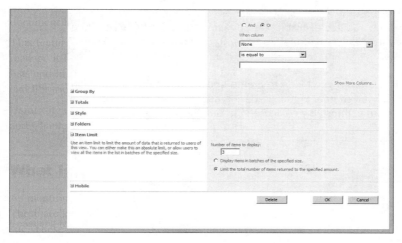

FIGURE 8.33
Specifying the item limit on a view.

If you want to let the users see the old announcements, you can choose the Display Items in Batches of the Specified Size option. That makes the view show the items in pages and allows the users to go back and forth between the pages, showing only the number you specified at a time (see Figure 8.34).

FIGURE 8.34
An announcement list showing the announcements in groups of three.

Create Mobile Views

Scenario/Problem: Today, many people have mobile phones or other small mobile devices capable of displaying websites. However, the size of the device's screen and its resolution limits the users in how much they can see.

Solution: It is often a good idea to create special views that show information in a more compact way, to enable mobile device users to see that information more clearly and more comfortably navigate in it (see Figure 8.35).

FIGURE 8.35

A mobile view for an announcement list is designed to be easier for mobile device users.

SharePoint attempts to identify whether the device is a mobile device and then switches to a default mobile view that is optimized for that purpose. Each mobile view has a special URL that the mobile device is redirected to, whereas nonmobile devices see the view as if it is a regular view.

To specify that a view should have a mobile URL, scroll to the Mobile section in the view creation page and expand it using the plus sign next to the section title.

You can create a view and specify it to be the default mobile view for the list (see Figure 8.36), or just leave it as another new view in the list.

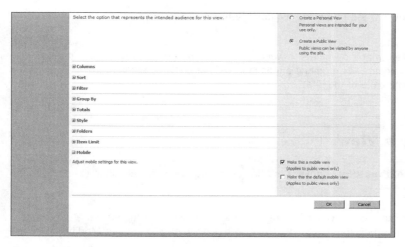

FIGURE 8.36
Creating a mobile view.

If you don't have a mobile device yourself, and you want to see what the view looks like after it has been created, you must manually type the URL that SharePoint has created for the mobile view. To know what that URL is, go into the view modification page and scroll down to the Mobile section. The URL for the mobile view appears there as text (see Figure 8.37).

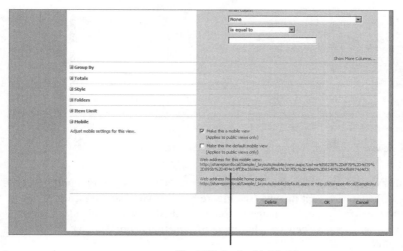

The URL for the Mobile View

FIGURE 8.37
The URL of the mobile view is displayed when modifying the view.

To learn how to modify a view, see the following section.

> **TIP** To see what the whole site would look like from a mobile device, use the second URL that appears when editing a mobile view. That URL is the link to the mobile view of the home page of the site.

Modify a View

> **Scenario/Problem:** You want to change the settings for an existing view.

Solution: The easiest way to change a view is to switch to the view that you want to modify and then use the view picker drop-down menu to choose Modify This View (see Figure 8.38).

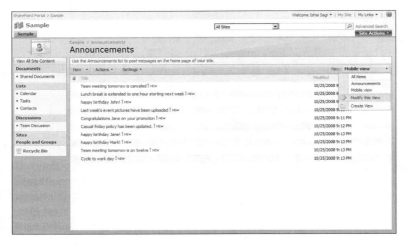

FIGURE 8.38
To modify a view, use the view picker menu option Modify This View.

Selecting this option opens the view editing page, which enables you to modify every setting about the view, except its type (see Figure 8.39). If you want to switch a view to a different type (for example, change it from a standard view to a calendar view), delete the view and create a new one. For more information about deleting a view, see the next section.

To change the view's filename,
type the new filename here.

FIGURE 8.39
To change a view's file name, use the Web address box.

One difference between the view creation page and view editing page is that in the view editing page you can define the name of the file that the view uses.

Delete a View

Scenario/Problem: You want to delete a view because it might be obsolete, or you want to create a view with the same name but with a different type and you need to delete the existing view before you can achieve that.

Solution: To delete a view, navigate to the view's modification page (see the preceding section), and then use the Delete button at the top of the page. You are then prompted to confirm that you want to delete the view. If you confirm, the view is deleted.

CHAPTER 9

Authoring Pages

SharePoint pages are files that enable you to modify the content that they display. These pages include the home page of the site and other pages that you can add to the site's document libraries. By default, a SharePoint site has only one page that you can edit: the home page. However, you can create many more pages and add links to them. Usually, the additional pages are in document libraries in the site.

This chapter explains how you can create new pages in a site and how you can edit and author the content in those pages. It covers topics such as editing controls, which are controls that exist on some pages to enable you to specify their content, and some common web parts that you can add to the pages.

Create a New Page

Scenario/Problem: Often, as a site manager, you want to add more pages to a site. These pages can be used to show information you don't want to display on the home page of the site and can be focused to specific uses, such as articles (where each article is a page) or new items (where each news item is a page).

Solution: You add pages to SharePoint sites by creating new pages in document libraries. Publishing sites make it easier to add pages by providing action menus that enable you to create new pages in a document library called Pages. In nonpublishing sites, however, you must create a document library to hold the pages. The following sections show how you can create pages in both types of sites.

Create a New Page in a Nonpublishing Site

In a standard site, to create pages in addition to the default home page, you must create a document library to hold those pages. To do so, create a document library (see "Create a New Document Library" in Chapter 7, "Creating Lists and Document Libraries") and select that the Document Template for the document library is a web part page. Then, to create a new page, simply click the New button in the document library to open the Create New Page page (see Figure 9.1).

The New Web Part Page page enables you to pick the name for the file that will be created and the layout for the page. Selecting a different layout changes the image on the left, showing you a preview of the layout.

After you click Create, the new web part page opens in editing mode, allowing you to add web parts to its web part zones (see Figure 9.2).

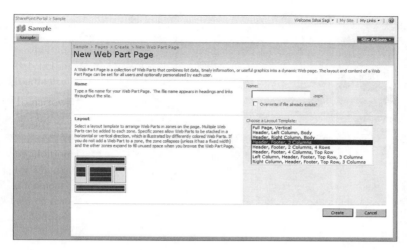

FIGURE 9.1
Creating a new web part page.

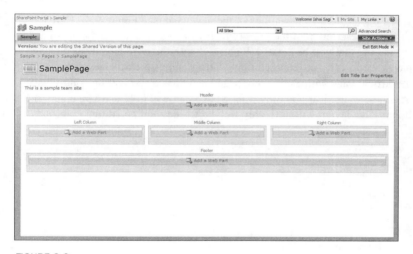

FIGURE 9.2
A newly created web part page, with empty web part zones.

Create a New Page in a Publishing Site

Creating pages in a publishing site is easier because a publishing site already has a document library dedicated to pages. Plus, it has a menu option under the Site Actions menu to create a new page. To create your new page, simply open the Site Actions menu and click Create Page (see Figure 9.3).

FIGURE 9.3
The Create Page option in the Site Actions menu.

In the page that opens, define the settings of the new page (see Figure 9.4). Here, define the title and description of the page (which will be displayed on the page) and the name for the file that will be created. Finally, choose the page layout for the page. Different page layouts offer different editing controls and web part zones. For example, the Article Page with Body Only page layout has a text editing control and no web part zones, so use it if you only want a page that will hold text you enter. The Blank Web Part Page layout will have only web part zones and no editing controls.

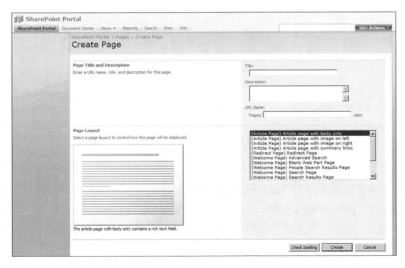

FIGURE 9.4
The Create Page settings page.

Because page layouts can be created by developers or removed by administrators, you might see more or fewer options for layouts. Review the options available and choose the one closest to what you want to achieve with your page. Remember that a page is just a file in a document library, and you can always delete the page if you chose the wrong layout—the same as you would delete any other file in a document library. (See "Delete a File or List Item" in Chapter 6, "Creating and Managing Files, List Items, and Forms in SharePoint.")

Edit a Page

Scenario/Problem: As a site manager, you want to change what is displayed on a specific page in a site.

Solution: To change the display, you must view the page in editing mode—a mode that enables you to edit the page. You can make such changes after you switch to editing mode. (You learn how to make each specific change, such as changing text or a picture or a web part, later in this chapter.)

When you have the permissions to edit a page, and if the page is not currently checked out by someone else, edit the page by navigating to it in the browser, opening the Site Actions menu, and choosing Edit Page (see Figure 9.5).

FIGURE 9.5
Open the Site Actions menu and choose Edit Page to get to the page edit mode.

If the page is in a document library that requires check-out before pages can be edited (which is the default in publishing sites), you can edit the page only if it is currently checked in. If the page is checked out, the Edit Page menu option will not be available until that page is checked in.

When the page is in editing mode, the page looks different than how it looks normally, showing the web part zones (where you can add web parts) and, in some pages, editing controls (see Figure 9.6).

Editing Toolbar

Picture Editing Control   Text Editing Control   Web Part Zone

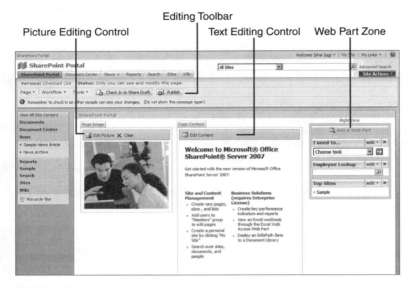

FIGURE 9.6
In editing mode, a page shows different options.

When you are finished editing the page, save your changes. Depending on whether the page is in a managed pages library, this is done in a different manner. If the page is not in a pages library, you can just click the Exit Edit Mode button on the top-right corner of the page. If the page is in a pages library, click the Publish button. For more information, see "Publish a Page," later in this chapter.

Use the Text Editing Control in a Page

Scenario/Problem: When authoring a page, you want to enter or change the text that appears on the page.

Solution: Some pages have text editing controls embedded in them. These controls enable you to type rich text in them, including pictures, links, tables, and other kinds of text. The following sections explain how you can use this type of control to add or change these elements.

> **TIP** Some pages do not have a text editing control. To add text to or edit text in those pages, use the Content Editor web part, as explained later in this chapter.

Edit Text

To edit text in a text editing control, either click the Edit Content link on the top of the control or just click anywhere in the control. When you perform either of these actions, the rich text editing toolbar appears, allowing you to add special text elements, as shown in Figure 9.7. Use the toolbar and control as you would use any word processor; for example, to make part of the text bold, highlight it and click the Bold button (labeled B).

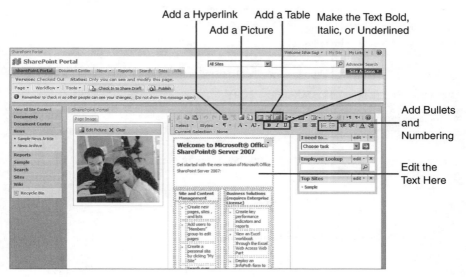

FIGURE 9.7
When you're editing text in a rich text control, the editing toolbar is displayed.

Add a Hyperlink

To add a hyperlink to the text, highlight the part of the text that you want to make a hyperlink and click the Hyperlink button. Clicking this button opens a dialog that enables you to pick where the hyperlink will link to (see Figure 9.8).

Besides choosing how the hyperlink behaves—opening in a new window or displaying a tooltip—select what the hyperlink will point to by either typing the link in the Selected URL box or clicking the Browse button. Clicking this button opens another dialog showing you the current site and allowing you to navigate through the different document libraries and lists until you find what you want to link to (see Figure 9.9).

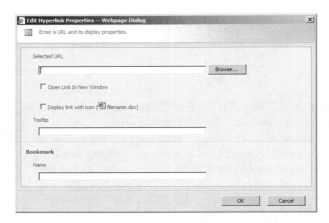

FIGURE 9.8
The dialog for adding a hyperlink.

Use the up button to view other lists and libraries in the site.

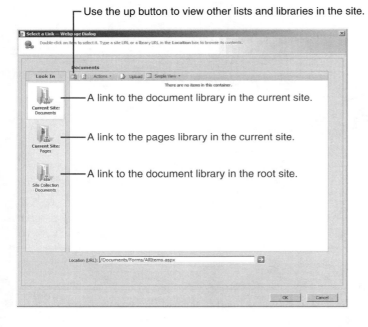

A link to the document library in the current site.

A link to the pages library in the current site.

A link to the document library in the root site.

FIGURE 9.9
The dialog for browsing for a hyperlink target.

By default, the dialog shows three links on the left, linking to the document libraries: the one in the current site, the one in the root site, and one link to the pages library in the current site. You can use these links, or if you want to navigate to another place in the site or in another site, click the Up button in the toolbar. This shows you all the document libraries and lists and even subsites (see Figure 9.10). Double-click any site, list, or library to view what is in it, or click a site, list, library, or the items in them to add the link to the selected item to the Location box at the bottom of the dialog. Click OK to make the hyperlink point to the item you selected.

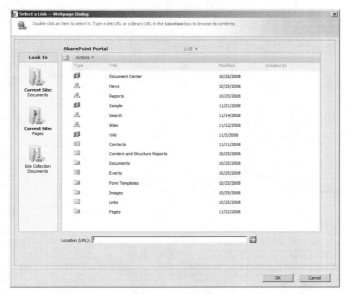

FIGURE 9.10
Navigating a site for the hyperlink target.

Add a Picture

To add a picture to the text editing control, place the cursor where you want the picture to be added and click the Picture icon in the toolbar. This opens a dialog in which you can select the picture to add as well as define the picture's settings (see Figure 9.11).

You can either type the link to the picture in the Selected Image box or click Browse to show the dialog that browses to the picture (see Figure 9.12).

In this dialog you can select the picture by clicking it once and clicking OK, or navigate through the sites to find the picture you want. The links on the left side go to the picture library in the current site and to the one in the root site. If the picture you are looking for is in a different location, click the Up button, which will show you all the contents of the site. Then navigate through the site and subsites and look in different picture libraries (or document libraries) to select the picture you want. To select a picture, either double-click it or click it once and click OK.

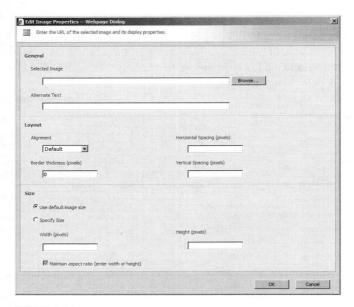

FIGURE 9.11
The dialog to add a picture.

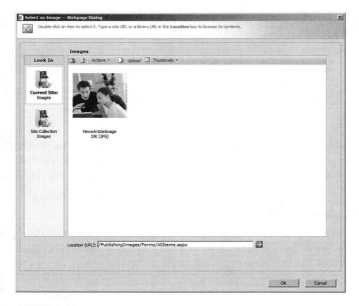

FIGURE 9.12
The dialog to browse to a picture.

Add and Edit a Table

To add a table in a text control, place the cursor where you want the table to be added and click the Table icon. Clicking this icon opens a dialog that lets you specify the settings for the table—how many rows, how many columns, the width and the height, as well as formatting (see Figure 9.13).

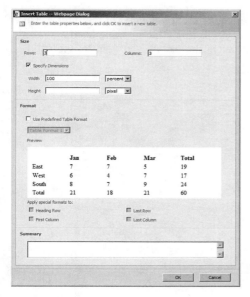

FIGURE 9.13
The dialog to add a table.

After the table has been added, edit it by clicking the Edit Table icon, as shown in Figure 9.14, and add or remove rows and columns by using the Table Operations button.

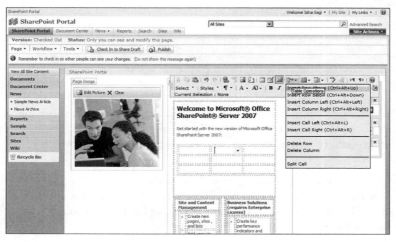

FIGURE 9.14
The menu options to edit a table.

Use the Picture Editing Control in a Page

Scenario/Problem: When authoring a page, you want to change the picture that appears on the page.

Solution: Some pages have a picture editing control embedded in them (see Figure 9.15). This control is used to simply display a picture. The following sections explain how to use this editing control to select the picture you want for the page.

The Picture Editing Control

FIGURE 9.15
The picture editing control.

TIP Some pages do not have a picture editing control, and the pictures displayed in them are stored in web parts. For information about how to modify web parts, see "Use the Image Web Part" and "Modify a Web Part" later in this chapter.

You can either clear the control (removing the picture) or edit it. To clear the control, click the Clear button. To edit it, click the Edit Picture button. Clicking this button opens the editing dialog, which enables you to set the properties of the picture (see Figure 9.16).

In this dialog you can specify a different picture to be displayed in the control by either typing the link to the picture or clicking Browse to view the pictures available in the current site. This process is exactly the same as the one for adding a picture to the text editing control described previously in this chapter.

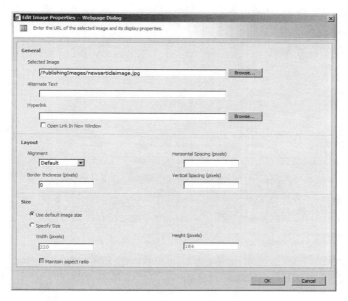

FIGURE 9.16
The Edit Image Properties dialog for the picture editing control.

Add a Web Part

Scenario/Problem: When authoring or editing a page, you want to add different kinds of content to different sections of the page.

Solution: Some pages enable you to add web parts to them. To add a web part to a page, decide to which zone you want to add it and click the Add a Web Part button in that zone. You are able to move the web part to another zone after it has been added. The Add Web Parts dialog enables you to select which web part or web parts to add to the zone (see Figure 9.17). The dialog shows all the web parts available for you in this site. Some sites offer different web parts than others.

The list of web parts begins with the choices of the lists and libraries in the current site, under the Lists and Libraries section. Choose one to add a view of that list or library to the page. The other web parts, under the All Web Parts section, are designed to display other kinds of data. For more information on some of the most commonly used web parts, see "Use Built-in Web Parts" next in this chapter.

FIGURE 9.17

The dialog that enables you to select web parts to add to the page.

Select the web parts you want by using the check boxes on the left and clicking Add to add them. Some web part zones add the web parts side by side, although most web part zones add the web parts you select below the existing web parts.

Use Built-In Web Parts

Scenario/Problem: When authoring or editing a page, you want to add different content to different sections of the page.

Solution: The following sections explain some of the choices you have when adding a web part to a page. Although there are many more web parts for you to choose from, the ones described here are the most common ones.

Use the List View Web Part

The List View web part is not called by that name in the Add Web Parts dialog. Instead, you see lists of all the lists and libraries available in the current site as web parts (refer to Figure 9.17). By selecting one of them and adding it to the page, in fact, you are adding a List View web part to the page.

After you add the web part to the page, it displays the items in the list or library that you selected. Depending on the type of list, the view that is displayed by default might be different. Links lists show the links in a bulleted list, whereas document libraries display the type of document, name of the document, and name of the last person to modify it.

If you want to change what is displayed, you can do that from the web part's settings pane (see Figure 9.18). To get to the pane, click the Edit button on the web part's title bar to open the Edit menu, and then select Modify Shared Web Part. For more information about how to modify a web part and get to its editing pane, see "Modify a Web Part" later in this chapter.

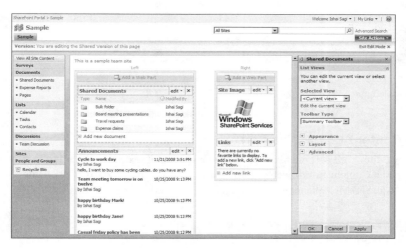

FIGURE 9.18
The List View web part editing pane.

The web part settings for the List View web part enable you to select different views for the web part to display out of the list of views that were created for the list or library. You can also create a view just for the web part by clicking the Edit the Current View link if you want the web part to display a view that was not created in the list or library.

You can also select the toolbar type for the web part. This setting defines whether the web part will display a Summary toolbar. This means that the web part will display a link at the bottom for adding a new item to the list or creating a new document in the library. Or it will display a full toolbar link in the regular list views, complete with New and Upload buttons, as well as Actions and Settings menus (see Figure 9.19).

The last option for the toolbar type is to have no toolbar at all.

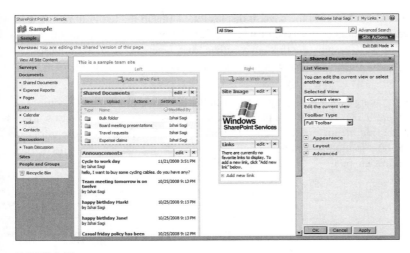

FIGURE 9.19
The List View web part with a full toolbar.

Use the Content Editor Web Part

The Content Editor web part enables you to type any kind of text in it, including scripts. To add a Content Editor web part to a page, select it from the list of available web parts, under the Miscellaneous section (see Figure 9.20).

FIGURE 9.20
Choosing the Content Editor web part.

After you add the web part, it does not appear with any text (see Figure 9.21). Instead, you see an instruction telling you that you need to add text (content) to the web part by opening the tool pane for the web part. To do so, click the link in the text. If, in the future, you would like to change the text, see "Modify a Web Part" later in this chapter.

FIGURE 9.21

The Content Editor web part before any content has been added to it.

When you click the link, the tool pane for the web part opens, allowing you to enter content in it (see Figure 9.22).

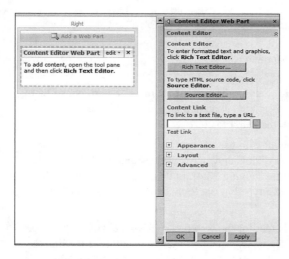

FIGURE 9.22

The tool pane for the Content Editor web part.

There are three different ways to specify the content for the web part. The first is to use the Rich Text Editor. To do this, just click the Rich Text Editor button in the tool pane. This results in a dialog that allows you to type rich text, complete with hyperlinks, images, and tables, and even a spell checker—just like a basic word processor (see Figure 9.23).

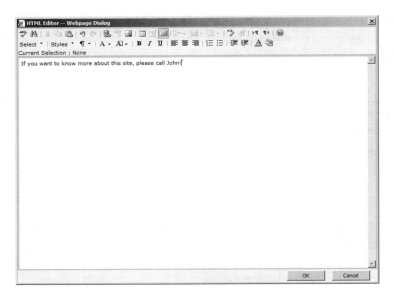

FIGURE 9.23
The Rich Text Editor in the Content Editor web part.

When you're finished typing and formatting the content for the web part, click OK to close the dialog. The page refreshes, and the content that you typed is displayed in the web part. At this point click OK on the panel to close it.

The second way to specify the content is to use the source editor. To do so, click the Source Editor button, which opens a dialog showing you the source HTML code that makes the content for the web part (see Figure 9.24). In this dialog you can see the source code of anything that you have typed in the Rich Text Editor and edit it using regular HTML syntax.

Finally, you can specify that the content for the web part will not be part of the web part, but instead will be brought from an external text file. To do so, type the link to the file in the Content Link box (see Figure 9.25). This file can be in SharePoint or in another site. Be sure to link only to a file that all the users of the site have permissions to view; otherwise, they will not be able to view the page.

CAUTION   Do not use this feature of the web part to link to office files or other types of files. Only text or HTML files are supported by the web part

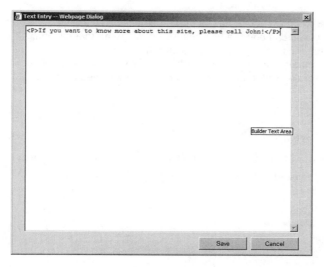

FIGURE 9.24
The source editor in the Content Editor web part.

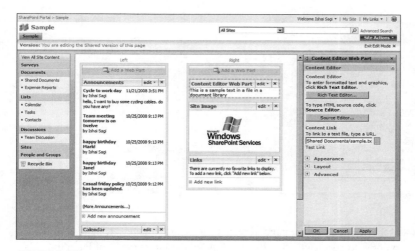

FIGURE 9.25
Specifying a file in a document library to be the content of the web part.

When you are done specifying the contents, click OK for the tool pane to save your changes.

NOTE The Content Editor web part is different from the text editing control in several ways. For one thing, you can edit the text in it only through the tool pane of the web part. But one of the most significant things about this web part is that changes to the web part's content are not tracked in the page's version history. So even if you restore an old version of the page, the web part will have the latest text that was entered in it.

Use the Image Web Part

The Image web part enables you to display just an image. To add an Image web part, select it from the list of available web parts under the Miscellaneous section (see Figure 9.26).

FIGURE 9.26
Selecting the Image web part.

After you add the web part to the page, it doesn't have any image set; instead, it offers instructions on how to specify the image: by clicking the Open the Tool Pane link. To specify the image, click the Open the Tool Pane link. If you need to change it later (after you have chosen an image), see "Modify a Web Part" later in this chapter.

When the tool pane is open, you can specify what image should be displayed, as well as some settings for how it will be displayed (see Figure 9.27).

FIGURE 9.27
The tool pane for the Image web part.

The first setting is the link to the image. Just type (or paste) the link into the Image Link box. Click the Test Link hyperlink above the box to make sure the link you typed is correct and points to the right picture. If the link is fine, the picture opens in a new window, which you can then close (see Figure 9.28).

FIGURE 9.28
An Image web part displaying the selected image.

In the Alternative Text box, type the text that you want to appear in the web part if the user who is browsing the site is using a browser that doesn't support images or has that option turned off. This text also will be displayed when the user hovers the mouse cursor over the picture.

Use the Content Query Web Part

The Content Query web part is one of the most useful web parts. It is used to display information in the current site or in other sites in the current site collection, based on a query. For example, if you want to show an aggregation of all the announcements from all the sites, this web part does it. It is a quite complex web part with a lot of options, some of them requiring a developer to configure, but most of them are easy to set up, as shown here.

The Content Query web part is available only in publishing sites and is not available in sites that are not at least under a root publishing site.

The Content Query web part is usually under the Default category in the web part list (see Figure 9.29). To add it to the page, select the web part in the list and click the Add button.

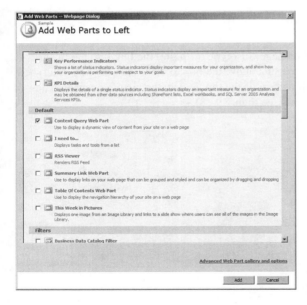

FIGURE 9.29
Selecting the Content Query web part.

After it is added, the web part displays, by default, the last 15 created pages from all the pages in all the pages libraries from all the sites in the current site collection (see Figure 9.30).

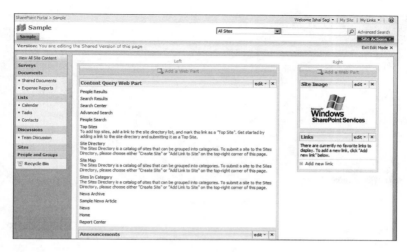

FIGURE 9.30
The Content Query web part showing the last 15 created pages from all sites.

To modify the query that the web part performs and display a different kind of content, click the Edit button in the top-right corner of the web part and select Modify Shared Web Part from the menu that appears (see Figure 9.31). This selection opens the tool pane for the web part.

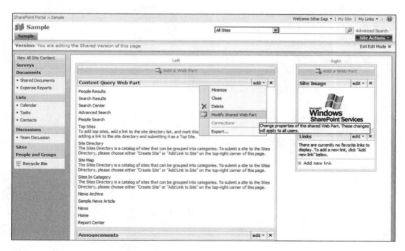

FIGURE 9.31
Getting to the Content Query web part tool pane.

In the tool pane, expand the Query section. You then see the options to specify what content should be displayed and from where (see Figure 9.32).

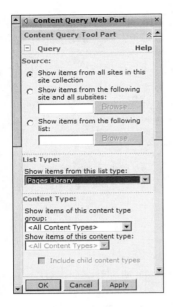

FIGURE 9.32
The Query section of the Content Query web part's tool pane.

You can specify whether the query will be on all sites in the site collection, from a specific site and its subsites, or on just a specific list. For the last two options, use the Browse button to open a dialog that enables you to select the site or list in question (see Figures 9.33 and 9.34). Then click OK to return to the Content Query web part configuration pane.

FIGURE 9.33
Selecting a site for the Content Query web part.

FIGURE 9.34
Selecting a list for the Content Query web part.

In the List Type selection box, you can define what kind of list type the web part should look in for its content. This includes document libraries, pages libraries, picture libraries, and all other list templates.

The Content Type section enables you to select what content types the web part will limit its query to. If you don't want to specify a specific content type, leave it at the default All Content Types. Otherwise, you can limit it to a group of content types (for example, all the document content types) and to a specific content type. To do that, select the content type group (for example, document content types), and then either select All Content Types in the second drop-down (see Figure 9.35) or select the specific content type that you want.

The next options that you can set are the filters (see Figure 9.36). You can specify that the web part will display only list items or documents that have specific values in specific columns by setting up to three filters on the web part. To do so, scroll down in the tool pane to the Filters section, and under Show Items When, select the column that you want, the kind of filter that you want, and the value to filter on. For example, select Company is equal to Adventureworks.

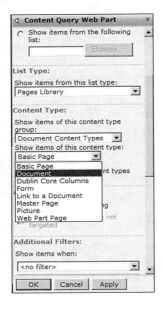

FIGURE 9.35

Selecting a specific content type for the Content Query web part.

FIGURE 9.36

The Filter section in the Content Query web part with a filter specified on the company column.

Modify a Web Part

Scenario/Problem: When editing a page, you want to change the settings for existing web parts on that page.

Solution: The following sections explain how to get the web part to editing mode and cover some of the common settings you can modify for that web part in that mode, such as modifying the web part's title, its display settings, and the web part's position in the page.

To modify a web part of any kind, switch the page to editing mode (See "Edit a Page," earlier in this chapter), and then click the Edit button on the top-right corner of the web part you want to modify. If you have permissions to edit the web part, the option Modify Shared Web Part is available in the menu (see Figure 9.37). Selecting this option opens the tool pane for the web part. Some web parts have different tool panes with different settings, but all of them have some basic settings that you can modify.

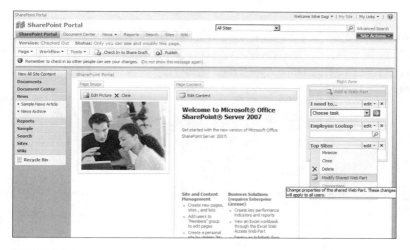

FIGURE 9.37
To modify a web part, open the Edit menu and select Modify Shared Web Part.

Modify the Web Part's Title

To modify the web part's title, expand the Appearance section in the web part's tool pane (see Figure 9.38). The first option in the Appearance section is the title of the web part. Simply type in the title that you want and click OK to save it.

FIGURE 9.38
Expand the Appearance section in the tool pane.

Modify the Web Part's Title Bar and Border Settings

To modify whether the web part displays the title bar and whether it displays a border line around its contents, expand the Appearance section in the web part's tool pane and scroll down to the Chrome Type selection (see Figure 9.39).

FIGURE 9.39
Selecting the chrome type for a web part.

The chrome type can be one of these options:

▶ **None:** The web part does not display a title bar or border. This is typical for Image web parts where you want the picture to appear without a title bar above it and without a border around it, as if it is part of the page and not in a web part (see Figure 9.40).

FIGURE 9.40
The Image web part with the None chrome type.

▶ **Title and Border:** The web part displays the title bar and a border around the content (see Figure 9.41).

FIGURE 9.41
The Image web part with the Title and Border chrome type.

▶ **Title Only:** The web part displays the title bar without a border around the content (see Figure 9.42).

▶ **Border Only:** The web part does not display the title bar but does display a border around the content (see Figure 9.43).

FIGURE 9.42
The Image web part with the Title Only chrome type.

FIGURE 9.43
The Image web part with the Border Only chrome type.

Modify or Remove the Link for the Web Part's Title

In some web parts, you want the title to be a link that the users can click. To set that link or remove it (some web parts have a link by default), expand the Advanced section in the web part's tool pane and scroll down to the Title URL box. In this box, as shown in Figure 9.44, type the link that you want for the web part's title or clear the box to remove the link.

Move a Web Part in a Page

To move an existing web part in a page, switch the page to editing mode (see "Edit a Page" earlier in this chapter), and then just drag and drop the title of the web part to the location where you want it to appear. To do so, just hover the mouse cursor over the web part's title; then hold down the left mouse button and, without releasing it, move the mouse cursor to the place where you want the title—either in the same web part zone or in another.

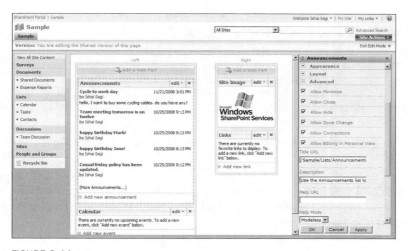

FIGURE 9.44
The Title URL box controls the link for the web part's title.

The location of your mouse cursor is displayed by the title of the web part that you are moving. When you are hovering the mouse cursor over a web part zone, the place in that zone where the web part will be added is signified by a bold line above or below or between the existing web parts already in that zone (see Figure 9.45). When you have the mouse cursor where you want the web part to be, just release the mouse button.

The bold line shows where the web part will be moved.

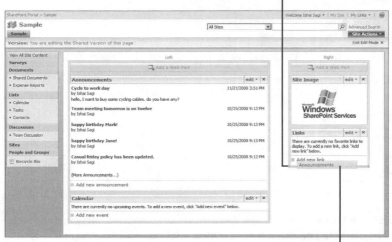

The title of the web part shows where the mouse cursor is.

FIGURE 9.45
Dragging and dropping the announcements web part.

Reuse a Web Part (Export/Import)

Scenario/Problem: After you have configured a web part to your liking, you want to save that web part and use it again in another page with similar settings.

Solution: The following sections explain how to export the web part and then import it to another page.

After you have configured a web part to your liking, you might want to save it and use it again in another page with similar settings. To do that, you must export the web part and then import it to the other page.

Export a Web Part

Exporting a web part is actually saving the web part's settings as a file to your computer. To do that, switch the page that has the web part to editing mode (see "Edit a Page" earlier in this chapter) and open the web part's Edit menu to select the Export option (see Figure 9.46). However, some types of web parts do not allow themselves to be exported, and that option does not appear in the menu. In those cases you should look in the options in that web part's tool pane to see whether there is an option to allow the web part to be exported because some web parts have that option.

FIGURE 9.46
The Export option is available under the Edit menu.

After you select the Export option, a File Download dialog appears, allowing you to save the web part to your computer. Save the file anywhere on your computer so you can import it later (see "Import a Web Part," next).

Import a Web Part

To import a web part that you have previously saved to your computer, open the page in editing mode (see "Edit a Page" earlier in this chapter) and click the web part zone where you want the web part to be added, as if you are adding a new web part. However, when the dialog with the list of web parts appears, instead of selecting a web part from the list, click the Advanced Web Part Gallery and Options link at the bottom of the dialog.

Selecting this link opens the web part gallery as a pane on the right side of the screen, showing the list of web parts in the pane (see Figure 9.47). At the top of the pane is the Browse drop-down menu. Click it and select Import from the options.

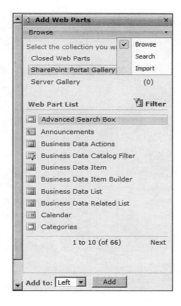

FIGURE 9.47
Click Import in the Browse drop-down menu.

The Import pane enables you to browse to a file in your computer that you exported previously (see Figure 9.48).

Browse to the file you want to reuse and click the Upload button. The web part is then displayed as an option below the button, under the Uploaded Web Part heading (see Figure 9.49).

FIGURE 9.48
The Import pane.

FIGURE 9.49
Uploading a web part file.

To add the web part to the page, either click the Import button at the bottom of the pane, or drag and drop the web part to the place in the web part zone where you want it to be. To do that, just click the web part's title, and while holding down the left mouse button, move your mouse cursor over to the location where you want the web part to be added. While you drag the web part, the web part's name is displayed where your mouse cursor is going, and when you are hovering over a web part zone, the location where the web part is added is marked with lines (see Figure 9.50).

The lines mark where the web part will be added in the zone.

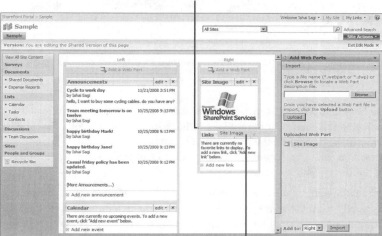

The location of the mouse cursor is
displayed as the title of the web part.

FIGURE 9.50
Dragging and dropping a web part.

To place the web part in the desired location just release the mouse button. The web part will be added to the location you chose, as shown in Figure 9.51.

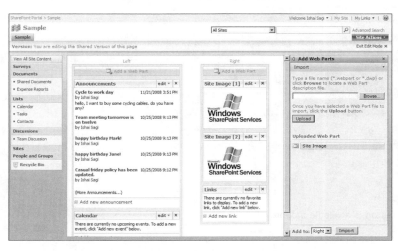

FIGURE 9.51
The new web part is added to the page.

Publish a Page

Scenario/Problem: When a page is located in a document library that requires publishing—something that is common when using the publishing features (where all pages in a site are in the Pages library)—you must publish the page for users to be able to see it.

Solution: This section explains how to publish a page in a library that requires publishing.

Publishing can be accomplished from the document library itself, just like publishing any other file that is in a document library (see "Check In and Check Out a File or List Item" in Chapter 6). You check in the page and then publish it, going through any approval process that might be required. (Again, refer to Chapter 6 for more information about the publishing and approval process.)

However, unlike publishing regular files, publishing pages is unique in that you can publish them directly from the pages themselves. When you are editing a page that requires publishing, a page editing toolbar appears at the top of the page, with buttons designed to assist you in publishing the page (see Figure 9.52). If the library where the page is located does not require approval, simply click the Publish button to publish the page for everyone to see.

The Publish Button   The Page Editing Toolbar

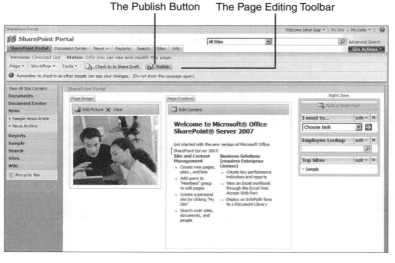

FIGURE 9.52
The Publish button is available if approval is not required.

However, if the library does require approval before publishing, you see the Submit for Approval button instead, as shown in Figure 9.53.

The Submit for Approval Button

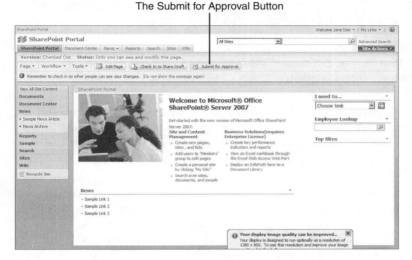

FIGURE 9.53
The Submit for Approval button is available if approval is required.

When you submit for approval, most users are not able to see your changes, but the people with permissions to approve items in the document library can view your changes and approve or reject them. If an approver approves the page, it is published for other users to view. Approvers who navigate to the page see a toolbar allowing them to approve or reject the page from the page itself, as shown in Figure 9.54.

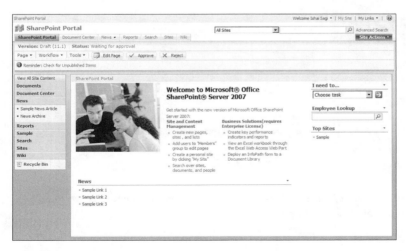

FIGURE 9.54
An approver gets buttons to approve or reject a page.

Discard the Check-Out of a Page

Scenario/Problem: Often you start editing a page and then either change your mind or regret a change and want to roll back and start again.

Solution: To start over, just discard the check-out of the page. This section explains how to accomplish that.

The option to discard a check-out is available only when the page is in a document library that tracks versions and requires a check-out, such as in publishing websites. Pages that are not in such document libraries do not give you the option, and any change you make is saved; therefore, you must manually roll it back.

To discard the check-out of a page, use the built-in Discard Check Out option for that page from the library view, exactly as you would discard a check-out of a file in a document library (see "Check In and Check Out a File or List Item" in Chapter 6). However, an easier and more accessible way to discard the check-out of the page is through the page editing toolbar. When the page is open, click the Page menu in the page editing toolbar to open the menu; then select the Discard Check Out option, as shown in Figure 9.55.

FIGURE 9.55
Use the Page menu to get to the Discard Check Out option.

If the page editing toolbar is not shown, click Site Actions and choose Show Page Editing Toolbar, as shown in Figure 9.56.

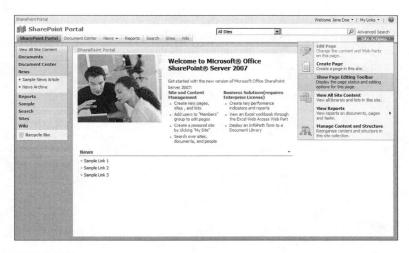

FIGURE 9.56
Use the Site Actions menu to get to the page editing toolbar.

However, if the toolbar does not appear, the most likely reason is that you are not logged on to the site as the person who last edited the page, and the page might be checked out to someone else. In this case the option to discard the check-out is not available.

Compare Versions of a Page

Scenario/Problem: Often you want to restore a page to a previous state (before some changes were made to the page), but you want to compare differences between the versions before making up your mind which one to restore.

Solution: Pages that reside in a document library that supports versioning enable you to restore previous versions of the pages, just like any other files in document libraries that support versioning. However, with pages you also get the option to view the changes that were made to them between each version and compare them.

NOTE Page changes that are tracked by versioning include adding and removing web parts and editing content in the page's editing controls, such as the text editing control and image editing control. However, changes made to the contents in the web parts on the page do not count as part of the page's contents and are not restored when you restore a previous version, nor are they shown in the comparison of versions.

To compare the changes between versions of a page, open the page's page editing toolbar by clicking the Site Actions menu and selecting Show Page Editing Toolbar, as shown previously in Figure 9.56. When the toolbar is displayed, open the Tools menu in the toolbar and select Compare Text Changes from the menu (see Figure 9.57).

FIGURE 9.57
Select Compare Text Changes from the Tools menu.

Selecting this option opens a page with a list of the versions in the left pane and the current text with change tracking in the right pane (see Figure 9.58).

FIGURE 9.58
The version comparison screen.

When a change is made to a piece of content in the page (for example, the text in a text editing control on the page), the section in the version comparison page shows the old value and the new value, indicating what editing was done (see Figure 9.59). New text is highlighted, existing text appears as regular text, and text that was deleted appears with a gray background and a line in the middle (strikethrough).

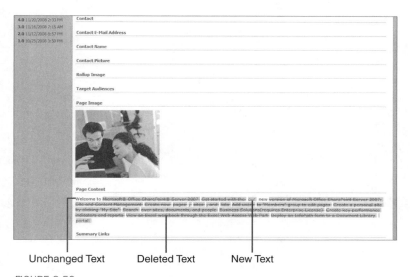

Unchanged Text   Deleted Text   New Text

FIGURE 9.59
The text in the text editing control was changed.

You can browse the other versions of the page by clicking the version date and time on the left, and delete or restore the version using the toolbar in the page.

CHAPTER 10

Managing Security

If you are in charge of managing a list or library, you should learn how to manage the security on either the list or library or on the single items in them. This chapter covers some basic tasks having to do with security of lists, libraries, and list items.

See What Permissions Are Set

Scenario/Problem: You want to see what permissions are given to whom in a list or library or on a specific list item. For example, you want to know who can read, write, or delete files in a document library. Alternatively, you want to know who has permissions to read a specific document or to edit it.

Solution: The following sections explain how to check what permissions were defined for files, list items, document libraries, and lists.

Check Permissions on Files and List Items

To check what permissions are set on a file or list item, you must have the right to manage permissions on the file or item. If you don't have the permissions, you do not see the option to manage them. The Manage Permissions option is in the drop-down box for the file or list item (see Figure 10.1).

FIGURE 10.1
Use the Manage Permissions option to see what permissions are set on a file or item.

Selecting this option opens a page that shows the permissions for the file or item you're looking at (see Figure 10.2). On this page you can see what permissions each user or group of users has on the file or item.

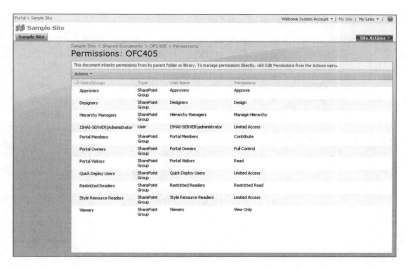

Portal > Sample Site

Welcome System Account ▼ | My Site | My Links ▼ | ⊛

🏠 Sample Site

Sample Site   Site Actions ▼

Sample Site > Shared Documents > OFC405 > Permissions
Permissions: OFC405

This document inherits permissions from its parent folder or library. To manage permissions directly, click Edit Permissions from the Actions menu.

Actions ▼

☐ Users/Groups	Type	User Name	Permissions
Approvers	SharePoint Group	Approvers	Approve
Designers	SharePoint Group	Designers	Design
Hierarchy Managers	SharePoint Group	Hierarchy Managers	Manage Hierarchy
ISHAI-SERVER\Administrator	User	ISHAI-SERVER\administrator	Limited Access
Portal Members	SharePoint Group	Portal Members	Contribute
Portal Owners	SharePoint Group	Portal Owners	Full Control
Portal Visitors	SharePoint Group	Portal Visitors	Read
Quick Deploy Users	SharePoint Group	Quick Deploy Users	Limited Access
Restricted Readers	SharePoint Group	Restricted Readers	Restricted Read
Style Resource Readers	SharePoint Group	Style Resource Readers	Limited Access
Viewers	SharePoint Group	Viewers	View Only

FIGURE 10.2
The manage permissions page.

The name of the file or title for the item appears in the page's title, after the word *Permissions*. This information helps you make sure you are viewing the permissions for the right file or item. The name of the user or group is in the first column, and the type (identifying whether it is a user or group) is in the second column. In the last column, you can see the permission set that the user or group has on the item or file. Depending on the configuration of your server, other columns with more information about the user or group also appear.

For example, in Figure 10.2, people in the Portal Visitors group can only read the file or item because they have only the Read permission, whereas Portal Owners can do everything to the file or item (including managing the permissions on it, deleting it, and so on) because they have the Full Control permission set. The user ISHAI-SERVER\Administrator is shown to have Limited Access permissions. This type of permission can mean different things in different sites but usually means read-only permission.

It is important to note that if permissions are given to a group and then separately to a user, if that user is a member of the group, the higher permission level wins. For example, suppose user A is a member of group B, and group B has Full Control permissions on an item. Although user A was given just Read access, because user A is a member of group B, that user also has full control of the item, and not just Read access. The same would apply if the situation were reversed: If user A has Full Access and that user is a member of group B, which has Read-Only access, the user still has full access to the item.

For more information about groups, see the section "See Who Is a Member of a SharePoint Group" later in this chapter.

Check Permissions on Lists and Libraries

To be able to check what permissions are set on a list or library, you must have the permissions to manage the list or library. If you do not have the right permissions, you do not see the option to manage the permissions. To get to the Manage Permissions option in a list or library, click the Settings button from the toolbar for that list. From the drop-down menu that appears, select Document Library Settings (if it is a document library) or List Settings (if it is a list).

Selecting this option takes you to the list management page. On this page find the Permissions for This List link or Permissions for This Document Library link and click it (see Figure 10.3).

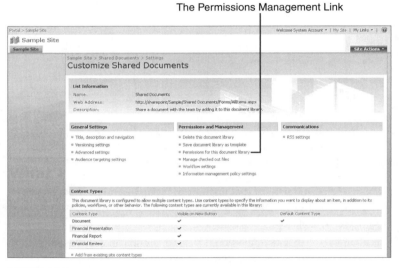

The Permissions Management Link

FIGURE 10.3
The list management page offers options for setting permissions.

Selecting this link takes you to the list or library management page (see Figure 10.4). On this page you can see what permissions each user or group of users has on the list or library.

The name of the user or group appears in the first column, and the type (identifying whether it is a user or a group) appears in the second column. In the last column, you can see the permission set that the user or group has on the library.

For example, in Figure 10.4, people in the Portal Visitors group can only read items in the list or library because they have only the Read permission, whereas Portal Owners can do everything in the document library (including managing the permissions on it) because they have the Full Control permission set.

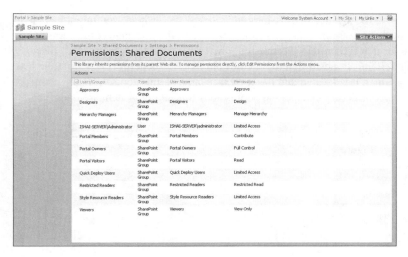

FIGURE 10.4
The list or library management page shows user and group permissions.

As with permissions on files or items, it is important to note that when a user is given more than one permission set—because that user is part of a group that has a different permission set—that user gets the higher permission set. In the example in Figure 10.4, if the user ISHAI-SERVER\Administrator is part of the Portal Owners group, that user has full control over the document library or list because the higher permission level of the group overrides the lower permission level of the user.

For more information about groups, see the section "See Who Is a Member of a SharePoint Group," later in this chapter.

Assign Permissions to a File or List Item

Scenario/Problem: You want to change the permissions a certain user or group of users has on a file or list item. Because permissions for items are inherited from the list or library they are in, the items or files have the same permissions as the list. Sometimes you want to set different permissions on documents or items than the ones for the list. For example, you want to upload a document to share with several colleagues, but not with other people who have access to the document library.

Solution: To assign permissions on a file or list item, you need to get to the manage permissions page of that file or list item. To get to this page, follow the instructions under "Check Permissions on Files and List Items" earlier in this chapter.

When you're on the manage permissions page for the file or item, you might be able to immediately change permissions, or you might have to first disconnect the permission inheritance for that file or item. Permission inheritance is on by default for all files or items in SharePoint. It means that the file or item inherits its permissions from the list or library in which it is located and has the exact same permission sets. If the permissions for the list or library change, the permissions for the file or item are updated automatically.

While inheritance is active, it is not possible to set a different permission level to the file or item (see Figure 10.5).

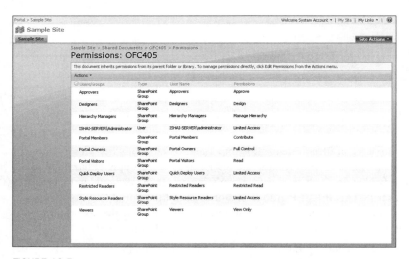

FIGURE 10.5
When a file or item inherits permissions from the list or library, you can only view the permissions.

To stop the file or item inheriting permissions, open the Actions drop-down menu in the manage permissions page and choose Edit Permissions (see Figure 10.6). The other choice is to manage the permissions for the parent, either the list or library. If you choose that approach, you are redirected to the manage permissions on a list or library page. For more information about managing permissions on lists and libraries, see "Change a User's Permissions on a List or Library" later in this chapter.

After you click the Edit Permissions option, a prompt appears, asking you to confirm that you want to disconnect the permissions inheritance from the list or library. The prompt also explains that after you do so, changes to the permissions of the list and library will not affect the file or item you are managing. This means, for example, that if a certain user is granted permissions to edit files or items in the list or library *after* you disconnected the inheritance of permissions, that user still will not be able to edit the specific list item or file that you managed unless you (or someone else) give that user the permissions to edit that document explicitly.

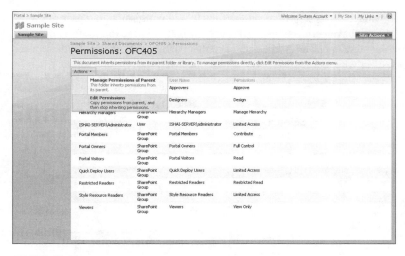

FIGURE 10.6
To disconnect the inheritance of a file or item, choose Edit Permissions from the Actions drop-down menu.

If you are sure that you want to manage the permissions for this file separately from the permission of the list or library, click OK. After confirming, the page changes and allows you to manage the permissions for the file or item.

If the file or item's permission inheritance was already disconnected in the past, by you or by someone else, you see the screen shown in Figure 10.7 when you click Manage Permissions for the file or list item.

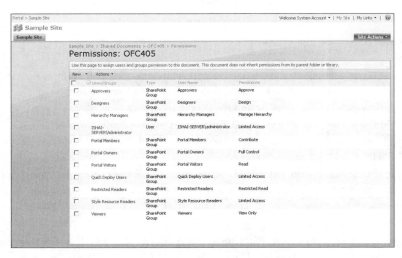

FIGURE 10.7
The edit permissions page for a list item or file when permission inheritance is disconnected.

Now you can manage the permissions on the file. To add permission to a user or group that doesn't already have permissions, click the New button in the top toolbar in the screen. Selecting New opens an Add Users page that enables you to select either a user or group and select what permission levels should be given (see Figure 10.8).

The Check Name Icon

Select a user by typing the name in this box.

Select a user by opening the address book.

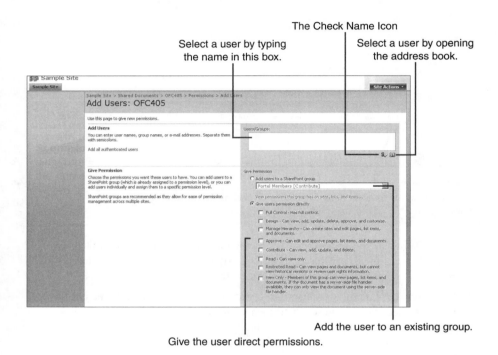

Add the user to an existing group.

Give the user direct permissions.

FIGURE 10.8
Adding permissions to a new user or group.

Under the Add Users section, type the name (or part of a name) or email address for the user or group that you want to add. Or click the address book icon to open the people search dialog, where you can search for people by typing their name or part of it. You can add more than one user or group at a time by separating the names with a semicolon. This is similar to when you are writing an email in Microsoft Outlook and you choose the person you want to send the email to.

If you use the Check Name icon and there is no exact match to the name you entered, a red underline appears beneath the name. You can then click the name to open a menu that shows users who are a close match to that name or select to remove the name.

For example, typing **John** and clicking the Check Name icon results in a red line under the name *John*. Clicking John shows that there is a user called John Doe. If that is the user you're looking for, click that name. If not, either click Remove to delete John from the text box or click More Names to open the search dialog (see Figure 10.9).

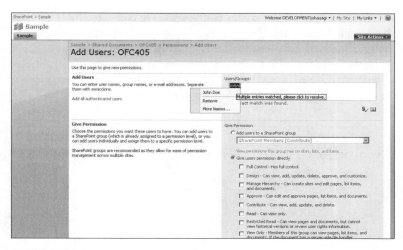

FIGURE 10.9
Typing part of a name in the text box.

The search dialog enables you to search for people. Just type part of the name of the person or group that you want, as shown in Figure 10.10, and click the Search icon. A list of possible matches appears. To select one of them, double-click the name, and it is added to the box at the bottom of the dialog. After you have chosen all the users and groups, click OK to close the dialog and return to the Add Users page.

FIGURE 10.10
Typing part of a name in the people search dialog.

After you have found the users and/or groups that you want to add to the list, select the permissions they should have by selecting one or more of the check boxes in the list of permissions under Give Users Permission Directly (see Figure 10.11). Selecting options here gives the users the permissions you selected. As before, the higher permission level wins; so if you give someone the permission to Read and to Contribute, the user can edit the file as well as read it because of the Contribute setting.

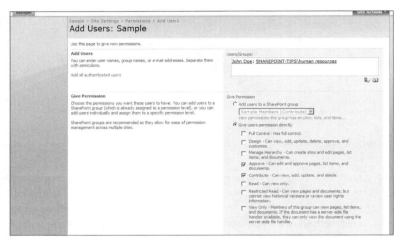

FIGURE 10.11
Setting permissions for a user and group.

Alternatively, you can add the users or groups to a SharePoint group. This means they will get whatever permission level the SharePoint group has. This is a useful mechanism to control permissions; for example, if you decide that all the users who have Contribute (edit) permissions on a document should now have read-only access, you would have to edit each user's permissions. Instead, using SharePoint groups, you can add users to a SharePoint group that has the Contribute permission level, and when a change is required, you change the permissions only on that SharePoint group, and not to each user separately. You can add both users and security groups to the SharePoint group.

To add users or groups to a SharePoint group, click the Add Users to a SharePoint Group option, and then select from the drop-down list what SharePoint group you want to add the users and/or security groups to (see Figure 10.12).

If the server hosting the SharePoint site supports sending emails, another option will appear allowing you to send email to the users, telling them that they have permissions on the file or item (see Figure 10.13). You have the option to select not to send the email, or if you select to send it, you can change the title and body of the email.

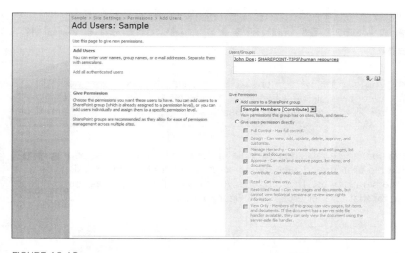

FIGURE 10.12
Adding users and groups to a SharePoint group.

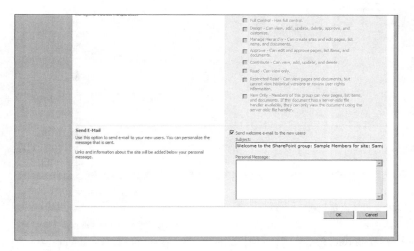

FIGURE 10.13
Sending an email to the users about their new permissions.

Change a User's or Group's Permissions on a File or List Item

Scenario/Problem: You want to change an existing permission that was granted to a user or group on a file or list item—perhaps to give that user more permissions or remove that user's permissions altogether.

Solution: To change permissions on a file or item, open the manage permissions page for that file or item and click the name of the user or group for which you want to change the permissions. This redirects you to a page that enables you to select permissions for that user or group (see Figure 10.14).

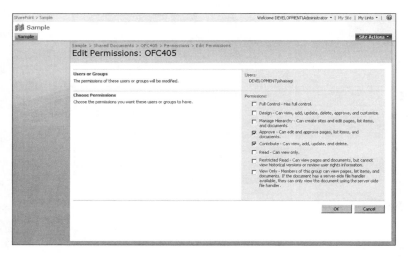

FIGURE 10.14
Changing a user's or group's permissions.

Here, you can select one or more permission levels. For example, if you select Contribute and Approve, the user will be able to both edit the document or list item and approve it, but will not be able to set the permission on the file or item. When you are done, click OK.

Assign Permissions on a List or Library

Scenario/Problem: You want to change the permissions on a list or library. For example, you want to add a user as a reader or as an author to the list or library.

Solution: To assign permissions on a list or document library, you need to get to the manage permissions page of that list or document library. To get to this page, follow the instructions in "Check Permissions on Lists and Libraries," earlier in this chapter.

On this page, you might be able to immediately change permissions, or you might have to first disconnect the permission inheritance for that list or library. Permission inheritance is on by default for all lists and libraries in SharePoint. It means that the list or library inherits its permissions from the site that it is in and has the exact same permission sets. If the permissions for the site change, the permissions for the list are updated automatically.

While inheritance is active, it is not possible to set a different permission level to the list or library (see Figure 10.15).

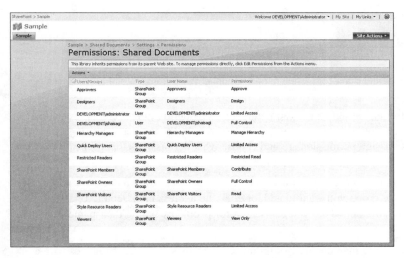

FIGURE 10.15
The manage permissions screen for a list when inheritance is enabled.

To disconnect the inheritance from the site, click Actions and choose Edit Permissions.

After you click the Edit Permissions option, a prompt appears, asking you to confirm that you want to disconnect the permissions inheritance from the site. The prompt also explains that after you do so, changes to the permissions of the site will not affect the list or library you are managing. This means, for example, that if a certain user is granted permissions to edit files or items in the site after the inheritance was disconnected, that user will not have the same permission levels on the list or library unless you explicitly change them on the list or library.

If you are sure that you want to manage the permissions for this list or library separately from the permission of the site, click OK. The page then allows you to manage the permissions for that list or library (see Figure 10.16).

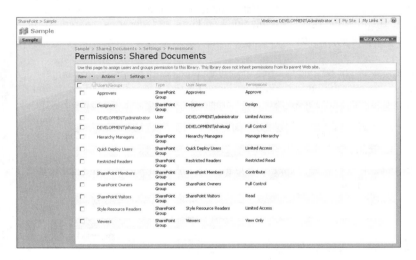

FIGURE 10.16
The manage permissions page when permission inheritance from the site is disconnected.

To add a user and assign permission, click the New button in the toolbar. Selecting New redirects you to a page where you can search for the user or security group that you want to assign permissions to and choose what permissions that user or group will be granted.

Under the Add Users section, either type the name (or part of a name) or email address for the user or group you want to add, or click the address book icon to open the people search dialog, where you can search for people by typing their name or part of it.

You can add more than one user or group at a time by separating the names with a semicolon. This is similar to when you are writing an email in Microsoft Outlook and you choose the person you want to send the email to.

If you use the Check Name icon, and there is no exact match to the name you entered, a red underline appears beneath the name. Click the name to open a menu that shows users who are a close match to that name or select to remove the name.

For example, typing **John** and clicking the Check Name box results in a red line under *John*. Clicking John shows that there is a user called John Doe. If that is the user you are looking for, click that name. If not, either click Remove to delete John from the text box or click More Names to open the search dialog (refer to Figure 10.10).

The search dialog enables you to search for people. Just type part of the name of the person or group that you want, as shown in Figure 10.10, and click the Search icon. A list of possible matches appears. To select one of them, double-click the name, and it is added to the box at the bottom of the dialog. After you have chosen all the users and groups, click OK to close the dialog and return to the Add Users page.

After you have found the users and/or groups that you want to add to the list, you can select what permissions they should have by selecting one or more of the check boxes in the list of permissions under Give Users Permission Directly (refer to Figure 10.11). Selecting options here gives the users the permissions you selected. As before, the higher permission level wins; so if you give someone the permission to Read and to Contribute, the user can change the list as well as read the items in it because of the Contribute setting.

Alternatively, you can add the users or groups to a SharePoint group. This means they will get whatever permission level the SharePoint group has. This is a useful mechanism to control permissions; for example, if you decide that all the users who have Contribute (edit) permissions on a document should now have read-only access, you would have to edit each and every user's permissions. Instead, using SharePoint groups, you can add users to a SharePoint group that has the Contribute permission level, and when a change is required, you change the permissions only on that SharePoint group, and not to each user separately. You can add both users and security groups to the SharePoint group.

To add users or groups to a SharePoint group, click the Add Users to a SharePoint Group option, and then select from the drop-down list what SharePoint group you want to add the users and/or security groups to (refer to Figure 10.13).

The last option on this page enables you to send email to the users, telling them that they have permissions on the list or library. You have the option to select not to send the email, or if you select to send it, you can change the title and body of the email.

Change a User's Permissions on a List or Library

Scenario/Problem: You want to change the permissions that a user or group has on a list or library. For example, you want to remove permissions altogether or grant more permissions.

Solution: To change permission on a list or library, open the manage permissions page for that list or library (see "Check Permissions on Lists and Libraries," earlier in this chapter) and click the name of the user or group for which you want to change the permissions.

Clicking the user name redirects you to a page that enables you to select permissions for that user or group (see Figure 10.17). Here, select one or more permission levels. For example, if you select Contribute and Approve, the user will be able to both edit documents or list items in the list or library and approve them, but will not be able to set the permissions on the files or items in the list or library. When you are done, click OK.

FIGURE 10.17
Changing a user's or group's permissions.

See Who Is a Member of a SharePoint Group

Scenario/Problem: SharePoint groups contain several users. You want to see who belongs to a group before you assign permissions to that group. You then want to add users to or remove them from a group; this task is explained in "Set Users' Permissions on a Site" in Chapter 14, "Managing Site Security."

Solution: SharePoint groups are defined at a site level, so to see who is a member of a SharePoint group, you need the right permissions on the site itself. If you have those rights, open Site Actions and select Site Settings (see Figure 10.18).

Selecting this option opens the settings page for the site (see Figure 10.19). Here, click the People and Groups link under the Users and Permissions header. The page that opens is the one used to manage security on a site (see Figure 10.20). The SharePoint groups are listed on the left navigation pane, under the Groups header.

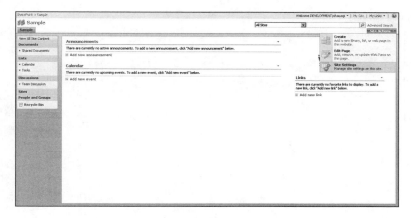

FIGURE 10.18
Select the Site Settings option.

The People and Groups Management Link

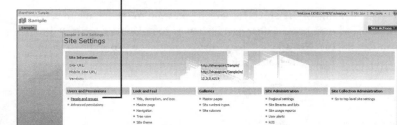

FIGURE 10.19
Click on the People and Groups link in the site settings page.

TIP Because the Site Actions menu might be hidden in some sites, to get to the manage site security page, add /_layouts/people.aspx to the end of the site path. For example, if your site is at http://sharepoint/sample, just type **http://sharepoint/sample/_layouts/people.aspx** in your browser to get to the page.

The SharePoint Groups

FIGURE 10.20
You can view the groups and who is in which group on this page.

Click the link with the name of the group for which you want to see the members. Doing so shows a list of members—either users (such as John Doe) or security groups (such as Human Resources). Not all users have display names set, so some of them might not have anything under the Name column, as shown in Figure 10.21.

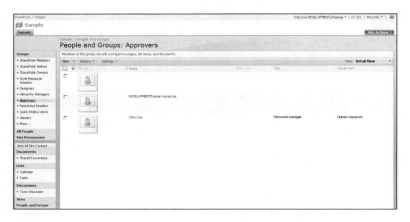

FIGURE 10.21
In the Approvers group the first user does not have a display name.

If you want to see who the user with the missing name is, just click that user's picture to open the user information page (see Figure 10.22).

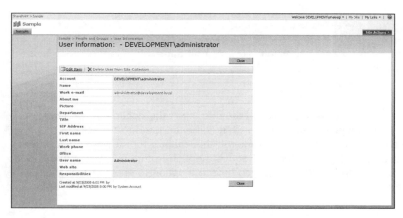

FIGURE 10.22
The User Information page for the administrator shows the user's details.

Configure Access Requests for Lists and Libraries

Scenario/Problem: You are managing the security of a list or library, and you want to configure the access requests for it. Access requests are sent when a user who doesn't have permission to a list or library wants to have permission. When users who don't have permission try to get to the library, if access requests are configured, they are presented with a page that enables them to request access (see Figure 10.23).

The Request Access Link

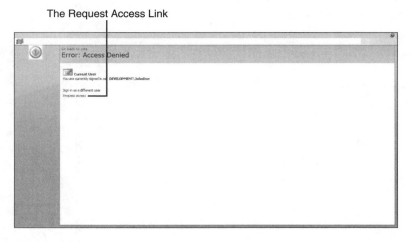

FIGURE 10.23
Users without access to a library see this page when trying to open the library.

As you can see, the users can then request access using the Request Access link. That request takes them to a page where they can explain why they think they should have access (see Figure 10.24). That information is then sent as an email to the library owner.

Solution: To enable or disable access requests, open the document library or list, and get to the manage security page for that library or list (see "Check Permissions on Lists and Libraries" earlier in this chapter for step-by-step instructions). On this page, click the Access Requests option from the Settings menu (see Figure 10.25). On the resulting page, you have the option to enable or disable access requests.

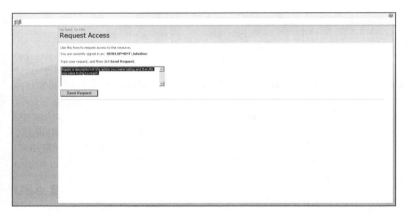

FIGURE 10.24
Requesting access to a document library.

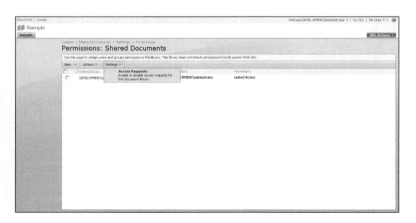

FIGURE 10.25
Select Access Requests to begin configuring access requests on a document library or list.

In some instances the Access Requests option is not available. The availability depends both on the server configuration and on the site configuration. If the option is grayed out and you can't change it, either the server administrator or site manager must change some settings.

The user who receives the access requests is defined at the site collection level. To be able to change that setting, you need permissions to manage permissions on the site. If you have those permissions, and you want to change the email address that will get the requests, select Site Settings from the Site Actions menu to get to the site management page.

If you started from a subsite, click the Go to Top Level Site Settings link. This redirects you to the page for managing the site collection (see Figure 10.26).

The Advanced Permissions Link

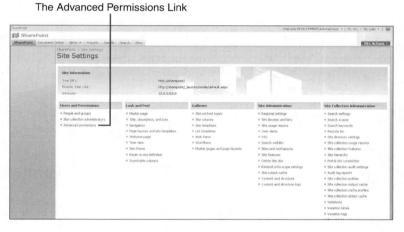

FIGURE 10.26
The Advanced Permissions link in the Site Settings page for a subsite.

Click the Advanced Permissions link under Users and Permissions to open the advanced permission management page. Here, you can open the Settings menu and select Access Requests (see Figure 10.27).

On the resulting page, you can set the email for the person (or a group) that access requests will be sent to (see Figure 10.28).

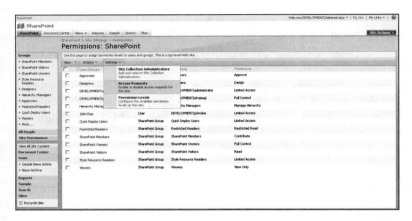

FIGURE 10.27
Select the Access Requests option.

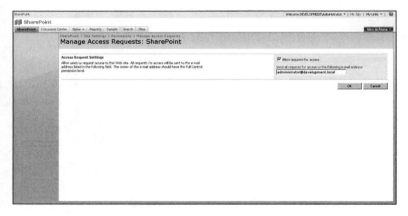

FIGURE 10.28
Select the person or group to receive access on this page.

CHAPTER 11

Workflows

Developers can create workflows to automate a process for files or list items. As an author or a contributor for a list or document library, you might be required to start a workflow or participate in one.

This chapter covers basic workflow-related tasks, explaining how to start a workflow, track its progress, and attach a workflow to a document library or list that you are managing.

Start a Workflow

Scenario/Problem: When a workflow has been attached to a list or document library, it either can be configured to start automatically when someone changes an item or file or can be configured to require the user to manually start the workflow. If it was configured to start manually, you might have to start it yourself.

Solution: If you want to manually start a workflow on a list item or file, open the actions drop-down menu for that list item or file and choose Workflows (see Figure 11.1).

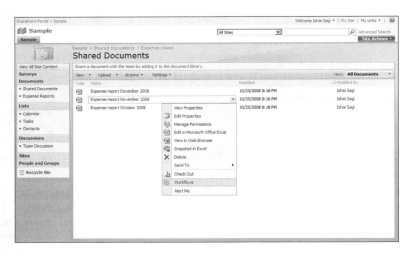

FIGURE 11.1
Open the actions menu for the list item or file and choose Workflows.

Selecting this option opens the Workflows screen that has the options to start one of the workflows associated with the list or document library on the specific item (see Figure 11.2).

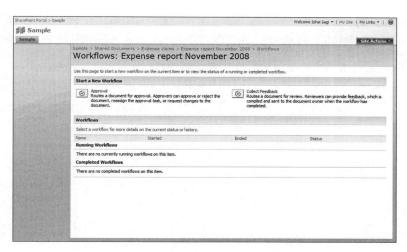

FIGURE 11.2
The Workflows screen.

Under the Start a New Workflow section, choose from the list of workflows that you can apply to the list item or file. Click the one you can to start; this opens the page that the workflow specifies as its "initiation" page (see Figure 11.3). This page will appear every time you initiate a workflow on an item, and each different workflow may have a different page. Some workflows do not have an initiation form at all.

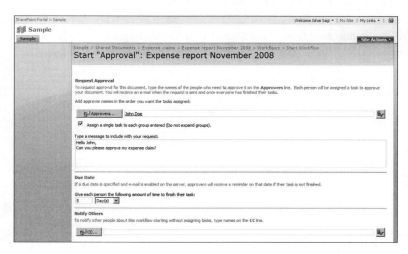

FIGURE 11.3
The Approval workflow's initiation page.

In the case of the Approval workflow, the initiation page asks you for one or more approvers from which you want the workflow to request approval, a number of days before the workflow reminds those users to approve again, and other people you want to notify of this item. It then creates a task in the tasks list in the site and assigns it to the approvers you select (see Figure 11.4). The task then sends an email to those approvers telling them of the task.

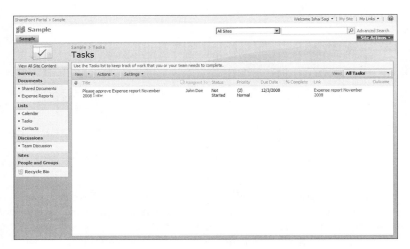

FIGURE 11.4
The Approval workflow creates tasks for approvers to approve.

After you fill in the initiation form, click Start. The workflow might take a while to start (see Figure 11.5). When it is complete, you are redirected to the list or library.

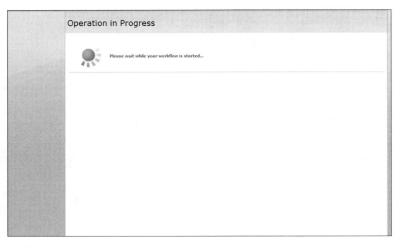

FIGURE 11.5
Waiting for the workflow to start.

Track the Progress of a Workflow

Scenario/Problem: You want to see the progress of a workflow that was started on a list item or file.

Solution: Open the actions menu for that item or file and choose Workflows (refer to Figure 11.1). The workflows page that opens shows you the running workflows and the completed ones at the bottom of the page, under the Workflows section (see Figure 11.6).

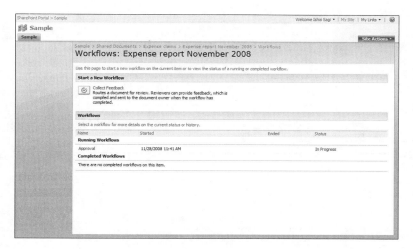

FIGURE 11.6
The running workflows appear under the Workflows section.

Click the name of the workflow or its status to get to the status summary page, relevant to the workflow on the current item (see Figure 11.7).

The workflow's status summary page shows you tasks that have been generated by the workflow and the history of the workflow progress (see Figure 11.8). More complex workflows have more steps to them, so viewing the history can be useful when you want to know who did what during the workflow runtime. For example, if the workflow was canceled, the history screen would show that information, allowing you to know who cancelled it. If there were any errors in any of the workflow steps, you can use this information to know why the workflow was not completed.

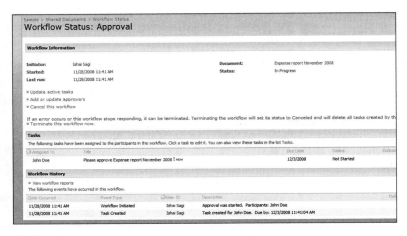

FIGURE 11.7
The status summary page for a workflow.

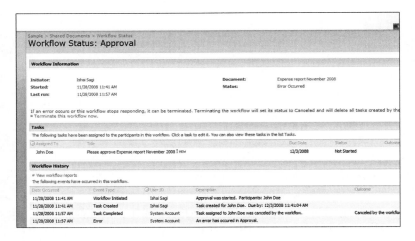

FIGURE 11.8
The status page for a workflow that was canceled with errors.

Some workflows offer quicker ways to get to the workflow status summary window. These workflows add a column to the list or library view showing the status in that view. For example, the approval workflow adds an Approval column to the views of the list or library, showing you the status of the workflow and enabling you to click the status to get to the status summary page (see Figure 11.9).

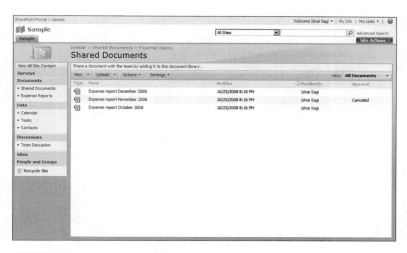

FIGURE 11.9
The approval workflow adds a column showing the status.

Associate a Workflow with a List or Library

Scenario/Problem: You want to assign a workflow to a list or library so that users can select it from the list of available workflows, or to define a workflow that will start automatically when a document or list item is added or modified in the library or list.

Solution: To attach different workflows to a list or library, you will need the manage list or manage library permission on that list or library. If you have those permissions, open the list's or library's setting page by clicking the Settings button in the toolbar and selecting Document Library Settings or Document List Settings (see Figure 11.10).

In the list's or library's setting page, click the Workflow Settings link under the Permissions and Management section (see Figure 11.11).

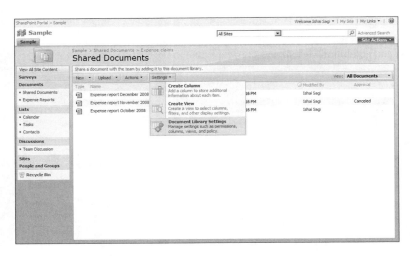

FIGURE 11.10
Open the list's or library's setting page.

The Workflow Settings Link

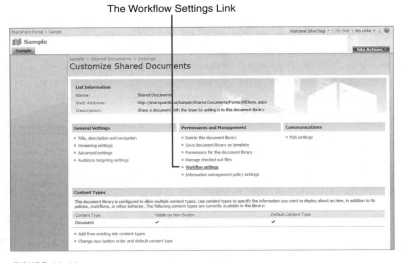

FIGURE 11.11
The Workflow Settings link in the document library or list settings page.

The Workflow Settings page for a list or library enables you to associate a workflow with that list or library (see Figure 11.12).

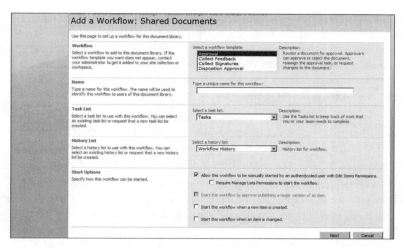

FIGURE 11.12
The Workflow Settings page for adding a workflow.

Here, you can define what workflow you want to create on the list or library by selecting from the workflow box that lists the available workflows. By default, the only workflows available in MOSS are the four built-in workflows:

- ▶ **Approval:** Allows starting an approval workflow on the list's or library's items, where approvers can approve or reject the document or list item, reassign the approval task, or request changes to the document.

- ▶ **Collect Feedback:** Allows starting a review workflow for a document or list item in the list or library. Reviewers can provide feedback, which is compiled and sent to the owner of the file or list item when the workflow has completed.

- ▶ **Collect Signatures:** Allows starting a workflow for collecting signatures that are required to complete a business process on a document. *Note:* This workflow can be started only from within a Microsoft Word 2007 or Microsoft Excel 2007 client, and then only from certain versions of Microsoft Office 2007 (Ultimate, Professional Plus, and Enterprise). If you cannot start this workflow from your Microsoft Office client, check the version of your Microsoft Office and upgrade if necessary.

- ▶ **Disposition Approval:** Allows starting a workflow to manage document expiration and retention. As part of the workflow, people involved with the file or list item are required to decide whether to retain or delete expired documents.

In WSS, only one workflow is available as a built-in workflow: the three-state workflow. This is the same workflow as the approval workflow described earlier and tracks the progress of approval of a document or a list item through three states: Active, Ready for Review, and Complete.

After you pick a workflow, choose a name for it. Because more than one workflow of any type can be attached to the document library or list, each must have a unique name so that the users can recognize it in the list of workflows. For example, a document library might require two approval workflows: one for expense claims and one for travel expenses. To create those two, you need to add them, both as approval workflows, but each one with a different name.

The next choice is what task list the workflow will use to create tasks associated with it. As you saw earlier in this chapter, the approval workflow creates tasks for approvers to approve the file or list item when the workflow starts. You can point each workflow to a specific task list or select that the workflow will create a new task list for itself.

The History List section enables you to define where the workflow will report its progress, for the purpose of storing the history. As you saw earlier in this chapter, when viewing a workflow's progress, you can see the history of steps that were done in the workflow. Here, you can define in which list that history is kept. By default, the history is kept in a hidden list called Workflow History that the users do not ordinarily see (see Figure 11.13). If you want to store the information in another list, you can define that here.

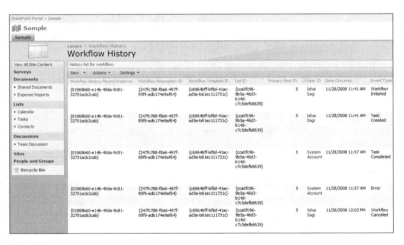

FIGURE 11.13
The Workflow History list is hidden from most users and has information about all the workflows.

Finally, the last section of the page, Start Options, enables you to specify when the workflow will start (see Figure 11.14).

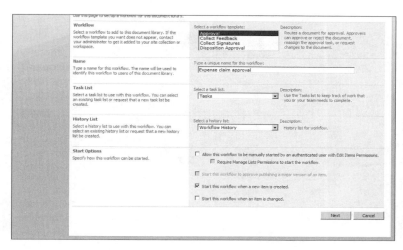

FIGURE 11.14
Creating a new approval workflow that will start automatically for new items.

With the first option users will be able to start it manually, whereas the third option will cause the list or library to start the workflow automatically when a new item or file is added to the list or library. As you can see in Figure 11.14, if you choose to let the users start the workflow manually, the users must have the Edit Items permission on the list or library; otherwise, they will not be able to start the workflow on any item. Select the Require Manage Lists Permissions to Start the Workflow check box to allow only managers of the list to be able to start the workflow.

The second option, Start This Workflow to Approve Publishing a Major Version of an Item, can be used only if the list or library has versioning set to allow major and minor versions. If this option is selected, this workflow will start when a user submits a file or list item for approval to get published as a major version.

The last option causes the workflow to start when an item or a file is changed in the list or library.

When you are finished configuring the workflow, click Next to open the workflow's association form (if the workflow has one). A workflow association form is different for each workflow type and is used to configure settings that are specific for that workflow type (see Figure 11.15). For example, the approval workflow's association form enables you to set whether the approval is done in parallel or in a serial manner. *Parallel* approval means that all the approvers get an email at the same time, whereas *serial* approval means the first approver on the list must approve before the second one gets the request to approve, and so on.

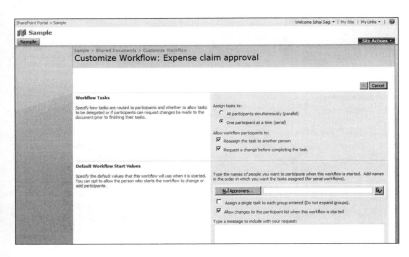

FIGURE 11.15
The approval workflow's association form.

When you are done setting the configuration for the workflow, or if there were no additional configuration settings, click OK. Your new workflow is added to the list of workflows the user can start, as shown in Figure 11.16, if you selected that users can start the workflow automatically.

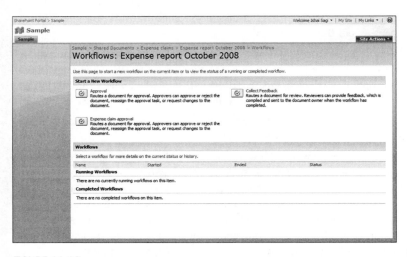

FIGURE 11.16
The new workflow appears in the list of available workflows.

PART III

Solutions for Site Managers

IN THIS PART

CHAPTER 12

Creating Subsites

If you are a site manager, you might want to create subsites under the site you are managing. For example, you might have a site called Projects, under which you will create a subsite for each project to hold the project's files and details. This chapter explains how to create subsites, including the different templates for subsites that come out of the box in SharePoint.

Additionally, this chapter includes some special instructions for the special Meeting Workspace subsites and how to use them.

Create a Subsite

Scenario/Problem: You want to create a site under an existing one. For example, you want to create a site for a team, or a blog site for a certain person, or a wiki site for a specific topic.

Solution: The following section explains how to create a site in general and then gives examples of creating three types of sites.

To create a subsite under an existing Microsoft SharePoint 2007 site, open the actions menu. Some SharePoint websites have an option to create a subsite directly in that menu, but in most you must choose the Create option (see Figure 12.1).

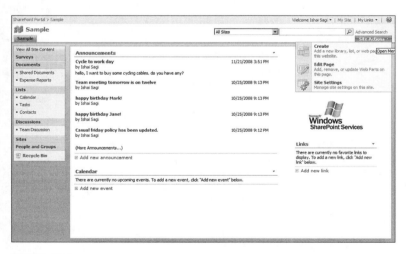

FIGURE 12.1
Choose the Create option from the menu.

Selecting this option opens the Create page for the current site (see Figure 12.2). The option to create a subsite, called Sites and Workspaces, appears under the Web Pages section of the page.

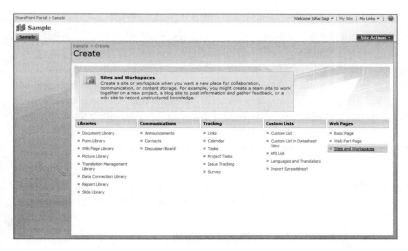

FIGURE 12.2
Click the Sites and Workspaces link.

After choosing to create a site, you are directed to the page where you can decide how the site will be called, what the link to it will look like, and what sort of site you want to create (see Figure 12.3).

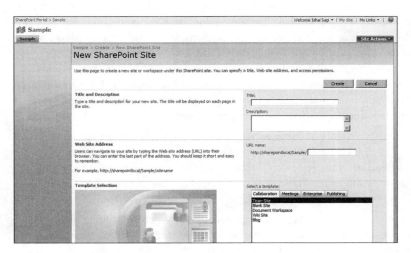

FIGURE 12.3
The site creation page.

The first option is the title of the site. The title will be displayed on the top of the site and in the navigation links pointing to the site. This title can be changed at any time from the site settings.

The second option is the site's description. This information will normally be displayed under the site's title or in the site's home page (depending on the design of the site) and can also be changed at any time.

The third option is the URL name for the site. This name determines how the link to the site will look. It is recommended that you consider this name carefully because, although it can be changed after the site is created, shortcuts that your users created and links that point to that site will break (without considerable work by the SharePoint administrator). This text should be as short as possible, and it is not recommended to use spaces or special characters in the URL name of a site.

> **TIP**   To change any of the first three settings in the site creation page, see "Change the Name, Description, Icon, or URL of a Site" in Chapter 13, "Customizing a SharePoint Site."

The next option, Template Selection (refer to the bottom of Figure 12.3), enables you to select which site template the site will be based on. This option enables you to pick from the list of available templates (every site can have a different list of templates that can be used under it) by simply clicking the one you want. The templates are grouped by type, so click the tabs for each group of templates and see what types are available in each group.

The next section in the page covers the Permissions options (see Figure 12.4). Here, you define whether the site will have the same permission set as its parent site (the site you are currently on) or will have unique permissions. If you are happy with the new site having the same permissions as the current site, leave the default setting, Use Same Permissions as Parent Site. However, if you choose Use Unique Permissions, you will have to set permissions on the site after it has been created. The permissions of the site can be modified at any time; see Chapter 14, "Managing Site Security," for more information about changing the site's permissions.

The Navigation Inheritance section enables you to specify whether the site should have the same top navigation bar as the parent site or should have a navigation bar of its own. This section lets you create subsites that look either like part of the top site or like separate sites altogether. These settings also can be changed later (see "Modify the Top or Left Navigation Bar" in Chapter 13).

The last section in the site creation page appears only in Microsoft Office SharePoint Server (MOSS) sites, where there is a site dedicated to storing links to other sites— what is known as a *site directory*. The last option enables you to automatically add a link to the new subsite to the site directory. To do so, select List This New Site in the Site Directory and optionally select how the site should be categorized. This setting is optional and can be changed later in the site directory site itself.

When you are finished setting the options for the new site, click the Create button to create the site. The new site will open, unless you have chosen the option to have unique permissions for the site, in which case the permissions setting page for the site will open first.

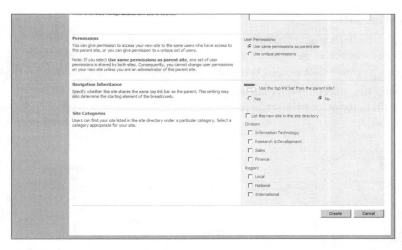

FIGURE 12.4
The site creation page (continued). Note that some of the options shown in this screen are available only in MOSS.

Create a Team Site

A *team site* is a simple site with a document library, an announcements list, a calendar list, a links list, a tasks list, and a team discussion board. To create a team site, select the Team Site template under the Collaboration tab (see Figure 12.5), fill in the other parameters, such as the site name and description, and click Create.

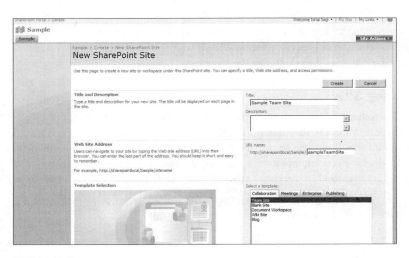

FIGURE 12.5
To create a team site, select the Team Site template under the collaboration tab.

Create a Wiki Site

A *wiki site* is a site for managing and sharing information on the site's pages, used mostly to share ideas and knowledge among many people. The Wiki Site template enables users who use the site to easily change the pages and create new pages.

To create a wiki site, select the Wiki Site template under the Collaboration tab (see Figure 12.6), fill in the other parameters for the site, such as the name and description, and click Create.

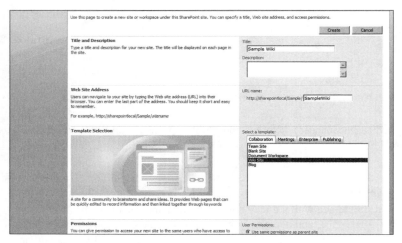

FIGURE 12.6
Creating a wiki site.

When the site is created, it will have only one page, the home page for the site. The page will have some default text explaining what a wiki is and an Edit button on the top, allowing users to edit the content of the page (see Figure 12.7).

Create a Blog Site

A *blog site* is another way to share information, usually in the way of articles or blog posts. Each article or post is very much like an announcement—a title and some text containing the information to be shared. However, the blog posts also offer the readers of the site the option to comment on them, and the posts can be categorized into categories that can be managed in the blog site itself as a separate list.

To create a blog site, select the Blog option under the Collaboration tab (see Figure 12.8), fill in the rest of the details, and click Create.

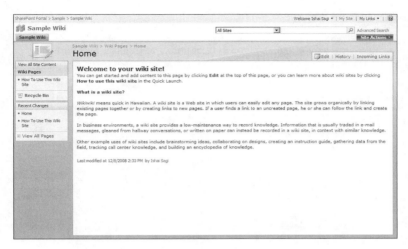

FIGURE 12.7
The home page of a new wiki site.

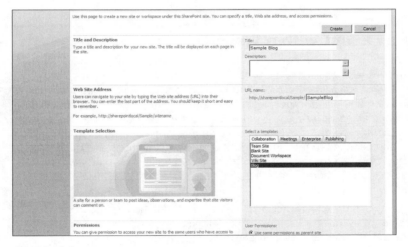

FIGURE 12.8
Creating a blog site.

After you create the site, the home page of the blog shows a sample post explaining what a blog is and displays a list of actions you can perform on the blog on the right, including creating a new post, managing the posts and comments, and so on (see Figure 12.9).

FIGURE 12.9
The home page of a new blog site.

Create an Event with a Website

Scenario/Problem: You want to create a site for an event. Events in calendar lists can have an associated subsite that is used to store more information about the event and help the people managing the event to get ready for it. For example, when planning a meeting, you might want to collaborate with other people on the agenda of the meeting. You also might ask several people who are scheduled to speak in the meeting to upload their presentations and supporting documents before the meeting so that the other attendees can read them on time. The attendee list for the meeting can also be managed on the site; it can list not just who was invited, but who actually came to the meeting.

This capability is not exclusive for meetings but can also be used to track information about an event—for example, a conference that requires some people to prepare to and collaborate their efforts for that.

Solution: To create an event site, you can use the regular method of creating a site, as explained earlier in this chapter, and choose one of the event meeting templates available under the Meetings tab (see Figure 12.10). This option creates an event site but does not link it to the calendar event item itself; that can be done later.

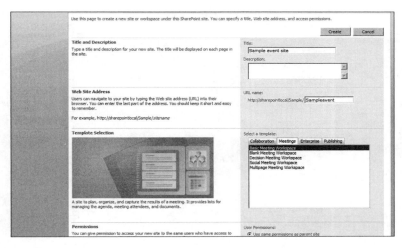

FIGURE 12.10
Choosing an event site template.

However, you can create the site directly from the calendar event item itself. Simply open the calendar event item for which you want to create a site, or create a new calendar event item (see Figure 12.11) and select the Workspace option before clicking OK.

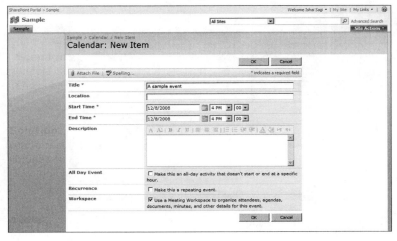

FIGURE 12.11
Creating a new calendar event item with the option to create a subsite for the event.

When you click OK, the following screen enables you to either create a new site for the calendar event item or link the calendar event item with an existing event site that you created earlier under the current site (see Figure 12.12).

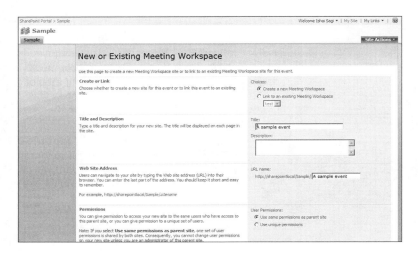

FIGURE 12.12
Creating an event site from a calendar event item.

If you choose to create a new site with the option Create a New Meeting Workspace, the option of choosing the site template appears after you click OK (see Figure 12.13).

FIGURE 12.13
Choosing an event site template.

After you select a template and create the site, a new site is created from that template. Different templates offer different lists in the site, but the most common one is the basic meeting workspace, offering management of objectives, agenda, attendees, and a document library to hold documents related to the event (see Figure 12.14).

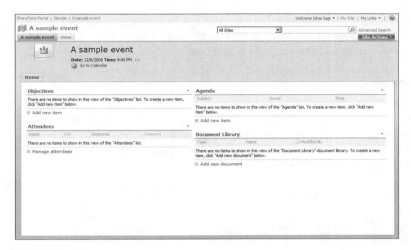

FIGURE 12.14
A new basic event workspace.

Create an Agenda

In a basic event workspace, you create an agenda by adding items to the Agenda list. A web part with the agenda usually appears on the home page, so to add an item, simply click the Add New Item link under that web part. The page for adding an agenda item then opens (see Figure 12.15). Here, you can specify the subject of the agenda item, who owns it, the time spot allocated to it, and any notes required.

FIGURE 12.15
Creating a new agenda item.

You manage the agenda as you would in any other list. For more information about managing lists (deleting or editing items, for example), see Chapter 6, "Creating and Managing Files, List Items, and Forms in SharePoint."

Invite Attendees

If you are the owner of the event workspace site, you can manage the attendees list of the event by clicking Manage Attendees under the Attendees web part on the home page. Selecting this option opens a special list to which you can add people as attendees, specifying whether each person replied to the invitation and if he or she is required to attend (see Figure 12.16).

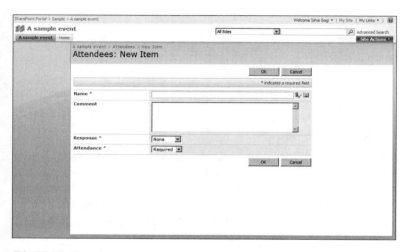

FIGURE 12.16
Adding a new attendee.

CHAPTER 13

Customizing a SharePoint Site

When you are in charge of a SharePoint site, you will want to customize it to fit your view of how it should look and behave. Such customization includes changing the site's title, the way the site looks (using themes), the page used as the home page for the site, the site's navigation, the site's search settings, and more.

This chapter covers these topics and explains how to accomplish some of the more common site customization tasks.

Open the Site's Settings Page

Scenario/Problem: You want to change a site's settings.

Solution: The following section explains how to get to the site setting page. For more information about changing specific settings, see the following tasks in this chapter.

To change settings, access the site's settings page by opening the Site Actions menu and choosing Site Settings, as shown in Figure 13.1. In publishing sites, this option is under the Modify All Site Settings submenu of the Site Settings menu.

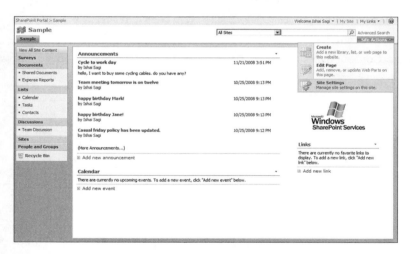

FIGURE 13.1
Opening the site's setting page.

Different types of sites have more settings than others (see Figures 13.2 and 13.3). A root-level site has more settings than a subsite, and publishing sites have additional settings. The settings available on the page will change based on the permissions you have on the site. For example, in a root-level site, the link to the settings for the site collection (see Figure 13.2) will be displayed only if you have site collection administrator privileges.

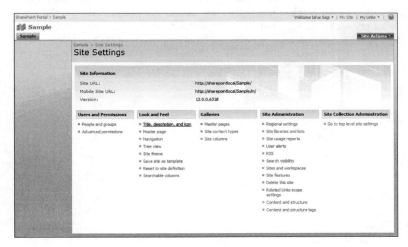

FIGURE 13.2
The Site Settings page for a subsite that is not a publishing site.

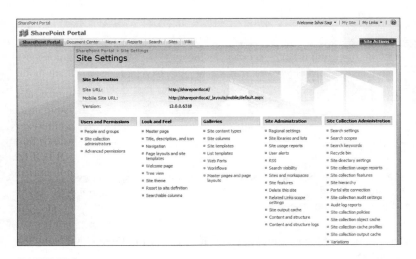

FIGURE 13.3
The Site Settings page for a root site that is a publishing site.

Change the Name, Description, Icon, or URL of a Site

Scenario/Problem: Every site has a name or title that is usually displayed in all the pages, usually above the top navigation bar and in the breadcrumbs navigation. The description of a site sometimes appears under the top navigation or in some of the pages, while the icon usually appears next to the title (see Figure 13.4).

You might want to change the title, description, or icon for a site.

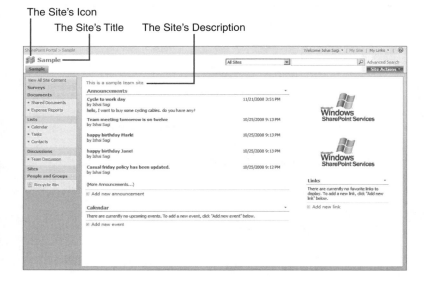

FIGURE 13.4
The title, icon, and description.

Solution: To change those settings, open the site's settings page, as explained earlier. In the site's settings page, click the Title, Description, and Icon link under the Look and Feel section of the page.

The Title, Description, and Icon settings page opens, as shown in Figure 13.5, allowing you to change the settings.

CAUTION Although you can change the URL name of the site from the Title, Description, and Icon page, it is not recommended that you do so after users have begun using your site. Any link or bookmark that users have created pointing to the site will be broken.

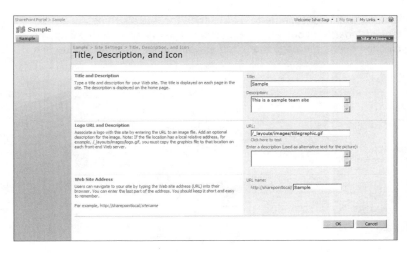

FIGURE 13.5
The Title, Description, and Icon link settings page.

Change the Look of a Site Using Themes

Scenario/Problem: *Themes* change how a site looks by applying different styles to the site. This includes different color schemes, fonts, and more (see Figure 13.6).

You might want to change how a site looks by using themes.

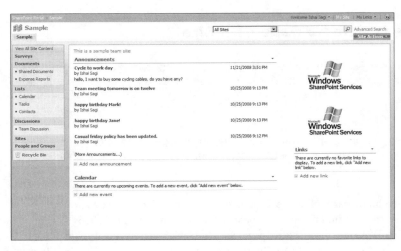

FIGURE 13.6
The sample site with the Verdant theme.

Solution: To apply a different theme to a site, open the site's settings page, as explained earlier. Under the Look and Feel section of the page, click the Site Theme link. This selection opens the page that enables you to pick a theme for the site (see Figure 13.7).

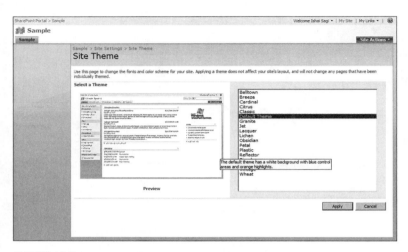

FIGURE 13.7
Picking a site theme.

When you click the available options for themes in the box, the image next to it is changed with an image showing a preview of how the site will look after applying the theme. You can always reset the theme back to the original by choosing Default Theme from the options.

Change the Home Page of a Site

Scenario/Problem: You want to change which page is opened when a user types in the address of the site or when the user clicks the site's link in the navigation bar.

Solution: In publishing sites you can choose which page in that site is the default, or home, page for that site. For information about creating pages, see Chapter 9, "Authoring Pages."

To change the home page, click the Welcome Page link under the Look and Feel section of the site (again, this option appears only in publishing sites). This selection opens the Site Welcome Page setting page, which enables you to specify which page should be opened (see Figure 13.8). Simply type in the link to the page in the site that you want to be the home page.

FIGURE 13.8
The Site Welcome Page setting page.

Modify the Top or Left Navigation Bar

Scenario/Problem: You want to modify the links shown on the top or left navigation bars. For example, you want to add a tab to the top navigation bar or remove a link from the left navigation bar.

Solution: To modify the links shown on the top or left navigation bar, open the site's settings page and click the Navigation link under the Look and Feel section of the page. The Site Navigation Settings page opens, as shown in Figure 13.9.

On this page you can define what links and headings each navigation bar will have—adding, removing, or changing the order of those links. The top navigation bar is referenced on this page as *Global Navigation*, and the left navigation bar is called *Current Navigation*.

In a subsite, this page has more options, as you can see in Figure 13.10. Here, you can set whether the site should display the same top or left navigation options as its parent site or should have its own set of navigation bar links.

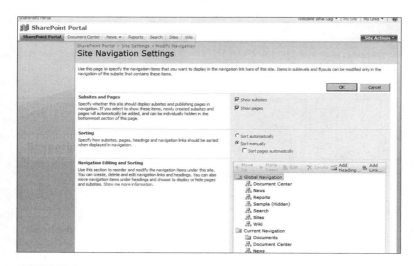

FIGURE 13.9
The Site Navigation Settings page.

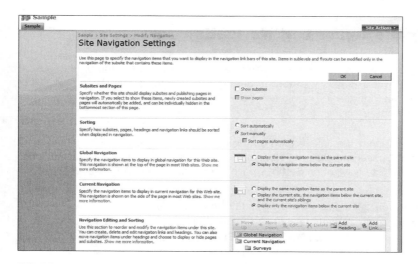

FIGURE 13.10
The Site Navigation Settings page for a subsite that is not a publishing site.

The first option on the page is whether the navigation bars should show subsites under the current site and whether it should show pages. This option is not available in nonpublishing sites because it relies on the Pages library that the publishing sites have by default. You can actually manage the links in each of the navigation bars under Navigation Editing and Sorting.

Add a Link to the Top or Left Navigation Bar

To add a link to either navigation bar, click the Global Navigation (for the top navigation bar) or Current Navigation node in the Navigation Editing and Sorting box, and
then click the Add Link option in the menu. This selection opens a dialog allowing
you to specify the link to be added (see Figure 13.11).

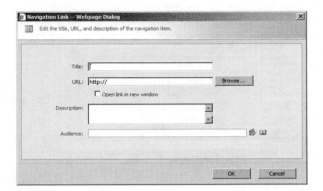

FIGURE 13.11
Adding a link to the navigation.

You can specify what text the link will display to the user in the Title box, and either
type in a link or browse to a page in the site using the Browse button. You can also
specify whether the link will be opened in a new window when clicked.

Edit a Link in the Top or Left Navigation Bar

To edit a link from either bar, click the link in the Navigation Editing and Sorting box,
and then click the Edit button on the toolbar. The dialog for the link's setting opens,
allowing you to specify how this link should behave (refer to Figure 13.11).

Remove a Link from the Top or Left Navigation Bar

To remove a link from either bar, click the link in the Navigation Editing and Sorting
box, and then click the Delete button on the toolbar.

Create a Site Column

Scenario/Problem: You want to create a site column.

Solution: To create a site column, open the site's settings page, as explained at
the beginning of this chapter, and then click Site Columns under the Galleries
section of the page. This selection opens the Site Column Gallery page, which
enables you to create new site columns or edit or remove the existing ones (see
Figure 13.12).

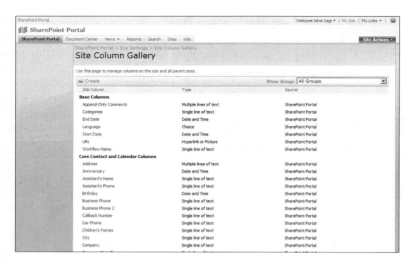

FIGURE 13.12
The Site Column Gallery page.

To create a new column, click the Create button on the toolbar. This selection opens a page that enables you to define the column's name and type (see Figure 13.13), as well as additional settings—just like creating a list column (see Chapter 7). The one difference from creating a list or library column in this page is that site columns can be added to a group to make finding the columns from the list of site columns easier.

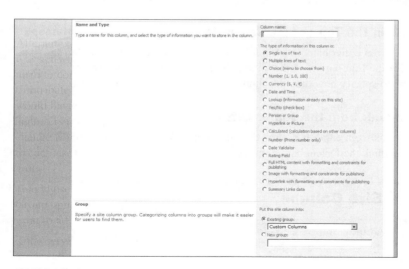

FIGURE 13.13
Adding a new site column.

The Group option enables you to either add the column to an existing group or create a new group by typing that group's name. By default, the columns you create are added to the Custom Columns group.

Create a Content Type

Scenario/Problem: As explained in Chapter 1, "About Microsoft SharePoint 2007," a content type is a collection of site columns and additional settings that can be created for a site. You want to create a content type and define what columns are included in the content type.

Solution: To create a new content type in a site, open the site's settings page, as explained at the beginning of this chapter, and click Content Types under the Galleries section of the page. This selection opens a page that enables you to create or modify content types (see Figure 13.14).

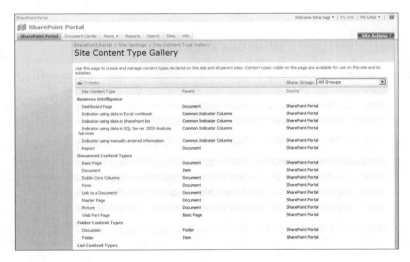

FIGURE 13.14
The Site Content Type Gallery page.

Click the Create button on the toolbar to create a new content type. The page shown in Figure 13.15 opens.

The first setting you need to set for a content type is the name for the content type, followed by its description. The name and the description will appear in the New drop-down in the document library or site when the user opens it to select a content type.

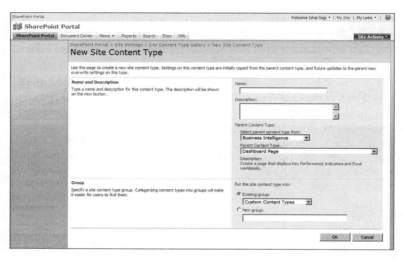

FIGURE 13.15
Creating a new content type.

> **TIP** It is always wise to name a content type in singular form; for example,
> "Corporate Financial Report" or "Board Meeting Presentation." The reason is that the
> name appears under the New button for document libraries and lists when you are
> creating a new item and signifies to the user that clicking the option will create a
> single document.

Next, select the parent content type. This step is important because most of the time
you will not want to start the content type from scratch but instead will want to rely on
an existing content type. Selecting the parent content type is also important because
changing it can (but not necessarily) affect the child content type. For example,
suppose you want to create a content type named External Contact that has the exact
same settings as the built-in Contact content type, but with additional columns to
capture the contact's company address and company description (see Figure 13.16).
Specifying that the new content type is the child of the existing Contact content type
means that you will have to specify only the columns you want to add on top of the
default Contact columns. Also, if in the future you decide that all contacts should have
an additional column—for example, Birthday—adding it to the parent content type
Contact can also add it automatically to the child External Contact, as shown later
under "Modify a Content Type."

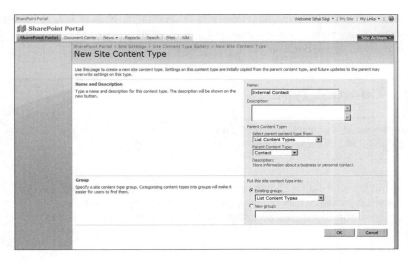

FIGURE 13.16
Creating a new content type named External Contact that inherits from the Contact content type.

After selecting the content type main settings, click OK to create the content type. This selection opens the page where you can define the additional settings for the content type—for example, add, edit, or remove columns; set workflow settings; and perform other advanced settings (see Figure 13.17).

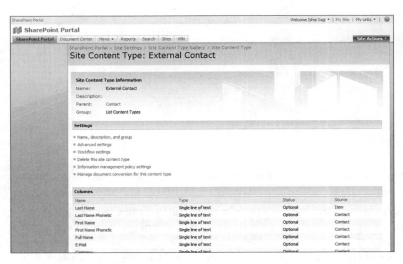

FIGURE 13.17
The settings page for a content type.

To add a column to the content type, scroll down to the bottom of the page, where you can find links to either create a new site column for the content type or add a column from the list of available site columns.

Modify a Content Type

Scenario/Problem: You want to modify an existing content type—change its name or perhaps add or remove a column and other settings.

Solution: To modify an existing content type, open the site's settings page, as explained at the beginning of this chapter, and click Content Types under the Galleries section of the page. This selection opens a page that enables you to modify content types (see Figure 13.18).

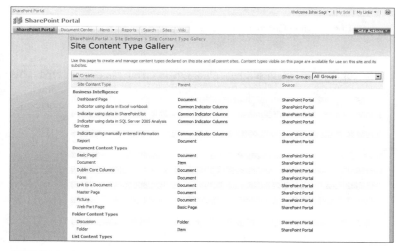

FIGURE 13.18
The site content types' gallery.

Click the name of the content type that you want to change so that you can change it to open the content type's setting page (see Figure 13.19).

To edit the content type, change any setting available on this page, including the content type's name, description and group, its workflow settings, its columns, and more advanced settings. With every setting that you change, you have an option to also update all content types inheriting from the content type. Updating them ensures that the change you made will also be made to other content types that were created with the current content type as their parent. For example, if you add a Birthday column to the Contact content type and you want the change to also affect any other content types that inherit from Contact, such as External Contact, select Yes under Update All Content Types Inheriting from This Type? when adding the site column (see Figure 13.20).

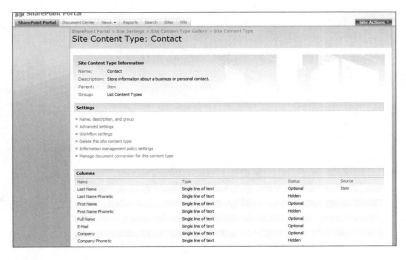

FIGURE 13.19
The Contact content type's settings page.

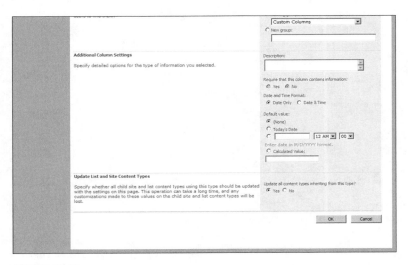

FIGURE 13.20
Adding a site column to a content type and updating the child content types.

CHAPTER 14

Managing Site Security

When you own a SharePoint site, you might want to restrict or allow different users to do different tasks. For example, you might want certain users to be able to add items to lists and upload files to document libraries, while leaving other users able to only read those items. You might want to give the permission to approve items and files to a group of people, or allow another group to create new lists and libraries or even manage the site together with you.

When you are managing SharePoint security, it is important to remember that you can set the permissions either for a specific user or group of users from the corporate directory or from other forms of external user databases (depending on the configuration on the server). The corporate directory groups or groups in other external databases are defined by the administrators of the corporate directory (and not as part of SharePoint), and you can give (or restrict) them access to your SharePoint site without having to manage the members of the group. For example, most organizations have a group for each division or team.

Furthermore, for security reasons you might want to create groups that you will manage on a site-by-site basis. These are called *SharePoint groups*, and SharePoint sites usually have several such groups set up—for example, the group of "visitors" who are allowed only to read content in the site, as opposed to the group of "members" who are allowed to add content to the site. Most of the time you should add users and groups to SharePoint groups, which will help simplify changing the permissions later.

This chapter explains how to manage the security aspects of SharePoint sites. All these tasks assume that you have the permission to manage the security of the site you are browsing.

Get to the Site's Security Settings Page

Scenario/Problem: You want to manage the security in a site.

Solution: The following section explains how to get to the site's security management page. Specific tasks in setting security are explained later in this chapter.

To get to a site's security settings page, open the site's Site Actions menu and click the Site Settings option. On some sites the Site Settings menu item opens to show other submenu items, where you can select People and Groups, which makes the process much shorter. If you don't have that option, just select the Site Settings menu option, as shown in Figure 14.1, and continue with the following instructions.

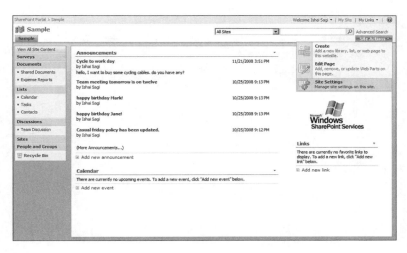

FIGURE 14.1
Opening the site's setting page.

In the site's settings page, click the People and Groups link under the Users and Permissions heading (see Figure 14.2).

The People and Groups Link

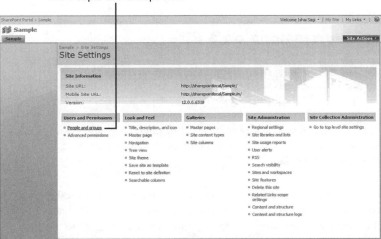

FIGURE 14.2
Click the People and Groups link to edit the permissions.

Selecting this link opens a page that enables you to manage the permissions for the site (see Figure 14.3).

FIGURE 14.3
The site's security management page.

On the left navigation bar, you can see the list of groups that exist in the site. Click them to view what users or security groups belong to them. Alternatively, click the All People link to see the list of all the people who were given permissions to the site, regardless of what group they belong to.

Set Users' Permissions on a Site

Scenario/Problem: You want to assign permissions on a site to a user or group, or add a user to an existing group.

Solution: To allow users to view a site to which they previously didn't have access, you can either add them to one of the SharePoint groups or add them to the site directly, and not to a specific group.

As mentioned earlier in this chapter, it is recommended that you always add users to SharePoint groups because doing so will make the permissions easier to manage in the future. To add or remove a user from a security group in a site, navigate to the site's security settings page, as explained earlier in this chapter. On the left side of the page, you can see the list of groups that exist in the site. Click any of them to add or remove users from those groups.

NOTE Because sites normally inherit permissions from their parent site (unless the site is a root site and doesn't have a parent) you might not be able to edit the site's permissions unless you break the site's inheritance using the Edit Permissions option in the Actions menu in the site's security page. However, be sure you do want to break the inheritance; otherwise, you might want to manage the security of the parent site and not the current site.

Add or Remove Users in a SharePoint Group

To add a person as a visitor to the site, add that person to the site's visitors group. Click the Visitors group link on the left to see the members of that group (see Figure 14.4).

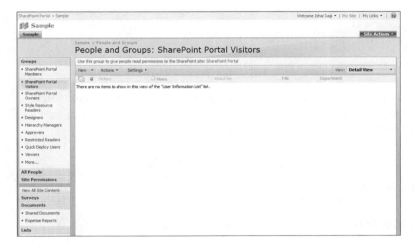

FIGURE 14.4
The site's visitors group.

To add a person to the group, click the New button on the toolbar. That selection opens a page that enables you to select one or more people that you want to add to the group (see Figure 14.5).

On this page you can either use the Add Users box to type the names of the people you want to add (separated with semicolons—for example, **John doe;Jane smith**), or click the address book icon to search and select the people from the directory.

After you select the people you want, either select the group to which you want to add them (the group from which you started the process—for example, the visitors group—is selected by default), or give those people permissions directly. If you do that, the people will have those permissions that you select on the site. If you ever want to change the permissions, because these people are not part of a group, you will have to change the permissions for each user separately.

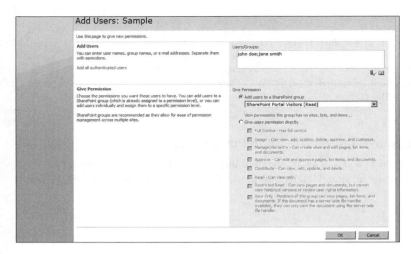

FIGURE 14.5
Selecting the users to add to the group.

When you are finished selecting the users and the group to which they should belong, click OK. The page showing the people in the group is updated to show the people you added (see Figure 14.6).

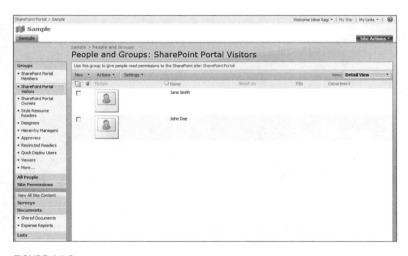

FIGURE 14.6
The users have been added to the group.

To remove people from the group, navigate to the page for that group and select the check boxes next to their names. Then open the Actions menu on the toolbar and select Remove Users from Group (see Figure 14.7).

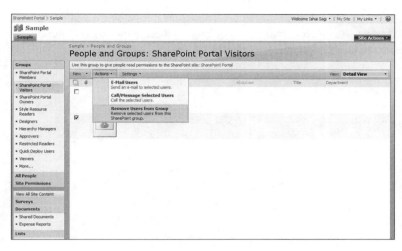

FIGURE 14.7
Removing a user from a group.

Add Users' Permissions Directly to or Remove Them from a Site

If you do not want to add a user to a SharePoint group in a site, but instead want to give that user a specific set of permissions unrelated to a specific group, navigate to the site's security page and click the All People link on the left navigation bar (see Figure 14.8).

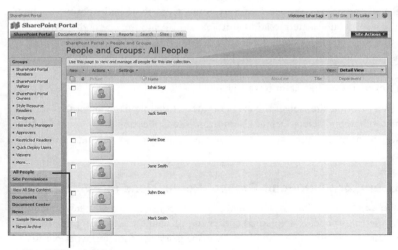

The All People Link

FIGURE 14.8
The All People page.

To add users to the site, click the New button. This opens a page where you can select the users and select what permissions they will have on the site by choosing the Give Users Permission Directly option (see Figure 14.9).

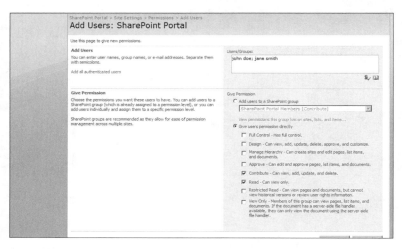

FIGURE 14.9
Adding users directly to a site.

You can either type the names of the people you want to add in the Add Users box at the top or click the address book icon to use a people search dialog to select the users. Then select the permission levels you want the people to have on the site; you can select more than one permission level—for example, Contribute and Approve—which will allow the users you selected to add list items and files to the site and approve documents that they or other people have added. Remember, the higher permission always wins, so the user or security group has all the permissions from all the permission levels. To learn how to create a customized permission level, see "Create Permission Levels for a Site," later in this chapter.

To remove users from a site, select the users on the All People page, open the Actions menu on the toolbar, and select Delete Users from Site Collection (see Figure 14.10). This removes the users from the site, including any SharePoint groups the users belonged to.

Change Users' or SharePoint Groups' Permissions in a Site

To change the permissions that are allocated to a user or group in a site, navigate to the site's security settings page, as explained earlier in this chapter, and then click the Site Permissions link on the left navigation bar. This opens a page showing what permission levels each user or group has been allocated in the site (see Figure 14.11).

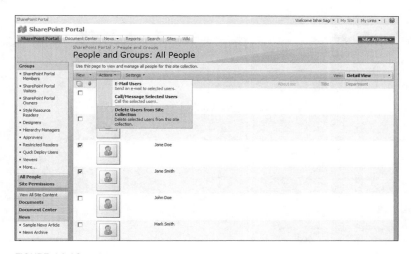

FIGURE 14.10
Removing users directly from a site.

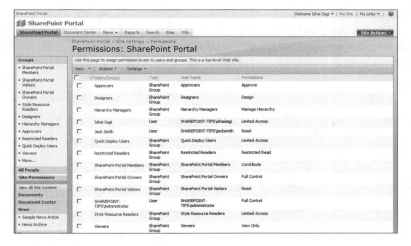

FIGURE 14.11
The permissions page shows the permissions each group or user has on the site.

To change the permission levels, select the users or groups that you want to change, open the Actions menu on the toolbar, and select Edit User Permissions from the menu (see Figure 14.12).

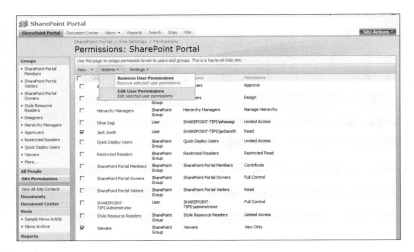

FIGURE 14.12
Select Edit User Permissions.

You then have the option to set what permissions those users or groups will have (see Figure 14.13). Select them, and click OK to set the permissions levels. To learn how to create a customized permission level, see "Create Permission Levels for a Site," later in this chapter.

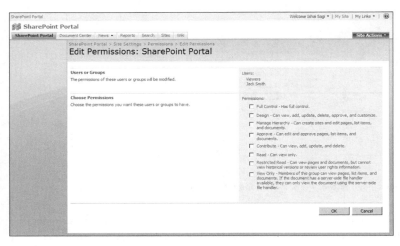

FIGURE 14.13
Select what permissions the users and\or groups should have.

Create a SharePoint Group for a Site

Scenario/Problem: You want to create a SharePoint group so that you can manage who is in the group, and then assign permission to everyone in the group to sites, lists, libraries, and list items.

Solution: By default, when you create a site, SharePoint creates some groups automatically for you to use in that site. To create a new SharePoint group, open the site security settings page, as shown earlier in this chapter, and then open the New drop-down menu by clicking the small triangle next to it to show the option of creating a new group (see Figure 14.14).

FIGURE 14.14
Select New Group from the New drop-down menu.

The page for creating a new SharePoint group has several options you can set for the group (see Figure 14.15). All these settings can be modified later by editing the group's settings.

The first option is the name for the group and its description.

The second is the owner of the group. This setting defaults to you, but you can choose any other user. Just make sure that user has permissions to access the site. The owner can add and remove users from the group, as well as change the group's settings, even if the owner doesn't have permissions to manage the site itself. This means you can make anyone an owner of a group without giving that user permissions to manage other aspects of the site.

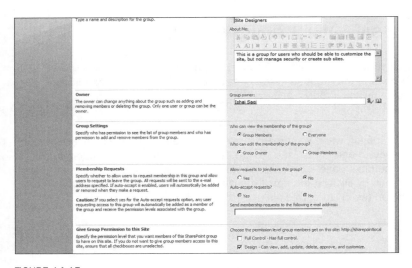

FIGURE 14.15
The new SharePoint group creation page.

In the Group Settings section you can define who can see the list of people who have been added to the group; the options are everyone or just the people who are members of the group. Also, you can define whether only the owner can add and remove members or whether anyone who is a member can do so (effectively making the group self-managing).

The next section on this page, Membership Requests, enables you to define whether people can send requests to join or be removed from the group. If you want to enable that option, you must specify an email address to which the requests will be sent. Users then have the option of sending requests to join the group when viewing it. You can also choose that if a user requests to join the group, the request would be automatically accepted.

Finally, in the last section of the page, you can define what permission levels the group will have on the site. To learn how to create a customized permission level, see "Create Permission Levels for a Site," later in this chapter.

Edit a SharePoint Group's Settings

Scenario/Problem: You want to change the settings for an existing SharePoint group.

Solution: To change a SharePoint group's settings, navigate to the site's security settings page, and then click the name of the group in the left navigation bar. Then open the Settings drop-down menu and click the Group Settings option (see Figure 14.16). The page that opens enables you to modify all the settings for the group (see Figure 14.17).

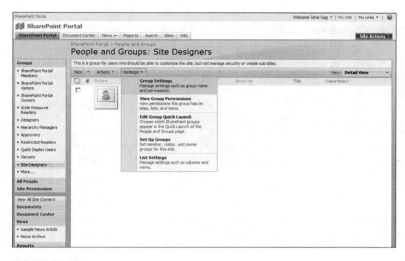

FIGURE 14.16
Getting to a SharePoint group's settings page.

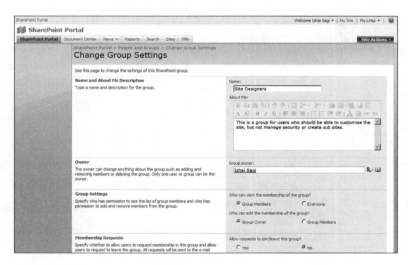

FIGURE 14.17
A SharePoint group's settings page.

Create Permission Levels for a Site

Scenario/Problem: Earlier in this chapter, you saw that to assign permissions to users or groups, you can choose from a predefined list of permission levels such as Readers, Contributors, or Approvers. If you want to create a permission level that allows different things from the existing permission levels, you can create a custom permission level. For example, you might want to create a permission level that enables users to view and delete items or files but not edit them. Or maybe you want to create a permission level that allows users to view the site and be able to create subsites, but not to be able to edit items in the site.

Solution: To create permission levels, open the site's security page and click the Site Permissions link on the left navigation bar. Then open the Settings drop-down menu on the toolbar and select the Permission Levels option (see Figure 14.18).

NOTE If you are working on a subsite, the permission levels are inherited from the parent site by default. Although you can still edit them (an action that will break the inheritance), make sure this is what you are actually setting out to do. If you want to make sure you are editing the permission levels in the top site, use the Manage Permissions of Parent option in the Actions menu of the site's security settings page to get to the parent site's security settings page.

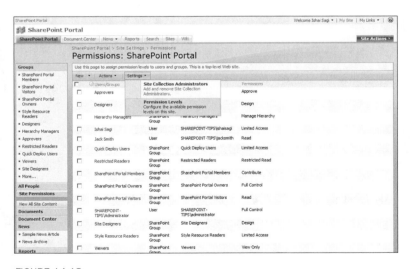

FIGURE 14.18
Opening the Permission Levels page.

On the Permission Levels page, you can see all the existing permission levels, and you can manage them from here (see Figure 14.19).

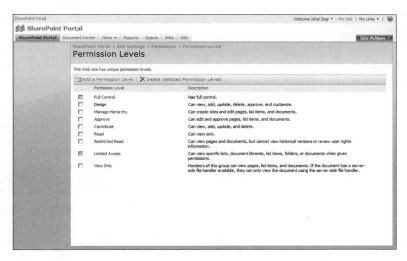

FIGURE 14.19
The Permission Levels page.

To create a new permission level, click the Add a Permission Level button on the toolbar. The Add a Permission Level page opens (see Figure 14.20). On this page you can define the name for the new permission level and what permissions set it should include. Simply select the permissions you want the permission level to include and click the Create button at the bottom of the screen.

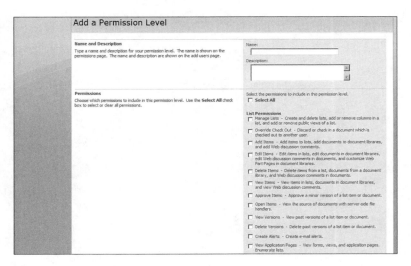

FIGURE 14.20
The Add a Permission Level page.

PART IV

Appendixes

APPENDIX A

Common Keyboard Shortcuts

Sometimes, using the keyboard instead of the mouse is more effective, especially if the graphical designer of the page moved things around and you are not certain where on the page they are. Knowing the keyboard shortcuts can help you get to where you want faster.

Like the structure of this book, this appendix is split between shortcuts for readers that will be useful to anyone using a SharePoint site, and shortcuts for authors/editors that will be useful only if you are adding or editing content in a SharePoint site. Also, some of these shortcut combinations work in all pages, while others are unique to certain types of pages, so each section lists where the shortcuts can be used.

Using Keyboard Shortcuts

The keyboard shortcut combinations are described in this book as a series of keys that you need to press. If you must press several keys at the same time, this is expressed with the + sign. If after pressing a certain key combination you must release the keys before pressing another, this is expressed with the "and then" phrase.

For example, if you want to switch a calendar view to the daily view (instead of the monthly view) the shortcut key is expressed as "Alt+Period and then Enter," which should be read as instructions to hold down the Alt key and the period key (.) at the same time and then release them and press Enter.

Keyboard Shortcuts for Readers

General Shortcuts

Skip to main content	Alt+J and then Enter
Help	Alt+6 and then Enter
Go to the search box	Alt+S
The Welcome personal link	Alt+L and then Enter
The My Links link	Alt+M and then Enter
Site Actions menu	Alt+/ and then Enter
View All Site Content link	Alt+3

Top Navigation

The first top navigation tab	Alt+1 (Enter to select)
Next navigation tab	Tab (Enter to select)
Previous navigation tab	Shift+Tab (Enter to select)

List or Library Views

New menu	Alt+N and then Enter
Upload menu	Alt+U and then Enter
Actions menu	Alt+C and then Enter
Settings menu	Alt+I and then Enter
View menu	Alt+W and then Enter

Calendar Views

Day view link	Alt+Period and then Enter
Week view link	Alt+Minus Sign and then Enter
Month view link	Alt+Equal Sign and then Enter
Previous day, week, or month	Alt+[and then Enter
Next day, week, or month in a view	Alt+] and then Enter

Keyboard Shortcuts for Authors/Editors

Editing List Items or File Properties

Cancel button	Alt+C
OK button	Alt+O
Save and Close (in a survey response)	Alt+S

In a Date Picker Control

Previous month	Alt+Shift+< and then Enter
Next month	Alt+Shift+> and then Enter

Editing Pages

Page menu in the Editing toolbar	Alt+G and then Enter
Edit button in a wiki page	Alt+I and then Enter

In the Add Web Part Dialog

Add button	Alt+O
Cancel button	Alt+C

All Site Content Page

Create button	Alt+N and then Enter
	Or, because the create button is selected by default when you load the page, simply press Enter when the page is loaded.
View menu	Alt+W and then Enter

Using the Rich Text Editor

Right-to-Left text direction button	Ctrl+Shift+<
Left-to-Right text direction button	Ctrl+Shift+>
Bold button	Ctrl+B
Copy button	Ctrl+C
Text color button	Ctrl+Shift+C
Center button	Ctrl+E
Numbered List button	Ctrl+Shift+E
Font menu	Ctrl+Shift+F
Italics button	Ctrl+I
Align Left button	Ctrl+L
Bulleted List button	Ctrl+Shift+L
Increase Indent button	Ctrl+M
Decrease Indent button	Ctrl+Shift+M
Font Size menu	Ctrl+Shift+P
Align Right button	Ctrl+R
Underline button	Ctrl+U
Paste button	Ctrl+V
Background Color menu	Ctrl+Shift+W
Cut button	Ctrl+X

APPENDIX B

Useful Links

This appendix contains a collection of useful links that you might want to use to get quickly to a certain place in a SharePoint site. In this list the placeholder {Site} is used for the site path. For example, if you want to get to the View All Site Content Page of a site, the link in the following list is written as {Site}/_layouts/viewlsts.aspx. To get to that page for a site with the path http://sharepoint, replace the {Site} placeholder with the path http://sharepoint and add the rest of the text to complete the link: http://sharepoint/_layouts/viewlsts.aspx.

Similarly, some links include the path to a specific page, in which case the placeholder {Page} is used. Simply replace the placeholder with the full path to that page.

Useful Links for Readers

The View All Site Content Page	{Site}/_layouts/viewlsts.aspx
My Memberships page	{Site}/_layouts/mymemberships.aspx
My Links page	{Site}/_layouts/myquicklinks.aspx
Add a link to My Links	{Site}/_layouts/quicklinks.aspx
My site	{Site}/_layouts/mysite.aspx
My alerts	{Site}/_layouts/MySubs.aspx
Site content and structure page	{Site}/_layouts/SiteManager.aspx
Search current site and below	{Site}/_layouts/OSSSearchResults.aspx

Useful Links for Authors/Editors

Manage content page	{Site}/_layouts/mcontent.aspx
List of last content you edited	{Site}/_layouts/myinfo.aspx
Create a new page (in a publishing site)	{Site}/_layouts/CreatePage.aspx
Web part page maintenance	{Page}?contents=1

Useful Links for Site Managers

Manage site settings	{Site}/_layouts/settings.aspx
Manage sub webs page	{Site}/_layouts/mngsubwebs.aspx
Manage navigation options	{Site}/_layouts/navoptions.aspx
Modify top navigation	{Site}/_layouts/topnav.aspx
Manage site security	{Site}/_layouts/people.aspx
Create new subsite	{Site}/_layouts/newsbweb.aspx
Manage alerts	{Site}/_layouts/ SiteSubs.aspx
Delete current site	{Site}/_layouts/deleteweb.aspx

Index

A

X-Y-Z

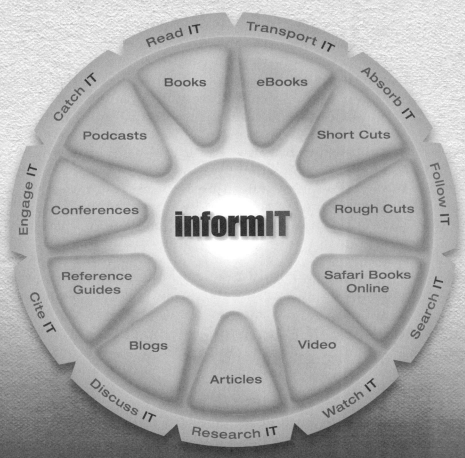

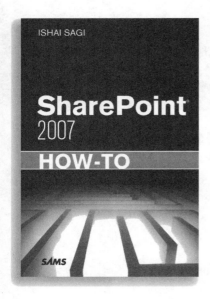

ISHAI SAGI

SharePoint 2007
HOW-TO

SAMS

 FREE Online Edition

Your purchase of **SharePoint 2007 How-To** includes access to a free online edition for 45 days through the Safari Books Online subscription service. Nearly every Sams book is available online through Safari Books Online, along with more than 5,000 other technical books and videos from publishers such as Addison-Wesley Professional, Cisco Press, Exam Cram, IBM Press, O'Reilly, Prentice Hall, and Que.

SAFARI BOOKS ONLINE allows you to search for a specific answer, cut and paste code, download chapters, and stay current with emerging technologies.

Activate your FREE Online Edition at
www.informit.com/safarifree

> **STEP 1:** Enter the coupon code: FGAOZBI.

> **STEP 2:** New Safari users, complete the brief registration form.
> Safari subscribers, just log in.

If you have difficulty registering on Safari or accessing the online edition, please e-mail customer-service@safaribooksonline.com